BLACKS
IN THE
WEST

Recent Titles in
Contributions in Afro-American and African Studies
Hollis R. Lynch, Series Advisor

The Oratory of Negro Leaders: 1900–1968
Marcus Hanna Boulware

Black Labor in America
Milton Cantor, editor

Refugees South of the Sahara: An African Dilemma
Hugh C. Brooks and Yassin El-Ayouty, editors

Bittersweet Encounter: The Afro-American and the American Jew
Robert G. Weisbord and Arthur Stein

The Black Infantry in the West, 1869–1891
Arlen L. Fowler

The Decline and Abolition of Negro Slavery in Venezuela,
1820–1854
John V. Lombardi

Political Philosophy of Martin Luther King, Jr.
Hanes Walton

The American Slave, Series 1, Vols. 1–7; Series 2, Vols. 8–19
George P. Rawick

Nigeria, Dilemma of Nationhood
Joseph Okpaku, editor

Private Black Colleges at the Crossroads
Daniel Thompson

Ebony Kinship: Africa, Africans, and the Afro-American
Robert G. Weisbord

Slavery and Race Relations in Latin America
Robert Brent Toplin, editor

Good Time Coming?: Black Nevadans in the Nineteenth Century
Elmer R. Rusco

Race First: The Ideological and Organizational Struggles of Marcus Garvey
Tony Martin

Silence to the Drums: A Survey of the Literature of the Harlem Renaissance
Margaret Perry

Internal Combustion: The Races in Detroit, 1915-1926
David Allan Levine

Henry Sylvester Williams and the Origins of the Pan-African Movement,
1869–1911
Owen Charles Mathurin

W. Sherman Savage

BLACKS
IN THE
WEST

Contributions in Afro-American and African Studies
Number 23

GREENWOOD PRESS
WESTPORT, CONNECTICUT ● LONDON, ENGLAND

Library of Congress Cataloging in Publication Data

Savage, William Sherman.
    Blacks in the West.

    (Contributions in Afro-American and African studies; no. 23)
    Bibliography: p,
    1. Afro-Americans—The West—History. 2. The West—History—1848-1950. 3.
Frontier and pioneer life—The West. I. Title. II. Series.

E185.925.S38   978'.004'96073   75-44657
ISBN 0-8371-8775-3

Library of Congress Catalog Card Number: 75-44657
ISBN: 0-8371-8775-3

First published in 1976
Second printing 1977
Paperback edition 1977

Greenwood Press, Inc.
51 Riverside Avenue, Westport, Connecticut 06880

Manufactured in the United States of America

To My Daughters
Eloise Sherda Logan
Inez Marian Allen

Contents

Foreword

That Dr. W. Sherman Savage should have devoted most of his long academic lifetime to the study of black pioneers in the American West is singularly fitting, for he himself has been one of the leading pioneers in the prolonged struggle to broaden mankind's frontiers of racial understanding and equality. His role, as he conceived it, has been not to voice violent demands or lead demonstrations, but to prove to the world that black men and women deserved a place in the annals of the past denied them by traditional historians. His remarkable success is demonstrated by his many publications, climaxed by this impressive volume.

Born in rural Virginia in 1890, Sherman Savage earned his undergraduate degree at Howard University in 1917, served in Europe during World War I in the menial capacities that prejudice then allotted members of his race, and in 1921 began the serious study of American history that was to occupy the remainder of his years. He launched his teaching career that year, but more important was his decision to pursue the advanced degrees that would qualify him as a scholar capable of commanding the attention of the profession. And this, in turn, meant graduate work in universities that seldom opened their doors to blacks, whatever the obstacles that stood in his way.

These were many. As a graduate student at the University of Kansas in 1921 and again in 1923 he endured uncomplainingly the affronts that were tragically common in those days, for there he could broaden his knowledge of the American past under such a master as Professor Frank H. Hodder, who directed his attention to abolitionism and encouraged his interest in black history. From Kansas he moved to the University of Oregon where he persisted in his studies despite officials who refused to provide him university housing and students who shunned his company. That was a lonely year for Sherman Savage but one well-spent, for he not only earned his Master of Arts degree in 1925 but was encouraged by Professor Dan Elbert Clark to focus his scholarly interest on the role of blacks in the conquest of the frontier. His next academic move was to Ohio State University where he studied with Professor Homer C. Hockett and completed his doctoral degree under Professor H. H. Simms, submitting an excellent dissertation that was published two years later by the Association for the Study of Negro Life and History as *The Controversy over the Distribution of Abolition Literature, 1830–1860*.

These steps up the academic ladder were sandwiched into a full program of teaching. Sherman Savage began his classroom career in 1921 when he joined the faculty of Lincoln University, a post that he held until his first—and obviously premature—retirement in 1960 at the age of seventy. For six years after his "retirement" he held a professorship at Jarvis Christian College, then spent four more as Visiting Professor of History at the California State University in Los Angeles. Not until 1970, after almost a half-century in the classroom, did he retire for the last time. Even this meant not leisure but more time for research and writing; since 1970 he has worked daily at the Henry E. Huntington Library, traveling two hours by bus from his Los Angeles home and laboring as industriously as he did when he began his investigations some fifty-five years ago.

His work has, over the years, focused increasingly on the role of blacks in the winning of the trans-Mississippi West. With remarkable foresight, he predicted his scholarly future in his first article, "The Negro in the History of the Pacific Northwest," which appeared in the *Journal of Negro History* in July 1928. "The purpose of this paper," he wrote, ". . . is to try, as far as possible, to find out how many Negroes were in the state [of Oregon] before 1850; what their influence was on the organization, whether the laws [against Negroes] were passed before Negroes were in the state or because it was feared they might come into that commonwealth.'' He was soon to broaden his geographic interest to include the entire West and his time span to embrace the period to 1890, but his basic purpose remained the same: to understand the role of blacks in the political, economic, and social development of the trans-Mississippi country, to explain their struggle for equality there, and to appraise the significant contributions they had made to the emergence of the western United States.

These broadened sights led him into a variety of investigations which were duly reported to his colleagues in a ground-breaking series of articles, largely in the *Journal of Negro History:* "Legal Provisions for Negro Schools in Missouri from 1865 to 1890" (1931); "The Negro in the Westward Movement" (1940); "The Contest over Slavery between Illinois and Missouri" (1943); "The Negro on the Mining Frontier" (1945); "The Role of Negro Soldiers in Protecting the Indian Frontier from Intruders" (1951); and "The Influence of William Alexander Leidesdorff on the History of California" (1953). Interspersed among these articles were others on varied aspects of black history, including an impressive volume, *The History of Lincoln University,* published in 1939.

Today, historians are producing an ever-increasing number of books and articles on black history, some of them touching on the part played by Negroes in frontier expansion. When Sherman Savage began his studies, however, such investigations were virtually unknown. He was, in the truest sense, a pioneer, blazing a path into an aspect of the past that had been too long neglected but that his successors were to follow. No prospector or cattle rancher or mountain man was more truly a frontiersman than Sherman Savage as he labored alone and selflessly to bring recognition to the blacks who had played such a significant role in the westering process.

This book climaxes a lifetime of study, for no lesser span would allow a scholar to investigate the masses of documents, newspapers, memoirs, and printed records that provide a solid foundation for Sherman Savage's conclusions. Today's readers, no matter how well versed in black history they may be, will be introduced to a variety of new faces and fresh information. True, the familiar figures are there—Edward Rose and James Beckwourth of the fur trade, John Wallace and Nat Love of the cattle frontier, Junius G. Groves of agricultural fame, William A. Leidesdorff of the business world, and others who have been singled out by scholars in the past. But so are many more largely unknown to history, for Sherman Savage's investigations have unearthed a whole *Who's Who* of blacks whose important contributions are scarcely remembered: Jacob Dodson, who pioneered with Fremont and other explorers; Biddy Mason, who, as nurse and midwife, brought many a Los Angelino into the world; Allen B. Light, who ranked among the great mountain men; George W. Bush, who gained fame as a "Potato King" in Washington; Peter Biggs, whose excellent barbering won him a position of influence in Los Angeles; John Wesley Fisher, who helped enlarge "Lucky" Baldwin's fortune by designing special shoes for his racing horses; and dozens more. This is the stuff of history, difficult to reconstruct but essential to the total story. Sherman Savage's dedicated research, revealed so spectacularly in the massive footnotes and bibliography in this volume, alone has made this remarkable book possible.

Readers, however, should be warned that he has refused to succumb to two temptations that would easily be understood, and even forgiven. His is not simply a collection of blacks' success stories, unleavened by any record of failure. He has been utterly frank where frankness is due; his chapter on black troops in the West records their disasters as well as their triumphs, their sins as well as their virtues, showing that the soldiers were humans capable of wrongdoing; his discussion of the cattle frontier makes the undisputable point that the first occupant of the Abilene jail was a black who deserved to be there. The truth, to Sherman Savage, is far more essential than racial glorification.

So is objectivity. Few scholars writing today have suffered the lash of discrimination as has Sherman Savage, particularly during his schooling at a time when separation of the races was decreed by both popular sentiment and the law. Yet the pages of this book mirror no bitterness, no universal condemnation of a society that doomed him to personal abuse. Instead, he lets facts speak for themselves, with their lesson made even more clear by his calm aloofness from controversy. This is not only good history but good human relations.

The publication of this volume is a landmark in the study of black history. It is also a landmark in the career of its author, but one that he refuses to recognize. This means no indifference on his part; he is simply too busy to pause in his historical investigations to celebrate a task that has been completed. A few months ago, when he celebrated his eighty-fifth birthday, some of us who are his daily companions at the Huntington Library hoped to stage a small celebration of the great day. Sherman Savage would have none of that. He was far too busy to waste time on festivities; more books must be written. May they all be completed, and may they all be as valuable as this one.

RAY ALLEN BILLINGTON
The Henry E. Huntington Library

Acknowledgments

A great deal has been written about blacks in the United States, but little has been written specifically about blacks in the West. This was revealed to me in a course in Western history which I took with the late Dr. Dan Elbert Clark of the University of Oregon. Since that time I have turned most of my attention to research on blacks in Western history. I was concerned with what influence they have exerted on this region of the United States.

Many organizations have assisted in this effort. Thanks are due the Social Science Research Council for a grant-in-aid; the American Philosophical Society; Lincoln University for a sabbatical leave and typographical aid; librarians and staffs of the Henry E. Huntington Library, San Marino, California; the Library of Congress; the National Archives; and the Bancroft Library; University of California, Berkeley; the state libraries of Missouri and California; the city libraries of Los Angeles, San Francisco, Denver, St. Louis, Kansas City, San Bernardino, and Redlands; the state historical societies of Missouri, Kansas, Colorado, Wisconsin, and Minnesota; and the librarian and staff of Lincoln University, Jefferson City, Missouri.

Among the scholars who have contributed to this effort are Dr. Elmer Ellis, professor of history and former president of the University of Missouri, who read most of the manuscript; the late Dr. Ulysses S. Donaldson, instructor of commercial subjects at Sumner High School, St. Louis, who read the manuscript; Dr. Kenneth Porter, University of Oregon, who read part of the material; the late Mrs. Hazel McDaniel Teabeau, professor of English at Lincoln University; the late Dr. Ulysses S. Lee, Jr., professor of English, Morgan State College, Baltimore, who read the chapter on the black cowboy; Professor Sterling Brown of Howard University and Dr. Ray Billington of the Huntington Library, both of whom gave valuable suggestions. I owe special thanks to Dr. Gerald D. Browne, who helped in various ways to prepare the work for publication, including editing the manuscript.

Most of all, I wish to express my gratitude to the members of my family. They gave extraordinary assistance and continued encouragement without which the work could not have been completed. To many other persons who have assisted in sundry ways, my thanks. It goes without saying that the writer must assume responsibility for any errors that may appear in these pages.

BLACKS
IN THE
WEST

Introduction

The settlement and development of the West has been one of the most extensively studied topics of American history. A great deal of this interest was due to the influence of Frederick Jackson Turner and the frontier school. As a result of their work, almost every section of the frontier has been investigated in depth and much has been told us of the men and women who settled there. Conspicuous in its absence from the history of the West, however, was an account of black men and women. Indeed, many of the authors in early times wrote as though blacks had made no contribution at all. Fortunately, recent scholarship has brought us closer to the truth. Especially noteworthy in this respect are two studies: William Loren Katz's *The Black West* and Kenneth W. Porter's *The Negro on the American Frontier*.

The present study differs from those two in that it deals only with the West, thereby excluding the slave states. It is an effort to determine what influence, if any, blacks had on a region where their numbers were few. They were not drawn to the West in great numbers partly because there were no staple crops and partly because the region was far removed from the center of the black population.

Arkansas, Louisiana, Texas, and Missouri are all states west of the Mississippi, and in all of them blacks have, by their labor, made some contribution. But these states are part of the cotton kingdom, and as a result the black contributions in them have been thoroughly examined. We shall not, therefore, deal with three of these states, but we must treat the blacks in Texas because that state became the very center of the cattle industry. Any survey of the West must take into consideration the long drives which had their origins in Texas. A study of black cowboys by Philip Durham and Everett Jones has shown that black cowboys comprised one-fifth to one-fourth of those employed in the Texas cattle industry.

Missouri was a slave state by the provisions of the Act of Congress in 1820. Nevertheless, Missouri has been thought of as a western state by many persons who have treated its history. Following the Civil War, social practices in Missouri were not so sharply segregated as they were in the Deep South. Moreover, Missouri was the very heart of the westward movement: Independence has been regarded as the jumping-off point of both the Oregon and Santa Fe trails; the headquarters of the fur companies were located in St. Louis; and the terminus of the Pony Express was located at St. Joseph. But despite all this we shall not deal with Missouri because H. A. Trexler's fine study, *Slavery in Missouri*, has covered this field.

Our study does include one state east of the Mississippi, however—Wisconsin. Because Wisconsin is so closely related to Minnesota, it is difficult to separate the history of the two. They were the only states or territories in this group to have blacks among their population as early as 1840, according to census reports. Their importance grew in proportion to the rapid expansion of the fur trade, which was consequent upon the migration of trappers and traders into the region.

It may seem surprising that Illinois is not also included, since it too played a very important part in the westward movement. The first producing lead mines were in this state and in southeast Missouri, and blacks were brought into this area to work in these mines and to serve in many other capacities. But the story of blacks in Illinois has already been told by W. D. Harris in *The History of Servitude in Illinois*. While there is room for a new in-depth study of blacks in this state, such a study cannot be undertaken here.

This survey includes, then, the following states: Wisconsin, Minnesota, Iowa, North and South Dakota, Nebraska, Kansas, Oklahoma, New Mexico, Colorado, Wyoming, Montana, Idaho, Utah, Arizona, Nevada, California, Oregon, and Washington. It takes as its beginning the year 1830. The general movement of the population into western territory really began after that year, and while a few blacks were in the West before 1830, none is recorded until the census report for 1840. Congressional activity regarding the distribution of public land influenced many people to move west. Some free blacks undoubtedly moved west because of the solace it afforded them. In some areas there were laws against the introduction of slaves, and such laws as there were against free blacks in other areas were by no means as severe as those in the states of the Deep South. On the whole, however, the agitation against slavery, which became noticeable about 1830, seems not to have been the root cause of black migration. Rather, the westward movement of black people is best seen as a part of the westward movement of America. The black population was largest in the states where the general population was largest, indicating that the same factors which attracted the general population attracted blacks.

The date selected for the close of our study is 1890. By then many things had happened; after this time America was a different country from what it had been before. And of all areas of the country, the West had changed the most. The transcontinental railroads had been completed, making it easier for people to go west. In some quarters there had been the demand for the regulation of the railroads, which resulted in the passage of the Interstate Commerce Commission Act. All of the West was organized by 1890. With the exception of the territories of Arizona, New Mexico, and Oklahoma, this region of the country had become a group of states. While there was an abundance of land, most of the good arable land had been claimed. After 1890 it was no longer possible to keep the six-inhabitants-per-square-mile apportionment of the arable land. In short, by 1890 the frontier had closed.

1 • The migration of blacks to the West

Blacks moved west for various reasons, including the love of adventure as well as the desire for economic and political improvement. They were part of the general westward movement of Americans, although, prior to emancipation, slavery provided an additional impetus. In subsequent chapters we shall examine in greater detail the diverse functions blacks performed in the West, as well as the political and social struggles they faced. While in the present chapter we must take some notice of these things, our immediate purpose will be to sketch the shape of the black movement westward.

A bare outline is to be seen in the table of black population growth. The increase for the period under consideration is striking, for in the three decades following the close of the Civil War the black population increased by 33,109, and by the 1880s the number of blacks had more than doubled, reaching the mark of 72,575. By the turn of the century, the overall black population had increased to 165,432, as revealed by the census report. Because Oklahoma was not organized until the end of our period, records for it were not available before 1890. When records did become available, they showed that the black population there grew quickly, from 21,000 in 1890 to 55,000 in 1900. The factors which had been at work in other states in other decades were operating in Oklahoma: land was easy to acquire, and there were no firm rules and customs restricting blacks. The opportunities for black people who desired to get a start in business or in farming were excellent.

Prior to emancipation, some slaves escaped from Missouri to Kansas-Nebraska Territory, and a number of free blacks also settled in this area. But the proximity of Nebraska to Missouri made it easy for the slave traders to kidnap or entice free blacks out of the state and sell them into slavery. The territorial legislature of Nebraska passed a law making such an act a crime and set up penalties for its perpetration. Anyone who enticed or seduced a black by false promises or misrepresentations or who attempted forcibly to remove him from the state was guilty of kidnapping. The penalty for such a crime was imprisonment for a term left to the discretion of the presiding judge.[1] The act also applied if anyone employed a black against his will. However, in many cases the slave trader would be out of the state before his crime was even discovered. Thus the law which was created for the benefit of the black availed him little, but, like most laws, it might have acted in many instances as a deterrent.

The nearness of Kansas to Missouri made life for the black precarious in that territory also. There was always the danger that a slave trader might cross the border and take a black person back into slavery. Kidnapping of free blacks was a fairly profitable business because no money had to be paid to anyone for them. A census report for Kansas in 1865 showed a black population of 600. This indicates that blacks were not very numerous in Kansas at that time. Many who were leaving the slave states desired to go further than Kansas because it was too near slave territory.

Iowa was another territory bordering on Missouri, and it made an effort to control those blacks who went there. The regulation which the territorial legislature passed declared that after April 1843 blacks could pass freely through the territory, but no black or mulatto was to reside there unless he could produce a certificate of his freedom, authenticated by some court within the United States. The free black was also required to give as security a $500 bond which had to be approved by the commissioner of the county in which the person intended to live.[2] This was a great burden on those wanting to stay in Iowa; blacks who had been able to secure their freedom had little else, and only a few could meet the monetary requirement. If he could not meet its provision, the free black could be hired out until he accumulated enough money to post the bond.[3]

Iowa Territory above the Missouri Compromise Line had been organized with the provision that slavery was to be prohibited. The black population in the territory was small: in 1840 it was only 153, eighteen of whom were slaves.[4] Many citizens of the territory were from Missouri and other southern states, and they were apparently fearful that Iowa might become a haven for free blacks from other states. The members of the territorial legislature were determined that this should not happen. In 1851 the Third General Assembly of Iowa passed an act prohibiting the immigration of free blacks into the state. The law provided that, after its passage, no free black or mulatto should be permitted to settle in the state. It became the duty of all township and county officers to notify every free black who might immigrate to Iowa to leave within three days of the receipt of notice. Blacks who refused to go were to be arrested and taken before a justice of the peace or a county judge. If convicted, the individual was fined two dollars a day for every day he remained in the state after notice had been given. Then he was to be committed to jail until such fine should be paid or until he agreed to leave. The act did not apply to free blacks already living in the state because they had already complied with the territorial laws concerning certification and bonding.[5]

The new law was tested in the case of *Archie P. Webb vs W. Griffith*. Webb was born a slave in Mississippi but later secured his freedom, went to Arkansas, and then to Iowa. He was employed in Delaware Township, Polk County, where he diligently worked to obtain a livelihood. As required under the law of 1851, he was asked by the county sheriff to leave the state. However, Webb was sure that, whatever the difficulty, he could live better in Iowa than in a slave state, and so he refused to leave. He was arrested by order of the justice of the peace of Delaware Township, fined, and sent to jail because he could not pay the fine of twelve dollars and cost of two dollars and ninety-one cents. Webb was later released on a writ of habeas corpus issued by Judge John Henry Gray. Gray had been born in the border state of Maryland and had been educated in his home state and the state of Pennsylvania. He had previously come face to face with slavery and the slave question in his native state, and when the Webb case came before his court, the question of slavery was being agitated in the country and debated in the national Congress and state legislatures. Judge Gray, guided by the principle so ably expounded by Curtis and McLean in the Dred Scott case, held that blacks were citizens and the state of Iowa could not discriminate against its citizens.[6]

There were few blacks in the territories along the Rocky Mountains and Great Plains because there was little employment for them. The census does not show any blacks in this area in 1840. In 1850 twenty-two blacks were recorded in New Mexico, and Utah had a population of fifty, most of whom lived in Salt Lake City where they could find some employment. By 1860 the populations of New Mexico and Utah had increased to eighty-five and fifty-nine, respectively. In addition, Colorado showed a population of forty-eight blacks, and Nevada had forty-five.

Some blacks roamed over these territories and might be regarded as citizens-at-large because they did not settle very long anywhere, or certainly not long in this Rocky Mountain or plains territory. Such a person was Jacob Dodson, a free man who had worked in the family of Senator Thomas Hart Benton and later worked with John C. Fremont.[7] Dodson volunteered for this service because he had the spirit of adventure and he wanted to see the West. Fremont included him in his exploration parties because of Dodson's long experience and ability. Dodson was equal to any of the Californians in riding horses and lassoing wild cattle. After leaving the field of exploration, he married and settled in Washington, D.C., where he had lived before he began his journey with the Pathfinder of the West.[8]

Another black who wandered about this territory and who also served with Fremont was a man named Sanders. Sanders was free, but his wife had been a slave whom her master was willing to free, together with her children, for $1,700.[9] Sanders was able to pay the amount by prospecting for gold. He and his family may finally have settled in California.

Some blacks on the western plains before the Civil War helped in the construction and maintenance of forts. There is even a record of a black named George who, together with three or four Mexican men and one woman, operated a combination fort–stage depot in Arizona.[10] The forts helped the settlement of the West. Their purpose was to protect from Indian attack those who moved across the country. Crudely constructed, they were made of timber if possible, although any conveniently obtainable material was used. Many forts on the plains, for example, were adobe. The typical fort was surrounded by an outer court which prevented the immediate entrance of friend and foe alike. This plan enabled those within to observe approaching parties and to determine whether they were hostile or friendly. These forts were oases in a desert, serving not only as means of protection but as resting places and sources of supplies for trappers and traders.

Some forts were military, while others were trading posts. One of the military forts located on the frontier was Fort Snelling in Wisconsin Territory. At various times several blacks were brought to this fort by Major Lawrence Taliaferro; among them was Dred Scott, who later became a national figure.[11] The Blackfoot Post, built by Francis Chardon at the mouth of the Judieth River in Montana, was another military post. While building the fort in the winter of 1842, Chardon lost one of his workers, a black named Reese, who was killed by a band of Indians, perhaps the Blackfeet, whom Charles Larpenteur called "Blood Indians."[12] Chardon had confidence in and respect for his ability and vowed vengeance on the Indians. There was at least one other black at this fort, probably a free man since no mention was made of his master.[13]

It is certain that blacks helped in the construction of Bent's Fort, which was strategically placed to serve as a supply station for those who crossed the plains in order to make their homes in Oregon or California. Fur traders, trappers, and cattlemen all stopped here. A soldier with Doniphan's expedition reported that the fort was crowded with citizens, soldiers, traders, Santa Fe Indians, and blacks. Two blacks, Dick Green and his brother Andrew, were workers there, and they, together with a woman and a black blacksmith, were counted as part of its population. Dick and Andrew continued to work at Bent's Fort after they obtained their freedom in the late 1840s.[14] Because Andrew could speak the Cheyenne language, he served as an interpreter. Dick worked at various jobs, but in 1847 he was with his former master, Charles Bent, at Taos when the latter was killed by Indians. Dick later joined Colonel St. Vrain's company of trappers and traders and fought with noticeable courage at the storming of the Pueblo.

Next to Bent's Fort, Fort Benton was one of the most important forts on the frontier. It was located 3,500 miles from the Gulf by way of the Mississippi River. At least one black participated in its construction. When Major Dawson was transferred from Fort Union to Fort Benton in 1854, he decided that a brick fort was necessary for greater security from Indian attack.[15] One of the best brickmakers was a black named George. Dawson said that he could do as much work as any three other men at the fort at the time.[16] A list of the fort's inhabitants in 1862 included the names of three blacks: Phil Barnes and Harry Mills, both laborers, and Vanlitburg, a cook.[17]

There were also forts on the frontier which had been erected by the Indians for the protection of their wives and children and for their own defense in time of battle. Such a fort was held by the Crow tribe as early as 1840. Living there as a chief among the Indians was a black whom Parkman thought was James Beckwourth, although he may have been someone else. Whoever he was, in an encounter with the Blackfeet the black proved to be an inspiration to the tribe. He told his braves that the Crows made a great noise as if they expected to kill the living by the noise they made. The black leader was quite concerned about what the white traders might think of the Crows, and he told the tribe that white men would think that they spoke with crooked tongues and were cowards. He accused them of acting more like squaws than men, and he felt that they were not fit to defend their hunting grounds. He further told the Crows that, if they were afraid, he would show them a black man who was not, whereupon he leaped from the rock upon which he had been standing and, looking resolutely ahead, rushed forward toward the fort of the enemy as fast as his legs would carry him. The Crows were so stirred by his courageous words and his leadership that they entered the enemy fort and killed the Blackfeet to the last man.[18]

While crossing the plains, Zenas Leonard experienced many difficulties, including the loss of his horses, stolen by Indians. Leonard reported this to the black chief of the Crows, who said that the horses would be returned if Leonard would agree to give the Indians some small gifts. This was gladly done. According to Leonard, the black chief claimed that he first came to the country with Lewis and Clark in their expedition to the Pacific Coast and returned with the explorers as far as the Missouri River. After living there a few years, he returned to the Indian country with MacKinney, a trader on the Missouri River. The chief, according to his own statement, had been living in that country about a dozen years and had acquired a knowledge of the Indians' language and their manner of living.[19]

One of the most famous forts and trading posts on the frontier was Sutter's Fort. Its location in the Sacramento Valley was significant in the settlement of the West. Many expeditions stopped here for a much-needed rest after a long trip. The fort had been erected as a supply depot and an Indian agency, but the discovery of gold changed its whole history, as well as that of California. One of the problems which faced Sutter in building the fort was that of obtaining adequate and competent labor. In 1841 he was able to employ a half-dozen men to engage in the project, among them a black cooper.[20] When a census was taken of the inhabitants of the fort and its surroundings in 1846, the population consisted of more than 30,000 persons, including Indians, but there was still only one black, probably the same cooper.

Before the Civil War, most of the free blacks in the Far West were distributed among the Pacific Coast states. Some joined the westward movement to Oregon, and many others came with the gold rush. The law in Oregon, however, was prejudicial against blacks. When the provisional government was organized, the convention passed a resolution which made the laws of Iowa Territory the laws of Oregon. In cases in which the laws of Iowa did not apply to citizens of Oregon, common law was to operate.[21] A section for the control of free blacks was added to the state constitution. It provided that no free black or mulatto not residing in the state at the time of the adoption of the constitution should come or be within the provisional territory, hold any real estate, make any contract, or maintain any suit. The territorial legislature was to provide, by penal laws, for the removal, by public officers, of such blacks or mulattoes and was to make such effective regulation as to exclude them and to punish persons who should bring free blacks into the state to harbor or employ them.[22] This was a very drastic law, and for many years efforts made to remove it from the constitution proved unsuccessful. In 1900, for example, 1,907 people voted for repeal, while 19,999 voted to retain the measure. The view expressed by the *Morning Oregonian* was that there was no need for the repeal of that section of the state constitution because it was inoperative after the suffrage amendments were added to the United States Constitution.[23] Those who worked for repeal of the act realized that it was inoperative, but they desired nonetheless to see the provision erased from the laws of the state of Oregon. Another repeal effort was made in 1925 when the issue was again placed before the people in a general election. Again it failed. Finally, on November 2, 1926, the exclusion law was repealed.

But despite the law, blacks lived in Oregon. Evidently, enforcement was uneven. In 1857 a black man named Vanderpool was accused of violating the exclusion act, and a court ruled that he had to leave the state within thirty days.[24] Inasmuch as nothing more is heard of him, he probably left as directed. George Washington Bush came to Oregon in the expedition of 1844, but, because of the law against blacks and mulattoes, he did not remain long in the area.[25] Bush moved to what is now an area in the state of Washington, which at that time was considered Upper Oregon. It was thought then, by the British and some Americans, that the region north of the Columbia River would finally fall under British control. George Washington, founder of the town of Centralia, was another black who moved to Washington because of the Oregon law. Others apparently were not driven out. The presence of a black man who tried to earn a livelihood by piloting ships came to light in 1846 when the schooner *Shark,* a vessel registered by and bearing the flag of the United States, came into port at Baker's Bay, and the black pilot attempted to take her over to Astoria but instead landed her on the shoals.[26] In 1849 a black woman named Maurmia Travers had been brought to Oregon as a slave by Captain Llewellyn Jones of the United States Army. Jones was probably able to keep her in slavery because he was in the military service. According to him, Maurmia Travers was honest and conscientious.[27] In 1857 he gave her her freedom. An 1844 incident involving blacks and Indians revealed the former living on the Willamette River. Two blacks, James Saules and Winslow Anderson, hired an Indian for a specific time and agreed to pay for the work with a designated horse. Before the time of payment, Anderson sold the horse. Considerable confusion ensued; the Indian became unruly and was killed by white and black residents. Anderson was then forced to leave the territory.[28]

Washington was organized as a territory just before the Civil War, and there are only a few blacks for whom we have records there. The census of 1860, the first taken after Washington was organized, shows that only thirty blacks resided in the area. Most of them moved to Washington because of the laws against them in Oregon. One was Dick Saunders, who in 1855 was living in Cowlitz County. Congor Kelsey, a prominent citizen of Washington, said that he saw Dick many times and described him as of black complexion and as the husband of an Indian woman. Arthur and Henry Strong were two other blacks named in the 1860 census report as residents of Washington Territory. Both lived in Thurstone County, but their occupation is not clearly defined.[29] George Washington and George Washington Bush were two prominent black men who exerted considerable influence on the history of Washington. We shall have more to say about these men later.

California was the section of the West where most blacks settled before the Civil War. Nevertheless, the black population in this area was small in relation to the general population of California. The 1850 census report indicates that the state's population was 92,597, with men outnumbering women in every racial group.[30] This difference in sex ratio was probably due to occupational selection and the gold rush, which was at its height at this time. The black population in 1850 was scarcely 1,000. Most of the blacks in the Spanish territory were from states of the American Union. The largest concentration of blacks in the state was in Sacramento County, mainly because of the gold rush.[31]

Trade with China brought ships to the Pacific Coast, and many of their workers were blacks, both slaves and free men. Slaves had the chance to escape; free men had an opportunity to settle in a section which was not as hostile to them as the southern states were. There are instances of the appearance and settlement of blacks from ships as early as 1800. Captain Joseph O'Cain touched the shores of San Diego in January 1804, but he was refused provisions because he did not have the proper papers. The refusal had little influence on John Brown, one of the early blacks to come to this coast, for it was here that he deserted.[32] In 1816 the schooner *Albatross,* under the command of William Smith, arrived at San Diego where three blacks in its crew deserted and remained in the city in order to be instructed in Christianity. The names of two of them are given as Kanaska and

Bob, but the name of the third is unknown. They were among the first to settle in the western Spanish territory. Bob later studied Catholicism; he was baptized and christened as Juan Christabel.[33] Other blacks came to San Diego in April 1819 with the arrival of another schooner. A black man named Thomas Fisher came to the California coast supposedly around 1818. He apparently was captured from Bouchard's crew of pirates when they burned the mission and the town of Monterey in that year.[34] Another black named Fisher came to the Pacific Coast about 1846 as steward on a whaling ship. He became ill and was discharged. Later he served as Spanish interpreter for some of Kearney's officers near the Colorado River.[35]

These blacks and probably others came to the coast when the country was under the control of Mexico. There was apparently little or no slavery in the Spanish Southwest under the Mexican government. It could only have existed secretly because it was illegal after 1829. The United States treaty which obtained this territory from Mexico guaranteed to persons living in and entering this region all the privileges of American citizens. Thus, in this territory ceded by Mexico there were black citizens of the United States before the Civil War.[36]

By 1850 some blacks in California had attracted sufficient attention to be mentioned in the news. The death of Walter Street, at age twenty-four, is a case in point. Street was born in slavery but was manumitted because of his intelligence and his commendable character. At the time of his death he had won a large number of friends in San Francisco. His funeral procession moved from the corner of Sacramento and Leidesdorff streets, and the pallbearers—Captain C. R. Garrison, Captain R. M. Bowlin, Francis Poe, Judge Hall, and a man named Thurston—were men of distinction in the life of the city. The Right Reverend Bishop Kip of the Episcopal church conducted the funeral services at the Yerba Buena Cemetery where Street was interred. The large number of persons in attendance at this cemetery testified to the high esteem in which this black citizen was held.[37]

John Banning was an influential black man in the city of Los Angeles. He was able to earn a livelihood in the general drayage business, and because of his honesty and uprightness his services were sought by many, and he was liked by all who hired him. In June 1857, while engaged at his usual duties, his saddle went awry. As

Banning adjusted it, his gun discharged; the bullet shattered his leg, leaving a dangerous wound.[38]

A black woman who attracted considerable attention in the news was Biddy Mason.[39] Formerly a slave, she had been freed by a writ of habeas corpus, whereupon she moved to Los Angeles and remained there for the rest of her life. Biddy Mason engaged in the occupation of nurse and midwife to the best families of the city. Noted for her works of charity, she frequently visited the jail where she spoke words of encouragement to the prisoners. So devoted was she to such deeds of mercy that she became widely known as "Grandmother Mason."[40] In times of great distress for some unfortunates of the city, she would open an account at a store so that the poor could obtain supplies at her expense. But despite this unusual charity, she amassed considerable wealth. She bought a share in a large plot of land and later secured the rest of it, along with other properties, which increased in value with the growth of the city. At the time of her death, she possessed property valued at $300,000. Delilah Beasley commented: "She is the most remarkable person of African descent, who came to the Pacific Coast before the Civil War, and was associated with many of the significant civic movements. It was in her home that the First Negro African Methodist Episcopal Church in the city of Los Angeles was organized."[41]

Despite these signs of progress, there were some who felt that blacks were a hindrance to the development of California. Frank Soule, the author of *Annals of San Francisco,* commenting on the various racial elements in San Francisco, felt that Mexicans and Chinese, together with Indians and blacks, were generally an inferior lot. He believed, however, that, of nonwhite races, many blacks ranked first in morals, intellect, and achievements. Hinton Rowan Helper thought that free blacks chose to live in filth and degradation in the worst part of town. He failed to see that blacks lived in squalor because they were the poorest-paid workers and could afford nothing better and because of the general hostility and prejudice toward them.[42]

Writers such as Soule and Helper influenced others who felt that the best interest of the state would be served by keeping blacks out, or at least by seeing that no others came into the area. The editor of the *San Francisco Daily Globe,* for example, exerted what influence he could to keep blacks out of California. He argued that other states were barring the entrance of blacks and that most free blacks would come to California if they could find no other place to go. The state, therefore, would be overrun by free blacks. He also used the stock argument that the Negro race was inferior.[43] His view was shared by the majority of people in California, who opposed the free black and were determined that he should not remain in the state. A bill designed to regulate immigration of free blacks who might come to the state after October 1, 1858, was introduced into the California legislature. No black or mulatto would be allowed to come to the state to settle or reside. If a free black violated the provisions of the act, he was to be considered guilty of a misdemeanor. When convicted, the black was to be transferred from the state to whatever state or territory he might desire to enter, depending upon the laws of that state or territory. If the free black desired to go to a state or territory where blacks were not allowed, the sheriff of the county in which the trial was held was to be authorized to select the place to which the black should go. If the black did not have the means to go to that place, the sheriff was to hire him to the person who would enter a bond for the black to work for him for the shortest time. If the black was not sent as provided, then the prosecuting attorney and the judge were to declare the bond forfeited, and the black would be sent out of the state from the proceeds of the bond. The proposed act put a restriction of six months on the length of time a black could be hired out; this limitation was designed to keep employers from reducing free blacks to slavery. The first part of the bill was directed against free blacks who might come into the state; the second part was directed against those who were already in California.

The recorders of the several counties of California were to keep a book for the registration of free blacks and mulattoes. Every free black and mulatto over the age of fifteen was to be required, before the first day of the October following his fifteenth birthday, to apply to the recorder of the county in which he lived and request the privilege of registering as a free black. The registrar was to enter into the book provided by the bill the name and age of each applicant and, under his official seal, give the free black a certificate of entry. This certificate was to be renewable in the event of loss or destruction. The procedure was designed to detect whether a free black belonged in California or had come from some other state. If a free black did not have such a certificate as was provided by the proposed bill, it was to be taken as positive proof that he was from another state.[44]

The third section of the bill was directed against those free blacks and mulattoes who did not register. They would be guilty of a misdemeanor, and upon conviction they were to be fined a sum not to exceed $100. They would then be allowed to register one month from such trial or one month from the expiration of whatever sentence was given them.

The proposed bill also set a penalty for those who might bring slaves into the state for the purpose, direct or indirect, of freeing them. If a person ordered a free black to come into the state, he would come under the provisions of the bill. Such a person, if found guilty, was to be fined not less than $100 or more than $500. The law did not apply to any free black driven to the shores of the state by shipwreck or by the stress of weather. Under this provision, however, he could not remain more than six months. Neither did the law apply to persons who were on vessels of the United States or on those whaling ships in the coastwise trade plying to or from ports outside California. Even so, the bill applied to almost all free blacks in the state.[45]

The blacks of California were naturally fearful that the proposed bill might pass and become law. Their opinion was expressed by the Reverend J. J. Moore, a prominent black clergyman who spoke against it. He thought that those who sponsored such a bill had done so only because they had the power to do so and that they had produced no new arguments, nor had they shown any great intellectual ability. Moore asked the legislature as a whole to demonstrate its intelligence by not passing the bill.[46] Despite the efforts of the bill's proponents and the publicity in favor of its passage, it was defeated. One historian of California, Theodore Hittell, feels that the legislature should be praised for what it refused to do in time of great popular prejudice.[47] And it should be pointed out that earlier in its deliberations the legislature had made an effort to protect the free black from the slave trader. It had proclaimed, in a list of offenses against blacks, that every person who was guilty of hiring, persuading, enticing, decoying, or seducing by false promises, misrepresentation, or other means, any black, mulatto, or colored person to go out of the state for the purpose of selling such person into slavery or involuntary servitude, or for his own use, without the consent of the black or mulatto, should be guilty of kidnapping. If such a violator was convicted, he was to be imprisoned for a period of up to ten years.[48]

The close of the Civil War brought a new influx of settlers, and among them were blacks. In slavery, the black had been primarily an agricultural worker. After slavery, he continued to cultivate the land. The Homestead Act had been passed, and many blacks took advantage of the opportunity it gave them. The act was especially advantageous to soldiers who could apply their years of service in the Union Army toward fulfillment of the residence requirement for the homestead.[49] But it applied also to anyone who agreed to remain five years and make improvements on the land. Most blacks who wanted to settle on public land had to seek a homestead because they had no funds, having just come out of slavery. Some of those who could afford it used the method of preemption and paid one dollar and twenty-five cents per acre.[50]

The post–Civil War increase in the black population is especially striking in Kansas and Iowa. In Kansas their problems received great consideration because of the efforts of agencies promoting the West. Notable among these was the Singleton Movement, initiated by Benjamin Singleton of Morris County, Tennessee, which urged blacks to leave the South and relocate in the free or cheap lands in Kansas and the surrounding territory. The black population in Kansas increased from 627 in 1850 to 17,108 in 1870. In Iowa the black population increased from just a little more than 1,000 in 1860 to more than 5,000 in 1870. Largely responsible for the increase was the growth of the mining industry and the possibility of employment on rivers. The traffic of both passenger and freight ships on the Missouri and other rivers was very noticeable, and towns like Davenport, Dubuque, Clinton, and Burlington grew rapidly as a result.[51] There was also much overland traffic, and by this time the railroads were being built. Blacks worked on maintenance crews and handled freight. The one job in the railroad industry held almost exclusively by blacks was that of Pullman porters. Many of these porters settled in Iowa.

In many cases, strike breaking was the only way blacks could get employment in some industries and thereby gain entrance into some sections of the Midwest, which Hamlin Garland called the "middle border." Blacks came to Iowa in considerable numbers as strike breakers in the mining industry, which accounts for their presence at Buxton and Muchakinock. The town of Buxton was not a black town, but it boasted a large black population. In the 1890s the total population of Buxton was nearly 5,000, and half were blacks.[52] They had been brought into this region first by H. A. Armstrong, an agent of the Consolidated Coal Company, who attempted to settle the strike by bringing in blacks from Virginia, Kentucky, and Tennessee.

Buxton was one town in Iowa where blacks took a leading part. They built many things separately, including their own Young Men's Christian Association building, which was constructed before there was one for the white citizens of the community. Whether the two racial groups could not use the same building or whether the blacks preferred to use their own is not known. Blacks claimed that this YMCA was the greatest in the world. Blacks in Buxton also operated their own bank and many other businesses.[53] Other aspects of town life were integrated. At one time, for example, Buxton had a mixed high school, with a black superintendent and a black principal. Most of the teachers were blacks, and both races peacefully attended classes together.[54] The beneficial influence of the church was another important factor in the life of the community. The various denominations in the town coexisted; there were two Methodist churches, one supported by blacks and the other supported by whites, a black Baptist church, and a Swedish Lutheran church.

In several ways Buxton was an interesting and extraordinary town. It had the greatest number of professional men in the history of any town in the state, among them a black justice of the peace and a black constable. Although the town was on the middle border, it had neither policemen nor jails. Instead, the town council tried to keep order. They were not completely successful, however; an outsider, J. A. Switcher, on an occasional visit when the town was at its zenith, observed that it was a rowdy town and that murders and robberies were common. By the turn of the century, Buxton was only a ghost town. One church and a farm residence were the relics of the former greatness of the once industrial city that it had been.

Gold, which had influenced the settlement of California, also played a part in the settlement of Colorado. Gold was discovered there in 1857, and many blacks were in the throng that hurried to the Colorado gold field. Individual miners did not last long because quartz mining, which had to be done by large companies, was soon the dominant method. Still, blacks managed to find jobs around the camps and the emerging towns, and the black population in Colorado increased from only 48 in 1850 to 8,570 in 1900. Colorado is a good example of how an increase in the black population of any region of the West was proportional to favorable employment conditions. Conversely, such states as North and South Dakota, Idaho, Utah, and Nevada, which offered few opportunities for blacks, had small black populations.

The factors which drew blacks to the West, including the desire for new homes, better jobs, and more freedom, operated throughout this period. It is true that for many blacks, the West did not turn out to be the Promised Land. Into the new region white settlers brought with them old attitudes that were sometimes given the sanction of law. Nevertheless, the West did offer blacks relatively more freedom, and those who went there had a better chance than those who remained at home.

NOTES

1. *Revised Statutes of Nebraska,* Section 54.

2. *Revised Statutes of the Territory of Iowa,* 1843. This law was passed in 1839 at the first session of the Iowa Territorial Legislature, held in Burlington, Iowa.

3. Ibid., p. 99.

4. *Census Report of Iowa Territory,* 1840.

5. *Act of Third General Assembly,* Chapter 32, approved February 5, 1851.

6. Nathan E. Coffin, "The Case of Archie P. Webb, a Free Negro," *Annals of Iowa,* 3rd series., 11 (July-October 1913), p. 200.

7. Charles Carey, ed., *Journals of Theodore Talbot, 1843 and 1849–52* (Portland, Ore., 1931), p. 7.

8. Frederick S. Dellenbaugh, *Fremont and the Forty-Niners* (New York, 1914), p. 374.

9. John C. Fremont, *The Life of Col. John Charles Fremont, and His Narrative of Explorations and Adventures in Kansas, Nebraska, Oregon, and California* (New York, 1856), p. 342.

10. "Diary of Frank Aldrich," typed copy in the Huntington Library, San Marino, California, entry of October 6, 1876.

11. LeRoy Hafen and Carl C. Rister, *Western America* (New York, 1941), p. 390.

12. Charles Larpenteur, *Forty Years a Fur Trader on the Upper Missouri*, ed. Elliott Coues (New York, 1899), vol. 1, p. 217.

13. Annie Abel, ed., *Chardon's Journal of Fort Clark, 1834–1839* (Pierre, S.D., 1932), p. 255n.

14. George B. Grinnell, "Bent's Old Fort and its Builders," *Kansas State Historical Society Collections* 15 (1919–22), p. 52.

15. George R. Gibson, *Journal of a Soldier Under Kearney and Doniphan, 1846–47* (Glendale, Ca., 1935), entry for July 1846.

16. James Dawson, "Major Andrew Dawson, 1817–1871," *Historical Society of Montana Contributions* 7 (1910), p. 64.

17. Charles Russell, *Back Trailing of the Old Frontier: Story of Fort Benton* (Great Falls, Mont., 1922), p. 4.

18. Milo M. Quaife, ed., *Narrative of the Adventures of Zenas Leonard, Written by Himself* (Chicago, 1934), p. 241. Francis Parkman ascribes the affair to Beckwourth in *The Oregon Trail* (New York: Modern Student Library, 1924), p. 125. Quaife, depending on Dr. Wagoner, supposed that it was Rose.

19. John C. Ewers, ed., *Adventures of Zenas Leonard, Fur Trader* (Norman, Okla., 1959), p. 51.

20. George F. Wright, ed., *History of Sacramento County, California* (1880; rpt., Berkeley, Ca., 1960), p. 24.

21. F. I. Herriott, "Transplanting Iowa's Laws to Oregon," *Oregon Historical Society Quarterly* 5 (June 1904), p. 143. The common law as understood in England was based upon usage and universal reception.

22. *Portland Weekly Oregonian*, May 24, 1846.

23. Harvey Scott, *History of the Oregon Country* (Cambridge, Mass., 1924), vol. 5, p. 15.

24. *San Francisco Daily Alta Californian*, September 16, 1857.

25. See below, pp. 106-09.

26. *Oregon Spectator* (Oregon City), August 6, 1846.

27. Fred Lockley, "Some Documentary Records of Slavery in Oregon," *Oregon Historical Society Quarterly* 17 (June 1916), p. 108.

28. Report of the Secretary of War to Dr. Elijah White, Sub Indian Agent, January 26, 1844, letters of Dr. White in National Archives.

29. *Census Report of Thurston County, 1860*.

30. *Census Report of the City and County of Los Angeles, 1850*. The southern section of the area had a few blacks. Los Angeles City and County had only fifteen blacks and one mulatto woman.

31. Cardinal Goodwin, *Establishment of State Government in California, 1846–1850* (New York, 1914), p. 344. Mariposa County had 195 blacks, El Dorado 149, Calaveras 82, Yerba Buena 6, Tuolumne 63, San Joaquin 57.

32. Hubert Bancroft, *History of California* (San Francisco, 1884), vol. 2, p. 248.

33. Ibid., p. 277.

34. Stephen C. Foster, "Los Angeles Pioneers of 1836," *Southern California Historical Society Publications* 6, Part 1 (1903), p. 81.

35. The name is spelled *Vizar* and *Fisar* at times.

36. William H. Brewer, *Up and Down California in 1860–1864*, ed. Francis P. Farquhar (New Haven, 1930), p. 45.

37. *San Francisco Daily Alta Californian,* November 20, 1850.

38. *Los Angeles Star,* January 24, 1857.

39. See below, p. 135.

40. *Los Angeles Times,* February 12, 1909.

41. Delilah L. Beasley, *Negro Trail Blazers of California* (Los Angeles, 1919), p. 107.

42. Hinton R. Helper, *Land of Gold: Reality vs. Fiction* (Baltimore, 1855), p. 168.

43. *San Francisco Daily Globe,* April 8, 1858.

44. Ibid., April 9, 1859.

45. Ibid., January 18, 1858.

46. *Sacramento Daily Union,* April 1858.

47. Theodore H. Hittell, *Brief History of California* (San Francisco, 1898), vol. 2, p. 806.

48. California, *Laws of the State of California, Act of the Legislature, 1833, Offenses against Persons,* Section 55.

49. Herndon Smith, comp., *Centralia, the First Fifty Years, 1845–1900* (Centralia, Wash., 1942), p. 17.

50. Charles Larpenteur, *Forty Years a Fur Trader on the Upper Missouri,* vol. 1, p. 217.

51. Leola Nelson Bergmann, "The Negro in Iowa," *Iowa Journal of History and Politics* 46 (January 1948), p. 38.

52. Jacob A. Swisher, "The Rise and Fall of Buxton," *Palimpsest* 26 (June 1945), p. 192.

53. *Iowa City Reporter and Leader,* February 20, 1910.

54. Swisher, "The Rise and Fall of Buxton," p. 181.

2 • The slavery issue

Slavery in the West

When men began to move west, the area was regarded as free territory that would not be disturbed by slavery. Many people felt that
slavery could not exist in the West because it would not be profitable. The commodities that had made it profitable in the South—
cotton, rice, sugar cane, and tobacco—were not grown in the West.
Both Henry Clay and Daniel Webster assured the country that there
could be no slavery in the West because of geographical prohibitions.
They did this with firm conviction in the debate on the Compromise
of 1850, which, when passed, resulted in self-determination within
the territory on the slavery issue. Others spoke against slavery in the
West on moral grounds. This position was represented by a former
citizen of a slave state, writing in the *Californian,* who opposed the
introduction of slavery in California and other parts of the West because, to him, slavery anywhere was wrong. He felt that blacks had
equal rights to health and happiness and that every individual's duty
to society was to be employed in such a way as to support himself.[1]

Many of the governments established in the West had adopted the
slavery provision and related ideas of the Ordinance of 1787, which
set up a territorial governing system for the Northwest. The provision
of that ordinance which dealt with slavery was Article VI. It stated

that "there shall be neither slavery nor involuntary servitude in said territory, otherwise than in punishment of crimes whereof the party shall have been duly convicted. Provided always, that any person escaping into same, from whom labor or service is lawfully claimed, such fugitive may be lawfully reclaimed and conveyed to the person claiming his or her labor or service."

Nevertheless, slavery did exist in the West, largely because of slave owners who moved to the frontier and brought their slaves with them. Many of those who migrated west were from the southern states of Virginia, Kentucky, Tennessee, and the Carolinas. In Oregon in 1850, about 30 percent of the population had come from southern states. These persons were determined to perpetuate slavery in this new territory, and they persisted despite all opposition.

The controversy over slavery in the West was therefore an extension of that issue in the East. The North was determined that slavery should not be established in the new states and territories which were formed out of newly acquired land, especially the section north of the original Missouri Compromise Line. The South was equally determined that its slave economy should be established and perpetuated in as many ·as possible of the states which were formed from this acquired land. The South hoped that a sufficient number of its own citizens would go to these new states to gain control of their governments in order to maintain the South and its point of view.[2]

The matter of slavery in Missouri was settled with the admission of that state into the Union. But Nebraska and Kansas were admitted after the Kansas-Nebraska Bill was passed by Congress. There were two main reasons for this bill: the building of the Pacific Railroad to the West and the extension of slavery. It was an attempt to effect a compromise between the free and the slave interests of the American Union by prohibiting slavery in Nebraska but acknowledging its possibility in Kansas.

According to the census report of 1860, the black population of Nebraska was eighty-two. When the Civil War began, the black population was still less than a hundred, and a large number of these were free blacks. There were, however, a few slaves in Nebraska. From 1854 to 1857, the territory of Nebraska was divided into six districts, and a yearly census was taken to ascertain how many persons lived in each district and in the territory as a whole. The 1854 census showed four slaves in District One and nine in District Two.[3]

The report for 1855 showed five slaves in Richardson County in the southern part of the territory near Kansas and Iowa; Atoe County, in the same general area, had six. According to the 1856 report, there were five slaves in Atoe County, two in Richardson County, and four in Omaha County.[4] It is possible that there were other slaves who were not reported. Several instances of blacks at Fort Phil Kearney are known. For example, a black woman was brought to the fort by a Mrs. Carrington, the wife of an army officer stationed there. Supposedly, there was a need for slaves to furnish the domestic service around the post, and the woman served as a maid to Mrs. Carrington.[5] Another black woman was a servant of the wife of a Lieutenant Ward, and Captain Ten Eyck had a black slave who served as his butler.[6]

The incidence of slavery in Kansas was greater than that in Nebraska. The first census, in 1855, revealed 193 slaves, and in 1856 the number had increased to 400. They were owned by fifty slaveholders who had moved into the state early and had sought to win Kansas for slavery. But there were also many persons in Kansas who opposed slavery. Some were "poor whites" or persons from the Deep South or the Southwest who did not own slaves. Elise Isely said that the Boston and Hutchinson families represented a cross section of those who came from slave states but were opposed to slavery.[7]

The presence of slaveholders and the Kansas-Nebraska Bill notwithstanding, the constitution of Kansas included a section on slavery providing that there should be no slavery or involuntary servitude in the territory except as punishment for those who had been convicted of a criminal offense.[8] The statutes of the territory of Kansas also provided for slaves in bondage. Any person who was held in slavery had the privilege of petitioning the district court judge for leave to sue as a poor person in order to establish his right to freedom. He was required, however, to give the ground upon which he claimed his freedom. The court then would decide if the ground was sufficient.[9] The slave was not to be removed from the territory nor be harshly treated until his case was heard. The drawback of such a law, as far as the slave was concerned, was that it placed the burden of proof on him, in the interest of protecting the slave owner as well.[10] Lacking formal education or outside assistance, he was usually helpless.

Another act of the territorial legislature of Kansas made it plain that no person who was conscientiously opposed to holding a slave or who did not admit the right to hold slaves in the territory could sit as a juror in a trial when any violation of the act dealing with slaves was being tried.[11]

There were some slaves also in Iowa because of its nearness to Missouri. State records document such cases as that of the black who was given to a bride at the time of her marriage to George Wilson of Agency, Iowa. The condition of the gift was that the boy, Henry Triplett, must be taught a trade and be given his freedom at the age of twenty. This was carried out faithfully, and he was apprenticed to a blacksmith named Stephens. Triplett subsequently became a minister in the Methodist church, but he always revered his former master, Wilson.[12] According to information furnished by his son, George Wilson owned another slave, a black woman whom he held on his farm at Agency and at Dubuque at various times. She was unruly and Wilson could do little to control her. In the southern system, her master would have made an attempt to break her spirit. But in Iowa such action would scarcely have been attempted. Wilson decided upon another method; he traded the slave woman for a pair of mules and never bought another slave.[13] In Linn County in 1860 there was a case concerning a woman named Henrietta. Like many other slaves, she had no other name.[14] Henrietta was born in Virginia and was probably sold to her master in Iowa, although there is a possibility that she had been reared in her master's family and brought to Iowa by them.

The territorial laws of Iowa specified that slavery or involuntary servitude should exist only as punishment for convicted criminals. Fugitive slaves were another matter, however. Slaves frequently escaped from Missouri into Iowa, and the citizens of northern Missouri were so much concerned about them that they formed an organization to help the slave owners in that section reclaim their property. In 1860 four slaves belonging to T. W. Dobyns, John Furgenson, and Chester Cotton escaped to Iowa and were traced as far as Henry County where the trail was lost.[15] Although slavery was prohibited by law, then, it did exist, and the problem of escaping slaves was very serious. One writer reported that as many as 10,000 slaves escaped from the South each year. This figure may be high, but it is known that a large number did escape annually right up to the Civil War. Slavery was therefore a prominent issue in Iowa. Henry Clay

Dean, speaking of the Democratic party in Iowa, claimed that it had lost two governorships, two United States Senate seats, and both houses of the state legislature for three successive sessions because it had not concerned itself with the black question.[16]

In Wisconsin and Minnesota there was little demand for slavery. In fact, there was strong opposition. Henry Dodge and the Gratiot brothers were among the greatest influences in its abolition in Wisconsin and Minnesota. David Giddings, a relative of the famous Joshua R. Giddings, was another fearless fighter against slavery. When the Wisconsin state constitution was drafted, it gave suffrage to all white men over twenty-one years of age, but Giddings moved that the word "white" be stricken so that all males, without regard to race, should vote. The section on black slavery was submitted separately. Both sections failed at that time, however.[17].

There were those who migrated to Wisconsin and Minnesota from southern Illinois, Missouri, and southern states. In some cases they brought their slaves with them to perform domestic service.[18] One instance involves Major Lawrence Taliaferro, an Indian agent for many years at Fort Snelling. He inherited a number of slaves, whom he took with him to Fort Snelling after his appointment.[19] Among the slaves brought from Virginia was Harriet, who was purchased from Taliaferro by Dr. John Emerson in order that she could become the wife of Dred Scott.[20] Taliaferro leased his slaves to officers at the fort, which accounts for the way he could keep a number of slaves with so little for them to do. Later, the major freed his slaves, who were valued at $30,000.[21]

In Colorado as well, only a few slaves were found. The soil and climate there were not amenable to the kinds of crop which blacks had traditionally worked. Still, some of the first blacks recorded in Colorado, in the census of 1860, were probably slaves. One writer, for example, says that Joel Estes, discoverer of the beautiful park which bears his name, had with him several black slaves.[22]

Likewise, there were few blacks, slave or free, in Utah. In the three decades from 1850 to 1880, the black population of Utah increased by only nine. Consequently, the black has exerted little influence in Utah. Some mention might be made of the Mormon church's position with respect to slavery, however. The Mormons had moved from the Midwest, where they had first settled, because they had been badly treated there. They wanted to move out of the United States, but in this they failed because the United States acquired Utah Territory soon after they settled there. The Mormons wanted to go where their religious freedom would not be disturbed, but the freedom that they sought did not always carry with it political freedom or freedom for all blacks. Elder Orson Hyde, writing in the *Frontier Guardian,* felt that he was called upon to define the attitude of the church on slavery, for there were several men who had brought their slaves with them to their new location. Hyde explained that the slave could leave his master if he chose, for there was no law in Utah which authorized slavery, and no law could prevent slaves from leaving. He went on to say that when a slave owner in the South embraced the Mormon faith, the church decreed that it was for the slave to decide whether or not he wished to remain in the master-slave relationship. Nevertheless, the church left the slave a victim of existing laws, for it would not interfere with the law of the land. While regarding the selling of slaves as a sin, the church let moral responsibility for such an act rest with the individual church member. Hyde advised all the Mormon elders in the North and South to avoid controversies over the slavery question, and he told them that they should oppose no institution which the country recognized.[23] By this definition of its attitude on slavery, the Mormon church recognized the right of the slave to self-determination in his claim of freedom.

Richard Burton writes that slavery was legalized in Utah solely for the purpose of allowing the Saints to purchase slave children who might otherwise be abandoned or destroyed by their parents. He felt that some of the slave parents were so devoted to their children that they would destroy them rather than see them in slavery. Despite this, he was sure that there were only a few slaves in the territory. A most important factor, in his opinion, was the weather, which was not favorable to the crops which required slave labor.[24] He thought that another consideration was the cost of keeping slaves when there was nothing for them to do. Certainly, this was a factor in the whole slavery movement and was the reason why slaves were moved from the northern states to the southern states before the Civil War.

There were, however, some slaves in Utah, despite conditions that were not conducive to their presence in the state. A few slaves came to Salt Lake City with a company which set out from Mississippi on

January 10, 1847. The pioneers in the company were John Bank-
head, William Lay, and William Crosby, each attended by a
slave.[25] A list of slave holders in Utah supplies the names and other
information. Daniel Thomas, one of the original pioneers, brought
with him his slave servant, Toby. William Matthews brought his
servant, known as "Uncle" Phil. William Lay had with him Hank,
whose name appears on the plaque of the original settlers. William
Crosby owned two slaves, whose names, Oscar and Griff, also appear on the list of pioneers. James Flake also owned two slaves,
Martha and Green. Martha was acquired by Herbert Kimball, who
took her to California where he remained for a short time before re-
turning to South Carolina. Before his departure, however, he made
arrangement for James Flake to take possession of Martha, and she
became the wife of Green Flake.[26] Another pioneer slave owner was
William Smith, who owned Herman and Lawrence. All of these
men, together with their slave servants, were the pioneers who went
to Salt Lake City and had much to do with its organization and development.[27]

The record of what these blacks did when they obtained their freedom is not known in much detail. Green Flake moved from Salt
Lake City to Union, a small town in Salt Lake County. Later in life
he moved back to Salt Lake City and lived there for a time before
moving to Idaho Falls where he died on October 20, 1900.[28] Frank
Perkins, the slave of Ruben Perkins, settled in the West with his
master. Whether he remained a slave or became a free man in Utah
is not revealed in the available records. Ben Perkins, probably a
brother of Ruben Perkins, owned a slave named Ben, whom he sold
in Utah to a Texan named Sprouse. Sprouse tried to take Ben to the
South, but the latter escaped in the mountains near Denver and returned to Utah where he remained a free man the rest of his life.[29]

There were few blacks and correspondingly few slaves in Idaho,
Montana, Nevada, North and South Dakota, New Mexico, and
Arizona. Bancroft noted that the only slaves in Arizona, for example,
were a few domestic servants who were brought there from time to
time. A few others who belonged to the fur companies found work in
that industry. One case is recorded of a will, filed in 1818, in which
provisions were made for a slave woman, XY, to be given her liberty
at the death of her master.[30] This region was then a part of New
Spain, however, and the woman might have been an Indian.

Oregon was another state where there were not many blacks, yet few other states matched it in the controversy over slavery. The issue was political rather than economic, and it came into full view when the provisional government was established. A section added to the Oregon Organic Act excluded slavery from the territory, but there were those who felt that slavery ought to be extended to include Oregon.[31] One Oregonian, in an open letter published in the *Sacramento Democratic State Journal,* stated that there were many persons in Oregon who favored slavery.[32]

Oregon outgrew its provisional government and, looking toward statehood, operated under committees. In August 1857 a constitutional convention was called for the purpose of drafting a constitution. One of the first questions which faced that body was slavery. On August 18, 1857, Jesse Applegate of Umpqua County said that the members of the convention had been chosen by the people with the expressed or implied understanding that the slavery issue would not be decided by the constitutional convention but by the people themselves. He introduced a resolution to prevent the convention from discussing the subject. That body, he thought, was not capable of handling such a matter, and discussion would only engender bitter feeling among its members. It would destroy harmony, delay the business unnecessarily, and thus prolong its sessions. The second part of his resolution recommended that the committee on rules be instructed to declare out of order all debate on the subject of slavery, either as an abstract proposition or as a mere matter of policy.[33]

The convention made provision for submitting the whole question of slavery to the people; if the measure passed, it was to be be added to the constitution. The bill submitted to the voters stated that "persons lawfully held as slaves in any state, territory or district of the United States, under the law thereof, may be brought into the state and such slaves and their descendants may be held as slaves within the state and should not be emancipated without the consent of their owner." If the citizens voted against the measure, Section VI of the Northwest Ordinance, which stipulated that there should be neither slavery nor involuntary servitude in the state other than as a punishment for crime, would be added to the Organic Law.[34] The measure failed, and slavery was excluded from the territory.

Although the action of the convention seemed to exclude all possibility of slavery in Oregon, the same action had been approved earlier by the state legislature when it was organized. Despite this, slavery did exist in Oregon. One case was that of Lou Southworth, who came to Oregon with Benjamin Seals in 1853. Also in 1853, Amanda Wilhite came across the plains from Missouri and remained a slave in Oregon for many years, a gift from her master to his daughter. Amanda had been born in Liberty, Clay County, Missouri. She later became the wife of Benjamin Johnson, a slave who came across the plains at the same time.[35] Yet another instance of slavery in Oregon involved a man named Robin Holmes, whose children were held as slaves. Their owner, Nathaniel Ford, came to Oregon in 1845 and brought with him three slaves, two men and one woman. The woman married one of the men and became the mother of several children whom Ford continued to claim until 1853. Their parents, Robin and Polly Holmes, claimed their freedom, left Ford, and lived at Nesmith's Mill. When Ford denied them their children, Holmes sought a writ of habeas corpus to obtain possession of them.[36] Judge George Williams directed Ford to bring the children into court and to show cause for their detention.[37] The case came to trial in the summer of 1853, and the children were awarded to Holmes on the ground that slaves had been brought into Oregon where slavery could not exist according to the law and practice.[38]

Slaves are known to have been in California as long ago as the Spanish regime, although their presence then was exceptional. A case in point is that of the slave girl owned by the wife of a Spanish citizen named Ontonio Jose de Cot. Other citizens opposed the presence of the slave and insisted that she be removed from the country. Señora de Cot assured them that it was her intention to leave California as early as possible, and in all probability she did.[39] Bancroft speaks of a slave who had been brought into California from Peru in 1828 and who for some reason went back to Peru.[40] It is possible that she and the slave of Señora de Cot were the same person.

Some pioneers wanted to bring slaves into California from the southern states in the hope of producing cotton there. James Gadsden, famous for the purchase which bears his name, is representative of southerners who felt that cotton could be grown profitably in California's warm climate.[41] Such an ambition bore little fruit, however. For the most part, the slaves who were brought into California were body servants and domestic servants.

The gold rush, of course, made California a focus of public interest. Perhaps for this reason, slavery there received a good deal of attention. Before California came into the Union, slavery was a burning issue. The Compromise of 1850 made it a free state, but in 1852 the California State Legislature passed an act which allowed owners who had brought their slaves into the territory before it was admitted into the Union to keep them, provided they did not remain in California.[42] This action did not mean that the state legislature had sanctioned slavery but that California would not free the slaves who had been brought in before 1850. The owners were given a stipulated time by which to remove their slaves from the state. Some owners complied with the law within the time specified, while others completely disregarded the law, holding their slaves almost until the Civil War.

In many of the California papers, advertisements appeared which offered black slaves for sale. Perhaps this was in order to comply with the law which demanded that owners get rid of their slaves if they wished to remain in California. In 1851, for example, a slave holder advertised in one of the Sacramento papers that he had for sale a black named Julius Caesar, whom he would sell for $100. He asked the abolitionists or persons who were opposed to slavery to buy him, but whether Caesar was bought or given his freedom outright is not known.[43]

The case of Charley Bates is evidence that the California law did not protect all blacks there. Bates had been the slave of a man from Mississippi who brought several slaves into California with the idea of giving them their freedom in two years. Not trusting their master, all the slaves except Bates ran away. Bates remained the full two years, secured his freedom, and moved to Stockton. One day he was seen by one of his former master's creditors, who filed against him as chattel property and put him up for sale. He was bought by an abolitionist for $750.[44]

The case of Alvin Coffey is another which shows that the law was not always enforced. Coffey was born about 1822 in Saint Louis County, Missouri, and remained there a slave, working for his master until 1849 when his master decided to leave Missouri and join the gold rush. By October 1849 they reached California and settled in a mining camp. Duval, the master, did not like the West and decided to return to Missouri. He took all the money which Alvin had been able to accumulate by working on his own after hours and then sold Alvin to a man named Tindle. This whole transaction was begun and completed in the state of California where slavery did not legally exist. Tindle in turn allowed Coffey to purchase his freedom for $1,500. Freed by his own purchase, Coffey devoted himself to business. He established a laundry, and in a few years he accumulated about $10,000. He was so successful in his business that he was able to make a loan of $2,000 to a minister who had lost his crop. Although the loan was never repaid, Coffey was sufficiently established in business to sustain the loss without apparent injury.[45]

There were two cases in San Jose that involved slavery in California. In one, a slaveholder named Ferguson had brought a black slave named Joe from Kentucky in the 1850s. Ferguson realized that there was always the danger that a slave holder might be taken to court in California, and this he was determined to prevent. He sold Joe to James Reed, for whom Joe worked for several years in San Jose.[46] The other case is of some importance from the point of view of the master as well as the slave, for it shows one man's humane response to the potential evil of the slave system. Judge Kincade came to town from Missouri, bringing with him two slave couples and their children. He soon realized that he did not need laborers in California and decided to sell one of the couples, Abe and Sarah, and their children.[47] The judge made sure, when he sold them, that the family would not be separated, since he shared the belief of those who felt that such separation was the worst feature of the slave system.

By 1859 most slave holders realized that, if they took their slaves into California, they were in danger of losing them. In that year, for example, Napoleon Byrnes of Missouri sold most of his slaves in his home state before he started for California. He did, however, keep two, whom he brought into California with him. One of them was known as "Uncle" Pete, who earned his livelihood by whitewashing buildings, a craft more in vogue then than now. "Uncle" Pete became a free man, but he seems to have been happy with Byrnes and his family. He constantly came back to visit his former master and insisted on waiting on the table on special occasions. He wanted to leave all of his earnings to Byrnes, but the latter kindly refused.[48]

Slavery in California was much like slavery in the acknowledged slave-holding states in that it was characterized by both good men and bad. There were benevolent masters who emancipated their slaves for a variety of reasons. One case of this sort occurred in Butte County, where Franklin Stewart freed a slave named Washington who for more than seventeen years had given faithful service in Arkansas and Missouri as well as California. Stewart made it known that he was entitled, by law and equity, to keep this slave and that he was freeing him of his own volition.[49] The transaction of emancipation was recorded in the court of Butte County, May 4, 1852. In the same county, A. G. Simpson freed his slave, Lewis Taylor.[50] Taylor seems to have been one of those slaves who came to California with their masters under an agreement that they would be freed after a specified period of service. The ironic feature of this case was that the master could not write; his slaves signed his name to documents which he authenticated by his mark. In Mariposa County, Thomas Thorn freed his slave, Peter Green, and the emancipation had a monetary condition attached to it. Peter was to pay Thorn $1,000 or serve for a year, beginning April 1, 1853. Which alternative Green selected is not known, but he did remain in the northern section of California and took a leading part in the Methodist church in Stockton.[51]

While slavery in the West was generally accompanied by humane treatment, the records do show some cases of brutality. In one such case in California, a master was observed beating his slave over the head with a stick because the latter had been associating with free blacks. The master was forcibly restrained from continuing his chastisement, but he threatened to take the black back and have him whipped. Friends of freedom instituted habeas corpus proceedings and secured a writ which was served on the master. However, when the case came to trial, the slave was awarded to the master, who took him back to the South.[52] This occurred in 1850, when the fugitive slave question was before the country. That question probably had a bearing on the outcome of the case.

Fugitive Slave Laws in the West

Because slavery in the West was generally prohibited by law, many slaves brought into the region sought their freedom through legal

means. It is true that there were slave cases adjudicated in the southern states, but they were not initiated by the slaves themselves, and
in any case the word of a slave was not taken against that of a white
man. In the West the burden of proof was on the slave owner to
show why his slave should not be freed.

But fugitive slaves created a problem of a different order. Although slaves escaped to all parts of the West, runaways were most
numerous in those states and territories nearest to the slave states.
Many slaves escaped from Missouri, for example, because it was
bordered on three sides by free territory. Incidents of the kind involving two slaves of A. J. Fredrick and R. H. Cabell were common.
Determined to go as fast and as far as they could, the slaves took
with them two horses which belonged to Fredrick and Cabell. On
September 16, 1856, an item appeared in the newspapers, offering
$200 for the return of either of these men or $500 for the return of
both. The slaves were never captured, and if there was ever a court
case, no record of it is available.[53] The Iowa Fugitive Slave Law of
1850 was an attempt to deal with problems of this sort, for under it
the slave owner could go after his slave and legally reclaim him.

The interpretation of the law varied from state to state, and even
from case to case, however. In some cases slave owners were able to
regain their slaves. When in 1859, for example, a slave named Peter
Fisher escaped from Kentucky to Kansas, he was found, arrested,
tried under the Fugitive Slave Law, and returned to his owners. An
abolitionist named Lewis Weld, who had joined Fisher on his way to
Kansas, was also arrested, but he was freed.[54] In one notable Iowa
case, the verdict went against the slave owner and did much to determine the relation of Missouri and Iowa over the slavery question.
The case involved a black man named Ralph who, as a slave in Missouri, had made a contract with his master to purchase his freedom,
which was to be granted at the end of five years on the payment of
$550 with interest. Ralph failed to make the payments and went to
Iowa where he was seized by his owner for debt. The case came before the Iowa Supreme Court, and Chief Justice Charles Mason rendered the decision by saying that Iowa Territory was free by the
congressional act of March 6, 1820, and that there was no alternative
but to give Ralph his freedom.[55] In yet other cases, the law was a
thin excuse for those who would administer justice according to their
own lights. On the morning of January 25, 1859, a man named Dey

took a slave through the underground railroad from Missouri to Kansas. Border ruffians seized the two of them and took Dey to Weston, Missouri, and later to St. Joseph where he was tried under Missouri, rather than Kansas, law. He was sentenced to five years at hard labor in the state prison at the capital, Jefferson City. However, a group of men who had been working to make Kansas a free state promptly crossed Missouri's border and rescued Dey.[56]

The Fugitive Slave Law of the state of Iowa made it possible for slaves to be arrested, but bystanders could not be forced to aid in that arrest. This was contrary to the National Fugitive Slave Law, which forced bystanders to give aid and assistance. Thus, when some slaves who had lived in Boone County, Missouri, escaped into Iowa and their owners brought suit against Ruben Jay, Sr., John Fisher, and Ruben Jay, Jr. for harboring them, Chief Justice Mason, at the end of a hotly contested trial, simply ordered the slaves to be turned over to their masters.[57] This was all that the court could do, for the provision of the Iowa Fugitive Slave Law was specific.

Slaves continued to escape into all the territories until the Civil War. A case in Milwaukee, Wisconsin, for example, was brought into court on a writ of habeas corpus because a black man named Charles had been claimed as a slave by Lindel Hayes. The judge discharged the black on the ground that slavery was contrary to the United States Constitution and the practice of the territory of Wisconsin.[58] Charles was brought into court a second time and charged with an attempt to commit assault on Hayes and resisting arresting officers. Again he was released.

Few cases of slavery were brought before the courts in the Inland Empire and the Rocky Mountain states. There were, after all, few slaves in these states, and in most cases those who were brought into the area were docile or they would not have been selected in the first place. The same does not apply to the Pacific Coast, however. For many years blacks came to the coastal states by ship, and of course the California gold rush accounts for the arrival of many others in that state.

In Oregon Territory slavery came before the court very early. Judge George Williams made it known that he was actively opposed to the bringing of slaves into Oregon. He felt that it would be destructive to the best interests of the men who came into Oregon to seek a livelihood. Williams warned the rich slave owners that they ran the risk of losing their slaves through legal proscription, and in the famous case of Robin and Polly Holmes he actually carried this out.[59] This was the only case of importance which came before the courts of Oregon Territory.

In 1860, on the eve of the Civil War, a slavery case, significant because of international implications, developed in Washington Territory. The case concerned the relationship between Charles Mitchell, a mulatto slave boy of Olympia, the capital of Washington Territory, and a well-known citizen of that territory, Major Talton.[60] According to Talton, Charles was not his slave but belonged to R. R. Gibson of Talbot County, Maryland. For five years prior to 1860, Charles had been hired by Talton and had worked for him during this time at Olympia.[61] In all probability, Charles was well-treated, for he made no complaint on that score. Undoubtedly he left because he longed to be free.

Slaves associated with free blacks who came to the city on ships from Canada and other sections of the United States. Charles knew some persons who worked on the *Eliza Anderson,* a mail ship that plied regularly between Olympia and Victoria, Vancouver Island, and way-ports. On September 24, 1860, he hid on board the *Eliza Anderson* and was not discovered until long after the ship had sailed.[62] When he was discovered, Captain John Fleming promptly put him under arrest and locked him in the lamp room. Two of the ship's crew and one of its passengers decided to sue for a writ of habeas corpus and filed affidavits before the Court of Civil Justice, Victoria. The crewmembers who filed were James Allen, a cook, and William Jerome, also a cook. Jerome claimed that he knew that the boy Charles had lived for some time in Olympia before his arrival in Canada, that Charles was a slave of Major Talton, and that he had tried to escape many times before but had not succeeded because he was so closely watched. Jerome further stated that he had been informed that Charles was being wrongfully detained on the *Eliza Anderson* by the ship's officers. This ship was American, and Jerome alleged that Captain Fleming felt that if Charles did not touch the soil of Canada, he could not claim his freedom and would therefore remain a slave.[63] The third affidavit was made by William Davis of Victoria, a passenger on the *Eliza Anderson.* Davis reported that the captain had tried to have Charles taken off the ship but could not and had been forced to bring him to Victoria. He also made the accusation that Charles was then locked up in order that he might not step on British soil.[64] It was known that if he did touch British soil, he would be free. The captain, Davis charged, did everything in his power to keep this from happening.

The case came before a court presided over by Judge David Cameron. The affidavits of Allen, Davis, and Jerome were read. Judge Cameron ordered the sheriff to take Charles into custody so that there would be no possibility of his escape or of his being spirited away. As the affidavits had asserted, the sheriff found Charles locked in the lamp room on the *Eliza Anderson.* The mate refused to give him up and said that he would repel any attempt to release him, but the captain intervened and ordered the slave released.[65]

The case, so far as Judge Cameron was concerned, was to be settled upon the broad principle of the Mansfield case, which ruled that when a slave touched the shores of England, he was automatically free. Charles therefore was given his freedom.[66] There is some doubt about this ruling, however, because foreign ships were expected to be exempt from the laws of the port. This was pointed out by Captain Fleming, who said that he surrendered Charles under the protest that the entire proceedings were a breach of international law. Fleming demanded that Charles be returned to his master.

A protest came also from Major Talton, under whose jurisdiction Charles had been, even if he did not own him. Talton wrote a letter to the acting governor of Washington Territory and asked him to bring the matter before the American government on the ground that he was an American citizen who desired that he might have justice and that the flag of the country might be vindicated. Talton argued that the British had violated the mutual understanding that they had with the United States regarding the right of search and seizure.[67] The acting governor, H. M. McGill, wrote to the secretary of state, Lewis Cass, and gave details of the case. He acknowledged that the American government generally held that, in the case of a merchant vessel which went, voluntarily or not, to a foreign port for trade, the vessel was exempt from the laws of the port. The governor felt that if such a vessel had a slave on board, a foreign government had no right to interfere and that the confinement of the slave, a fugitive from service, did not alter the case. He said that the law of England could not dissolve the relation of master and slave before the landing of the slave on British territory. McGill said that he had ordered the ship's crew to surrender Charles in order to prevent bloodshed. He made it known also that if there had been a warship nearby, he would have sent Charles to it for safekeeping.

Because of the relatively large number of blacks in California, the slave question came before the courts there more often than in the other states of the West. In its efforts to regulate slavery in the state, the California Legislature passed an act which gave the slave owner who claimed a slave the authority to procure a warrant for the slave's arrest. Any civil officer could be called upon, and he was forced to serve the warrant and make the arrest. If the slave owner could prove in court that the slave belonged to him, he was authorized by law to take the slave, by force if necessary, but he was required to remove the slave from the state.[68] The state constitution declared that neither slavery nor involuntary servitude could exist in the state of California, but the legislature provided for the punishment of those who helped slaves to escape. They were subjected to a fine, imprisonment, or civil damages which could be collected by the owner. This law was rigidly enforced between the years 1852 and 1854. Antislavery Democrats then amended the law, rendering it ineffective after April 15, 1855.[69]

Many persons in California had migrated from southern states where slavery was legal. Some of these southern pioneers were opposed to slavery in this new state because it meant competition for jobs. These same citizens were in favor of slave owners' being able to recapture any slaves escaping into California. This no doubt was partially the reason for the law which prohibited slaves from living in the state, and it was the reason why the legislature was ready to pass an enabling act to the California Fugitive Slave Law.

Several cases of owners who tried to secure their slaves and return them to servitude came before the California courts. One of these was the case of C. S. Perkins of Mississippi. Perkins claimed three slaves, Carter, Robert, and Sandy, who were seized on January 1, 1852, and taken before Justice of the Peace B. D. Fry. These slaves could be claimed under both the state and the national laws, which provided for the return of slaves who were fugitives from labor. The charge was vigorously denied by the slaves, each of whom claimed that he did not owe labor to anyone. The slaves declared that for several months they had been in the agricultural business for themselves. They sued for a writ of habeas corpus, which was finally brought before the California State Supreme Court on which Chief Justice C. H. Murray and associate justices Alexander Anderson and Solomon Hydenfelt sat. The writ was denied and the slaves were remanded to their master. In all probability they were taken back to Mississippi.[70]

A case similar in nature came before the court in Tuolumne County in 1854. A black man named Steve was claimed by his master under the California Fugitive Slave Law. On August 24, 1854, a justice of the peace issued a certificate of ownership to Steve's master, a man named Tucker. At the same time, Steve obtained a writ of habeas corpus, and the case was carried to the Tuolumne County Court. The judge there upheld the earlier decision, and Steve was remanded to the custody of the sheriff of the court while Tucker began arrangements to remove him to Arkansas. Steve managed to slip away, however, taking with him a gold watch belonging to Tucker's slave agent, O. R. Rosen, as well as thirty dollars in cash and a bank draft on Greenwood and Company of New York in the amount of $500. There is no record that he was ever captured.[71]

In 1853 a case of a different nature came before the court in Stockton. A black claimed as a slave was brought before the justice of the peace and fined $700 because he was not a slave in California, where slavery was illegal. A man named Alivino paid the fine with the condition that the slave would work for him for three years. Before the expiration of that time, however, the slave became restless and demanded his freedom. Alivino knew the laws of California and also the black's rights under the law, but he did not want to lose all of the money he had advanced. Therefore, he sued the slave for the cost of board, which he estimated at eight dollars per week, amounting to $1,248.[72] Whether he was able to obtain the money is not known.

One of the important cases of slavery which came before the courts in California was that of Robert Smith. In 1851 Smith started out from Hancock County, Georgia, with the strongest and best of his slaves and settled in Mississippi. He did not remain there long but moved westward, spending some time en route in Illinois and Missouri. Being a Mormon, Smith went on to the Mormon settlement in Salt Lake City. At the outset there were eight slaves, but by 1856 there were fourteen, among them the slave woman Biddy Mason. Smith went in search of gold but later moved to San Bernardino County, California. Because he had kept the slaves in California, contrary to the state constitution, Smith knew that they were legally free. He then decided to move to Texas, and he told the slaves that they would be free there since they were free in California. Biddy Mason was the first of Smith's slaves to doubt his many promises of freedom. When Robert Owen, one of the early black pioneers in Los Angeles, visited the slaves in Santa Monica Canyon, Biddy Mason made known to him her master's intentions, whereupon Owen had the slaves arrested and put in the county jail.[73] They were brought into court on a writ of habeas corpus, and the court decided that all of them over twenty-one years of age should have their freedom, while those under twenty-one should be placed under the jurisdiction of the court. "When the constitution was framed," the judge said, "those who had slaves were given a reasonable time to get them out of the state. The older slaves could not be held because the time for such holding had passed, and those who were born in California had never been slaves since they were born in a free state."

Also significant, because it came under both the national and the California fugitive slave laws, was the case of Archy, who was a slave boy. He served a man named Stoval; whose health led him to move from Mississippi to California in the summer of 1857. In January 1858, when Stoval was in Sacramento to board a ship for San Francisco and return to his home in Mississippi, the black boy was with him. But when the last boat for Sacramento was about to leave, Stoval discovered that Archy had disappeared. He left the ship, began a search for his slave, found him, and had him imprisoned in the State House. Messrs. McKune and Croker, attorneys in San Francisco, instituted habeas corpus proceedings before Judge Robinson in order to prevent Stoval from taking Archy out of the state.[74]

J. H. Hardy, counsel for Stoval, claimed Archy as a fugitive slave. If this claim could have been validated, Archy's case would have fallen clearly under both state and national laws, and the slave boy would have been returned to the South.[75] However, the case was appealed and came before George P. Johnson, United States commissioner for the District of Northern California. Johnson said that the return of fugitives from justice or labor was all that Congress had hoped to insure. Archy was neither. Johnson ruled that the case did not fall under the National Fugitive Slave Law and that therefore it was a matter for the courts. He then dismissed the case for lack of jurisdiction.[76]

The case then came before the district court over which Judge Robinson presided. Nothing was settled, and the case was carried to the California State Supreme Court. Here it was argued by attorney Hardy for Stoval and attorney Winnans for Archy.[77] The *Sacramento Democratic State Journal* of February 11, 1858, said that the case, which had been shifted about so much in the last few weeks, was about to be decided that day by the Supreme Court. The editor expected that a large number of people would be present to hear the decision. As he predicted, a huge crowd packed the court chamber.

The opinion in the case, written by Judge Burnett and Chief Justice Terry, was in favor of Stoval.[78] Archy was given into the custody of the chief of police.[79] Followed by the crowd, he was immediately escorted by several policemen to the station. On the way, Archy tried repeatedly to escape, but all attempts were futile.

The court decision created hostility between those who sympathized with Archy and those who felt that Stoval should have his property. Some feared that antislavery forces would attempt a rescue. To prevent this, Archy was placed in the city jail where he remained until February 14, 1858. Stoval realized the confusion that the case was causing and decided to leave Sacramento as soon as possible. On February 14, the *San Francisco Daily Globe* reported that Stoval and Archy had left Sacramento on the thirteenth by means of a two-horse wagon, and it was thought that their destination was Carson City.[80] The efforts of the antislavery men had failed.

The decision in this case was taken up and reviewed by the papers of northern California. The *Globe* editorially said that the decision of the court was that Stoval was not passing through the state but was in business. The slave was being given to his master because it was the first case which had come before the court under the law; after this, the law would be strictly enforced. The *Globe* questioned the court's

action in this respect.[81] The editor of the *San Francisco Chronicle*
claimed that he hardly knew how to comment upon the very singular
decision by the Supreme Court. He doubted whether a decision
which stultified itself was worthy of criticism, and he thought that
the court had added another bell and feather to its motley judicial cap
and had continued to build its reputation for being the greatest legal
clown of the age. The editor asserted that the decision demonstrated
that California was a slave state, and he attacked the Supreme Court,
"astride of which sat imbeciles as the supreme power of the state,
able to abrogate the Constitution, annul the law and defeat the will of
the people of the state." The editor singled out for special consideration Burnett, whom he called a jackass.[82] This harsh language indicates some of the reactions and passions exhibited toward the
California Supreme Court because of its decision in the Archy case.

But the case was not yet over, and other voices were to be raised.
On March 9, it reappeared with Archy Lee as defendant. How his
name became Lee is not known. Again, anxious spectators filled the
courtroom. Stoval claimed that while he was on a ship taking his
slave from California, D. C. Thomas and others had come aboard
and had forcibly taken possession of Archy. Stoval sued for Archy's
value, $1,500, and sought to reclaim him. The editor of the *Demo-
cratic State Journal* was moved to report that colored people had not
yet taken possession of the government. Later he claimed that he was
pleased to have been able to record that the country was still safe and
white men still ruled, but he added that it might be necessary to pass
a law to prevent further immigration of blacks.[83]

When the case was heard on the habeas corpus proceedings, Stoval's petition was denied and Archy was given his freedom. But a
United States marshal immediately arrested him and placed him in
custody under the National Fugitive Slave Law. Archy protested that
he had been freed by the court. In the furor, the blacks present attempted to free him by force. Despite this, he was finally carried to
prison.[84] The case was next to be heard before the United States
marshal for northern California.

Meanwhile, Archy instituted a case against Stoval in which he
claimed $2,500 for illegal detention in Sacramento, Stockton, and
San Francisco.[85] On March 19, 1858, an article in the *Globe* argued
that if Archy belonged to Stoval, the latter should be allowed to take

him home in spite of abolitionists and free blacks; if not, he should be free. Disinterested as this may seem, the writer went on to say that it was time that the white people of San Francisco asserted their rights and let free blacks and black worshippers know that in any circumstances they should occupy a back seat.[86]

For one reason or another, the case was postponed until the middle of April when it was again brought before Judge George P. Johnson. He gave Archy his freedom on the grounds that he had not escaped and therefore had not violated the laws of the state.[87] With this decision the issue, which had stirred up the whole state of California and had aroused much hostility, was finally settled. The Archy case is peculiar in that it fits none of those provisions which the state and the nation had established in order to control the relationship between master and slave. Archy received his freedom because of the laws enacted for the protection of slave property.

To summarize the issue of slavery in the West: while for the most part slavery was legally proscribed in the West, there were slaves there. Consequently, many of the problems which faced slaves in other states manifested themselves in the West as well. Slaves were brought to the West and sometimes were kept in defiance of the law. Some slaves who fled to the West in the hope of becoming free were tracked down, arrested, and taken back to slave states. And yet there was a fundamental difference. The South, in reducing the slave to the status of a possession, a thing, deprived him of his human voice. The slave could not speak out and argue his right to be free. In the West the black man could express himself in court and expect to be heard. Indeed, the burden lay not so much with the black man to justify his freedom but with the slave owner to justify slavery. As a result, a number of black people did pass from slavery to freedom, engaged in a variety of activities, and so took their place among all the people who settled the West.

NOTES

1. *San Francisco Californian,* March 15, 1858.
2. Seymour Dunbar, *A History of Travel in America* (Indianapolis, 1915), p. 1226.

3. *Territorial Papers of Nebraska,* vol. 1, 1854–1857.

4. *Census Returns,* 1856.

5. Grace Raymond Hebard and E. A. Brininstool, *Bozeman Trail,* vol. 2, p. 90.

6. Ibid., vol. 1, p. 294.

7. Elise Isely, *Sunbonnet Days* (Caldwell, Id., 1935), p. 81.

8. Constitution of Kansas, Bill of Rights, Section VI.

9. *Statutes of the Territory of Kansas* (1855), p. 381. This law became effective September 15, 1855.

10. Ibid., p. 171.

11. *Lawrence Daily Journal-World,* March 13, 1933, General W. H. Teors.

12. George Wilson, Jr., "George Wilson: First Territorial Adjutant of the Militia of Iowa," *Annals of Iowa,* 3rd series, 4 (January 1901), p. 571.

13. Ibid., p. 572.

14. Linn County, Iowa, U.S. Census Office, 8th Census, 1860 (Government Printing Office: Washington, D.C., 1864).

15. *History of Marion County, Missouri,* p. 218.

16. Louis Pelzer, "The History of Political Parties in Iowa from 1857 to 1860," *Iowa Journal of History and Politics* 7 (April 1909), p. 194.

17. Louise P. Kellogg, "The Story of Wisconsin, 1634–1848," *Wisconsin Magazine of History* 3 (1919–20), p. 230.

18. John N. Davidson, "Negro Slavery in Wisconsin," *Wisconsin State Historical Society Proceedings,* Fortieth Annual Meeting (December 8, 1892), p. 82.

19. James H. Baker, "Address at Fort Snelling in the Celebration of the Centennial Anniversary of the Treaty of Pike with the Sioux," *Minnesota Historical Society Collections* 12 (1905–08), p. 297.

20. John D. Lawson, ed., *American State Trials* (1914; rpt., Wilmington, Del., 1971), vol. 13, p. 220.

21. "Auto-Biography of Maj. Lawrence Taliaferro, Written in 1864," *Minnesota Historical Society Collections* 6 (1894), p. 235.

22. James Harvey, "The Negro in Colorado" (M.A. Thesis, University of Denver, 1941). This same evidence is given by Mrs. Ira Williams, granddaughter of Joel Estes.

23. "Slavery among the Saints," *Millenial Star* 13 (February 15, 1851), p. 63 (quoting remarks of Elder Orson Hyde in *Frontier Guardian*).

24. Richard F. Burton, *The City of the Saints and Across the Rocky Mountains to California* (New York, 1861), p. 297.

25. John Brown, "Pioneer Journeys: From Nauvoo, Illinois, to Pueblo, Colorado, in 1846, and over the Plains in 1847," arranged by John Zimmerman Brown, *Improvement Era* 13 (July 1910), p. 810.

26. Jack Beller, "Negro Slaves in Utah," *Utah Historical Quarterly* 2 (October 1929), p. 124. This accounts for her being listed as the slave of James Flake.

27. John Brown, *Autobiography of a Pioneer* (Salt Lake City, 1941).

28. Beller, "Negro Slaves in Utah," p. 125.

29. Ibid., p. 124.

30. Louis H. Warner, "Wills and Hijuelas," *New Mexico Historical Review* 7 (January 1932), p. 84.

31. William P. Lords, *Oregon Laws*, vol. 1, p. 83.

32. *Sacramento Democratic State Journal,* September 15, 1857.

33. *Journal of Constitutional Convention,* quoted in *The Oregon Constitution and Proceedings and Debates of the Constitutional Convention of 1857,* ed. by Charles H. Carey (Salem: State Printing Department, 1926), p. 79.

34. Charles H. Carey, ed. *The Oregon Constitution and Proceedings and Debates of the Constitutional Convention of 1857,* pp. 30-34.

35. Fred Lockley, "Facts Pertaining to Ex-Slaves in Oregon, and Documentary Record of the Case of Robin Holmes vs. Nathaniel Ford," *Oregon Historical Society Quarterly* 23 (June 1922), p. 112.

36. T. W. Davenport, "Slavery Question in Oregon," *Oregon Historical Society Quarterly* 8 (September 1908), p. 196.

37. Lockley, "Facts Pertaining to Ex-Slaves in Oregon," p. 112.

38. Davenport, "Slavery Question in Oregon," p. 196.

39. Theodore H. Hittell, *History of California* (San Francisco, 1897), vol. 2, p. 115.

40. Bancroft, *History of California* (San Francisco, 1884), vol. 2, p. 293.

41. M. Eva Thacker, "California's Dixie Land," *California History Nuggets* 5 (March 1938), p. 174.

42. *Laws of State of California, Acts of Legislature, 1853* (San Francisco: Franklin Printing House).

43. R. M. Baker, *Representative and Leading Men of the Pacific* (San Francisco, 1870), p. 304.

44. George H. Tinkham, *History of Stockton from its Organization up to the Present Time, Including a Sketch of San Joaquin County* (San Francisco, 1880), p. 132. This incident (involving Charley Bates) occurred soon after California came into the Union.

45. Delilah L. Beasley, *Negro Trail Blazers of California* (Los Angeles, 1919), p. 70.

46. "When San Jose Was Young," a series of articles prepared for the *San Jose News,* January 5, 1917–April 22, 1918.

47. Ibid.

48. Mary T. Carleton, comp., "The Byrnes of Berkeley: From Letters of Mary Tanner Byrne and Other Sources," *California Historical Society Quarterly* 17 (March 1938), p. 44.

49. D. L. Beasley and M. N. Work, comps., "California Freedom Papers," *Journal of Negro History* 3 (January 1918), p. 47.

50. Frank Gilbert, "History of California from 1513 to 1850," vol. 1 of F. Gilbert and Harry L. Wells, *History of Butte County, California* (San Francisco, 1882), p. 199.

51. Owen C. Coy, "Evidences of Slavery in California," *Grizzly Bear* 19 (October 1916), pp. 1–2.

52. *San Francisco Daily Alta Californian,* February 16, 1850.

53. Sheffield Ingalls, *History of Atchison County, Kansas* (Lawrence, 1916), p. 334.

54. Thomas A. McNeal, *When Kansas Was Young* (New York, 1934), p. 8.

55. Louis Pelzer, "The Negro and Slavery in Early Iowa," *Iowa Journal of History and Politics* 2 (October 1904), p. 471.

56. William E. Connelley, "The Lane-Jenkins Claim Contest," *Kansas State Historical Society Collections* 16 (1923–25), p. 56, note 14. The "Border Ruffians" were those persons who lived in Missouri but constantly made raids into Kansas, hoping to make it a slave state.

57. Letter to the editor of *Iowa Territorial Gazette and Burlington Advertiser* (Burlington, Iowa Territory), March 28, 1840, quoted in *Annals of Iowa* 11 (July-October 1913), p. 179.

58. *Milwaukee Sentinel Gazette,* July 1850.

59. Lockley, "Facts Pertaining to Ex-Slaves in Oregon," p. 109.

60. Robie L. Reid, "How One Slave Became Free: An Episode of the Old Days in Victoria," *British Columbia Historical Quarterly* 6 (October 1942), p. 251.

61. *Territorial Papers of Washington,* letter to H. M. McGill, Acting Governor of Washington Territory, from James Talton, September 30, 1860.

62. Reid, "How One Slave Became Free," p. 251.

63. Supreme Court of Civil Jurisdiction, Victoria, Canada. This statement was sworn at the office of W. W. Fyehott, September 25, 1860.

64. *Territorial Papers of Washington,* vol. 2, September 25, 1860, National Archives, Washington, D.C.

65. Reid, "How One Slave Became Free," p. 252.

66. The principle handed down in the Somerset Case, as rendered by Lord Mansfield, stated that slavery was so odious that it could be maintained only by the most positive municipal law. Slaves were freed when they touched the shores of England.

67. *Territorial Papers of Washington,* vol. 2, letter to H. M. McGill, September 30, 1860, National Archives, Washington, D.C.

68. Tinkham, *History of Stockton,* p. 135.

69. Ibid.

70. Ibid.

71. Edna B. Buckbee, *The Saga of Old Tuolumne* (New York, 1935), p. 211; *San Francisco Daily Alta Californian,* September 27, 1854.

72. Bates Collection, "Scrap Books," vol. 28 of unpublished manuscript, Bancroft Library, University of California, Berkeley.

73. *Los Angeles Times,* February 12, 1909.

74. *Sacramento Democratic State Journal,* January 8, 1858.

75. Ibid., January 9, 1858.

76. *San Francisco Daily Globe,* January 14, 1858.

77. *Sacramento Democratic State Journal,* February 11, 1858.

78. *Reports of Cases Determined in the Supreme Court of the State of California* (St. Paul, Minn.: West Publishing Co.), vol. 9, p. 171.

79. *San Francisco Daily Globe,* February 14, 1858.

80. Ibid.

81. Ibid., February 13, 1858.

82. *San Francisco Chronicle,* February 20, 1858.

83. *Sacramento Democratic State Journal,* March 18, 1858.

84. *San Francisco Daily Globe,* March 18, 1858.

85. Ibid.

86. Ibid., March 19, 1858.

87. Ibid., April 15, 1858.

3 • Blacks in the military

The United States had to organize and make safe for settlers the land it had acquired west of the Mississippi River. Roads which had been built for the purpose of connecting forts and camps soon bore the traffic of settlers and the mail; they had to be extended and kept open. Telegraph lines had to be erected. And the very best means of transportation—the railroad—had to be provided. The influx of settlers caused unrest among the Indians, and the railroad perhaps best symbolized the threat of the white man because it divided the buffalo which were so important to the Indian economy, made it easy for hunters to take a larger part in the destruction of these animals, and transported an apparently endless number of white men to dominate the land that for centuries had belonged to the Indian. The Indians were determined to drive out the white settlers and destroy the railroad. Some of those who had been on reservations left and took part in this hostility against all whites, both settlers and those employed in the West. The control of the Indians was a difficult task, for in many cases they had excellent leaders and made a strong fight against those whom they considered their enemies. To control the Indians, protect the settlers, and build and maintain the roads and telegraph lines were the jobs of the army, jobs in which black troops played a significant part.

In 1866 the army operated under a new policy resulting from an act passed by Congress on July 26 of that year. The act provided for an increase of six cavalry regiments, two of which—the Ninth and Tenth—should be black, and forty-five infantry regiments, four of which—the Thirty-Eighth, the Thirty-Ninth, the Fortieth, and the Forty-First—should be black.[1] In 1869 the four black infantry regiments were consolidated into two regiments. The Thirty-Eighth and Forty-First became the Twenty-Fourth, and the Thirty-Ninth and Fortieth became the Twenty-Fifth United States Infantry. After the reorganization, the Twenty-Fourth was sent to the West, while the Twenty-Fifth remained in the Southwest.[2] The Twenty-Fifth Infantry has received more publicity than the Twenty-Fourth. The former was active early in the Indian wars, and recent histories have kept the regiment's exploits before us. Dr. Arlen L. Fowler, in his *Black Infantry,* has given an excellent account of both these regiments.

Blacks at this time were enlisting in the army in large numbers. The pay of only thirteen dollars a month seems very small compensation for the kind of work that they were called upon to do in the army, but the amount these recruits would have been paid as farm workers in rural areas was also small. Moreover, blacks had just obtained their freedom, and because of conditions in the rural South, jobs for them were scarce. Enlistment provided a means of employment. As Dr. William H. Leckie has pointed out in *Buffalo Soldiers,* the army offered to many black men an opportunity for social and economic improvement which was difficult to achieve in a society almost closed to them.[3]

Some people believed that blacks would not make good soldiers, and the War Department was concerned that its black soldiers should be well trained. Most black recruits could neither read nor write. The Brevet Major General, Department of Texas, recommended that they be taught reading and writing, and he said that blacks in the army would be much better soldiers if they became more educated. They would be better citizens and politically equal to the whites in fact, as they already were under the Constitution.[4] The education of black troops had been provided for in the act of July 28, 1869. A chaplain, appointed by the President, was to be provided for each regiment.[5] The chaplain was to be responsible for the religious affairs of the regiment, and he was also to provide the black soldiers with an elementary education.

On June 20, 1870, the Twenty-Fifth Regiment was inspected prior
to being sent into actual combat. The officer in charge of this assignment was Brevet Major General James A. Charleston. He said
that the soldiers were well-trained and their clothing and equipment
were well-kept and in good order. From April 20, 1869, to June 20,
1870, there had been only eight deaths from all causes, according to
the inspection report. And in the black regiments, the desertion rate,
one of the greatest problems in the military service, was the lowest in
the army.

This is not to say that all black soldiers were exemplary. They
were capable of crime as well as courage and bravery. In Dakota
Territory, for example, an altercation developed between the citizens
of the town of Sturgis and the black soldiers of Company H of the
Twenty-Fifth Infantry. Fifty or more soldiers shot up the Abe Hill
Club and killed a cowboy. Four privates were identified and held for
trial, but they were not convicted because of lack of evidence.[6] At
Camlo, located on the Denver, Rio Grande, and Western Railroad, a
man named Edward Langlon was killed by a black soldier named
Henry Prince.[7] The records are not clear concerning the reason for
the crime, but Prince was arrested and punished with a prison term.
At Fort Concho, Texas, a black sergeant did not perform up to the
standards of a soldier when he failed to take his detail to the aid of
other soldiers in distress. He was court-martialed and sentenced to
twenty years at hard labor at a federal prison.[8] There is no indication, however, that the crime rate among black soldiers was greater
than that for white soldiers, and these examples of the culpability of
some blacks merely indicate that black soldiers behaved much like
soldiers in general, which is to say that they displayed the virtues and
vices common to humanity.

General Ulysses S. Grant was interested in the black soldiers, and
when the black regiments were formed, he directed General Philip
Sheridan, commander of the Division of the Gulf, and General William T. Sherman, commander of the Division of Missouri, to organize cavalry regiments in their respective divisions. He recommended two officers to command these regiments: colonels Edward
Hatch and Benjamin Grierson.

It was not easy to get officers for the black troops. There were no
black officers trained at that time since Congress had provided that

all regimental officers should be white, and many of the white officers did not want to serve with black troops even if offered a higher rank. Most of the officers were of poor quality. Both Hatch and Grierson complained about them and about the equipment being sent to the black regiments. But in spite of handicaps, Hatch was able to get some good officers, such as Lieutenant Colonel Wesley Merrit and Major Albert P. Morton.[9] Officers assigned to the black regiments had to take a special examination administered by experienced officers appointed by the secretary of war. Only those who had two years of field service in the Civil War were allowed to take the examination. One-third of those taking the examination had to hold the rank of captain or above, and one-third of these officers of higher rank were to be drawn from the volunteer regiments, probably because they could better handle the young men, especially the blacks, who were then joining the army.[10]

At the time the black regiments were organized, the chaplains appointed to them were white, perhaps because blacks had not applied. One of the first black chaplains in the regular army was Allen Allensworth. He was born a slave of A. P. Starbird in Louisville, Kentucky, April 7, 1852, and was named in honor of Bishop Richard Allen, the founder of the African Methodist Episcopal church. Young Allen's mother thought that a slave should in some way secure an education and grow up and be an important man like Bishop Allen. She could not read, but she felt that if reading was necessary for the advancement of white persons, then her son should also acquire the skill. She knew that it was against the law to teach blacks, but she told Allen to play school with the son of his master, to whom Allen had been given when young Starbird married. Little Tommie Starbird played school with Allen each day, and by this method he learned to read and write a little. This practice was discovered, however, and Allen was sent to live with a merchant, who made no provision for the continuation of his education. He obtained a spelling book and progressed on his own efforts. After the war he continued his struggle for an education at the Baptist Institute in Nashville.[11] He was active in education and religion in Tennessee, Kentucky, and Ohio, and he was pastor of several Baptist churches in these states.

On the suggestion of an enlisted black soldier, Reverend Allensworth applied for appointment as a chaplain in one of the black regiments. In such a case political help was needed, for black chaplains were specifically not to be appointed. One of Allensworth's strongest supporters was Senator Joseph Brown of Georgia. Allensworth pointed out to the senator an approaching vacancy in a black regiment and asked him to urge the President to appoint a black chaplain. This effort was endorsed by several ministers of both the Baptist and Methodist churches, as well as the leading citizens and political figures in Kentucky and Cincinnati, where he was at the time pastor of a Baptist church.[12] Brown took the matter up with the president, and by Special Order 428 from Headquarters of the Army, Adjutant General's Office, Washington, D.C., by the direction of the Secretary of War, Reverend Allen Allensworth was appointed chaplain in the Army of the United States. On July 1, 1886, he was to report to the commanding officer of the Twenty-Fourth Infantry stationed at Fort Supply in Indian territory.[13]

Allensworth was not the first black officer in the army, however. Henry W. Flipper had graduated in 1877 from West Point after several other black cadets had tried and failed. After graduation he was assigned to the Tenth Cavalry, stationed at the time at Fort Sill in Indian Territory. He served with this outfit until 1881, when Colonel William R. Shafter charged him with stealing funds from the Quartermaster Department. He was acquitted of that charge but was charged with action unbecoming an officer and was discharged from the army.[14] Flipper went on to become an outstanding mining engineer in Mexico. As an engineer practicing his profession in El Paso, Texas, he offered his services to the United States in 1898 in the Spanish-American War. He died in Atlanta in 1940.

The second black officer in the regular army was John H. Alexander, who graduated from West Point in 1887. He was assigned after graduation to the Ninth Cavalry as an assistant commissary officer in charge of the post exchange. In 1894 Lieutenant Alexander was relieved of his duties by a special order from the adjutant general of the army.[15] The reason for this is not available. He was praised by his commanding officer, Colonel Biddle, for the work he had been able to accomplish. Alexander became an instructor in military science at Wilberforce University at Xenia, Ohio, on March 26, 1894. He died from natural causes a short time after he moved to Ohio. There is little information on this officer, but he remained a second lieutenant for seven years. During the time he spent with the regiment, it was stationed in the Dakotas.

The last black man to enter and graduate from West Point before the turn of the century was Charles Young. He was able to remain in the army for more than three decades. After graduation he was assigned to the Ninth Cavalry, where he served until 1896. The attitude of the army had changed somewhat, and Young, unlike black officers who had preceded him, was assigned troops. In 1896 he was transferred to an otherwise all-white company of the Seventh Cavalry, where he remained for a year.[16] When the Spanish-American War broke out, Young was made a brevet major and was assigned to the Ohio volunteer black regiment. The troops of this regiment took an active part in the war in Cuba. His brigade took part in the charge up San Juan Hill with Theodore Roosevelt and his Rough Riders, and it was active in other contests in the war as well.

Among other assignments given Young was one with General John J. Pershing when he was in Mexico attempting to bring Villa under control. At that time he was with the Tenth Cavalry. When World War I came upon the United States, Young had rendered such good service during his career in the army that he was promoted to lieutenant colonel. At that time, army medical officials discovered that he had high blood pressure and was not fit to handle troops. To prove otherwise, Young rode his horse from Wilberforce University to Washington, D.C. The army still would not allow him to serve in combat, but it did assign him to special duty and sent him to Liberia to organize the troops of that country. This was his final duty. Young died in Africa in 1922. He had remained an officer longer than any other black man, and he had attained the highest rank of any black man up to that time.[17]

From the time they were fully organized, the black infantry regiments were sent to Texas. By 1880 most of the blacks had been sent from Texas and were fighting the Indians in the West. The Indians were becoming very troublesome. They did not trust the white men who were moving into their territory and occupying the land which had once belonged to them. The Indian's view of the white man's justice was expressed by Spotted Tail in a conference held at Camp Robinson in 1876. He insisted that if a contest over land were taken before a court presided over by a white judge, the land would be awarded to the white settlers.[18]

The job of protecting settlers who were moving into the West was a distasteful one to the soldiers of the Twenty-Fifth Infantry, although they preferred it to the unbearable conditions prevalent in some of the camps. The settlers had to move very slowly—only twelve to fifteen miles a day. Weather conditions, the amount of grass available, and the kinds of animals used (oxen were much slower than horses or mules) were factors contributing to the slow pace. Often the settlers were on foot because they had livestock. In some cases, the soldiers had to accompany trains of settlers for a hundred miles or more. When on escort duty such as this, and on scouting duty, the black infantry were usually mounted, for they ranged over such large areas that they would have been of little value on foot. A detachment of black infantry and cavalry detailed on scouting duty from Fort Davis on October 1, 1871, was away from the fort for twenty-nine days, during which time it traveled over five hundred miles through rugged country inhabited by hostile Indians.

Black troops were also very active in building roads for the benefit of the settler, the mail, and the express. The purpose at the beginning was to connect the forts and camps so that the army could move more effectively to control the Indians. Later, roads were necessary so that settlers could move to the West. The work was strenuous, and details were away from the posts where they were stationed for long periods of time. In one case, Company B of the Twenty-Fourth Infantry was engaged in constructing a road between San Felipe, Texas, and Fort Davis from September 26, 1870, to January 19, 1880.

Another strenuous duty was that of constructing telegraph lines. The War Department considered this necessary because the military posts were scattered all over the western part of the country and in many cases were widely separated from one another. Erecting the poles and stringing the wires were tremendous tasks. The work was assigned to the infantry, and a great deal of it to the black infantry. Like road building, this job kept the soldiers away from their posts for months.[19]

After a decade of service on the Texas frontier, the Twenty-Fifth Infantry was moved to a different section of the West. The Twenty-Fourth was sent to Indian Territory where it did much the same kind of work it had done in Texas and Kansas. In 1888 General Sherman felt that the Thirteenth Infantry, which had been in Arizona since 1880, should be relieved. This was done by transferring the Twenty-Fourth Infantry to its post.[20] Its headquarters was at Fort Bayard, New Mexico. The Twenty-Fourth served in this area until the Spanish-American War. The Twenty-Fifth Infantry was transferred to Dakota Territory. This was done despite the fears of some authorities that blacks could not stand the cold weather of the northern territory because their ancestors had come from a warm climate.[21]

The Twenty-Fifth had its headquarters at various posts. It was at Fort Randle, South Dakota, until November 1882, when the headquarters was transferred to Fort Snelling, Minnesota. In May 1888, the headquarters was transferred to Missoula, Montana. Four of the companies were stationed at forts Shaw and Custer, while the other companies were scattered about the territory.[22] The scenery in Dakota Territory differed from that in Texas, but the routine for the black soldiers was much the same. One new duty, however, was the wood detail. Wood was necessary for cooking and heating, and so trees had to be cut and hauled to camp. It was a task that required several men.[23]

One of the pressing problems facing the United States was that of keeping the settlers from settling on the land set aside for the Indians. The other problem was that of keeping the Indians from leaving the reservations and going on the warpath. It had been decided during the Jackson administration to remove the important tribes in the East to lands west of the Mississippi River. These tribes were assigned to Indian Territory, which today is part of Oklahoma. This was to be their land forever, and they were not to be disturbed by settlers. Many people regarded the Indians as semicivilized and thought that they would not make good use of this excellent land, and though the government was firm in its decision, white people were entering this land.

While many persons were interested in obtaining land in Indian Territory for settlement, others saw a means of making a profit from a migration to the land. Posters and placards gave information which was supposed to be of value to those coming to this territory. One poster was put up by Ames and Company of Independence, Kansas. The poster stated that the most convenient route to follow was from Independence to Carpenter City. There was, however, a drawback: the route passed through Arapaho Indian territory. Those who planned to take the route must be well-armed for protection, and Ames and Company had for sale 600 secondhand six-shooters, 1,100 double-barreled shotguns, and thousands of rifles.[24] This poster was a good advertisement for Ames and Company, but it also gave those who were willing to take the chance in using the route much information that they would need for their journey.

A poster by the Indian Territory Colonization Society, headquartered in Chetopa, Kansas, pointed out that there were 17,500,000 acres of land which were subject to homesteading. The organization offered to accompany any group which needed their services. Their poster also stated that reduced rates on the railroad could be obtained only through the Colonization Society. The most revealing information it gave was that Indians were glad to have the settlers come into the territory.[25]

Among the individuals who took a very active part in the effort to secure this land for settlers were David L. Payne and E. B. Boundinot. Payne formed a company in the early 1880s. Those who wished to join and go to the new land were asked to pay a fee of two dollars. Anyone who wished to participate in the project but did not wish to go to Indian Territory could pay twenty-five dollars, for which he would receive a certificate. Some people claimed that Payne took such payments for himself.[26] In 1879 E. B. Boundinot made a map of the Indian Territory and gave information on how the United States had secured this land. He insisted that it was public land and explained how citizens might obtain it.[27] This information was distributed throughout the country. It caused considerable excitement and had some influence on settlers moving to the West and becoming interested in Indian Territory. Boundinot insisted that the land was public because the United States had purchased it from Indian tribes. The national government had surveyed it, and so it was ready for settlement, he claimed. That it was purchased for that purpose was shown in the treaties with the Creeks and Seminoles.[28]

The migration to Indian Territory became a vexing problem to Indian agents and private citizens who worked in Indian agencies or had other authorized positions. The Indian agents were having trouble with what they regarded as lawless Indians. One of the problems was that of keeping the Indians on the reservation, for in many cases the Indians were not as well provided for as they desired. Other Indians, who had not been removed to reservations, were fighting to protect their land from the white settlers who were moving in. These conditions were more than the Indian authorities could handle, and they appealed to the army.

Typical of the complaints that reached the Bureau of Indian Affairs and the Department of the Interior regarding the intruders who were entering Indian Territory is one made by Levi Woodson of the Fox Agency to the commissioner of Indian affairs. Woodson stated that a wagonload of men, women, and children had just passed that agency, and he thought that they planned to settle in the area of the agency, about forty or fifty miles west of the Mexican Kickapoo station of the Sac and Fox Agency.[29] Other reports came into the various departments of the United States and even reached the commander-in-chief of the army, General William T. Sherman. Sherman thought that those who were going into Indian Territory could be induced to obey the law and leave when asked to do so if the law was given by high authority. Many of the officials of the United States, including army officials, felt that the problem had been very much exaggerated. This view seems to be supported by two Indian agents, J. L. Miles of the Osage Agency, and L. W. Marks, who had been sent to that agency to ascertain whether unauthorized persons had settled in the area. They reported that 200 such persons had had working arrangements to stay but had left when informed that they were on Indian land.[30] On April 26, 1879, President Rutherford B. Hayes issued a proclamation forbidding immigrants from settling on the land which had been set aside for Indians.[31] Intruders were to be kept out at all costs, even if troops had to be used.

A request for aid in the control of lawless Indians had been sent to General Sheridan by the Indian agent and the workers in Muskogee on a previous occasion, but there is no indication that troops were sent. Now, however, they were authorized by the President of the United States to carry out the provision of the proclamation if it was necessary. Through reports of officers in the field, the Secretary of War, Charles W. McCrary, had been informed of what was needed. He at once surveyed the troops in the area and found them sufficient to take care of the situation. At the time, there were at Fort Sill 124 men of the Fourth Cavalry and 16 of the Sixteenth Infantry; at Fort Reno there were 100 men of the Fourth Cavalry and 34 men of the Sixteenth Infantry; and at Fort Elliot there were 55 men of the Fourth Cavalry and 91 men of the Nineteenth Infantry. If additional troops were needed, they could be obtained from forts Hayes, Wallace, and Riley.[32]

People who entered Indian Territory were scrutinized regardless of the reason they gave for being there. They had to show proper authorization for their presence. For example, a common laborer, A. M. Singahai, was carefully questioned and was found to have a permit issued by E. A. Hayt, commissioner of the Indian Bureau, allowing him to work for Joshua McLaughlin of Arkansas, who owned a farm in Indian Territory.[33] But despite the efforts of Indian agents and other government officials, unauthorized persons entered. There were many who felt that all such persons should be kept out at all costs. Eleven people, headed by W. P. Adair, sent a letter to President Hayes complaining that white families were moving into the Cherokee land in Indian Territory. The letter also said that the Missouri, Kansas, and Texas Railroad had just brought in a load of blacks and asked that they be removed. It was also urged that all the provisions of the lands act be enforced.[34]

The migration to Indian Territory was no doubt influenced by the exodus to Kansas. The blacks who came to Kansas came in large numbers, most of them settling there. Some were not satisfied, however, and, hearing of the land in Indian Territory, decided to move there. The problem was becoming increasingly troublesome, and the national government had to make provisions for handling it. A resolution was introduced in Congress requesting the President to send to that body all the information which he had in his possession on the unauthorized persons going into the territory, if such would not be incompatible with the public interest and safety. Congress was concerned with what effort had been made by the administration to handle the matter.[35] The President, no doubt influenced by this resolution, issued a resolution of his own. He urged all unauthorized persons to stay out of the territory set aside for Indians and directed the proper authorities to keep them out. The President felt that unauthorized persons who were entering this territory knew the law and intended to take the land forcibly. He made it plain that the widespread rumor that the government would not disturb them was not true and that the law would be enforced.[36] Whether violators would be arrested or removed from the territory was not made clear.

In spite of the President's proclamation, people still went to this forbidden area, and some observers felt that not all was being done that could be done to bring the matter under control. A. B. Hunt, an Indian agent, criticized General Hatch and felt that he was not doing all in his power to remove the intruders.[37] Complaints of persons illegally entering this territory continued to reach the government from many sources. In 1880 Captain C. F. Towles sent a letter to the assistant adjutant of the Department of Missouri, complaining of the number of intruders in the territory. He had tried to handle the matter by ordering such persons to close their businesses and leave, but the situation was more than he could cope with and he was asking for more help.[38]

The complaint against General Hatch and the army does not seem justified; many persons were entering the territory from all directions, and some of them were confused because they were not sure what the law was. Many were anxious to secure this rich farmland, but only if they were legally authorized to do so. J. B. Welch of Elk County, Kansas, for example, wrote E. M. Marbel to ascertain the facts about land in Indian Territory. He lived only 200 miles from the territory, and he and his son had over 3,000 head of sheep and wanted to obtain some of the land in Indian Territory, but only if it was legal to do so. Marbel delivered his friend's letter to the Secretary of War, Robert Lincoln, to determine the attitude of the United States toward persons who moved into this territory.[39] J. C. Dater, of Defiance, Missouri, also wrote to Lincoln to ascertain if any citizen of the United States could settle in Indian Territory. Lincoln replied in the negative and made it plain that the military would not allow any unauthorized persons in that territory.[40] It was plain now that the army was to be used to keep out these intruders.

Among the units assigned to the task were the black soldiers, especially the cavalry, which was better suited to escort duty than the infantry. The Ninth Cavalry was one of the most active units in the work of keeping the intruders out of Indian Territory, largely because it had been organized and trained in Kansas, Indian Territory, and Nebraska, and was therefore close to the troubled area. In January 1883, companies F, C, and G of the Ninth Cavalry, stationed at Fort Sill, furnished escort to farmers who were forced to leave Indian Territory. Black soldiers were assigned to this duty, during which one of the worst storms in the history of the territory struck. On February second the thermometer registered five below zero; on the third it was eight below, and on the fourth, eleven below. There was a high wind, and the fine snow cut the faces of the intruders and the soldiers. Many of them were frostbitten. At the end of the tour of duty, ninety-two troopers were employed in this assignment, and fifty of these were not fit for duty for ten days after the farmers had been escorted out of the territory.[41]

While certain companies of the Ninth Cavalry were engaged in Indian Territory, most of the troops were on duty in Texas. In 1870 troops from Companies G and L, under the command of Captain Bacon, surprised and captured an entire Indian village, eighty-three head of stock, and all other supplies. Companies C, D, I, and K, under the command of Captain Dodge, skirmished with Indians in the Guadalupe Mountains.[42] When the problem of intruders in Indian Territory had been brought under control, additional Ninth Cavalry troops were assigned to Texas, where the Indians were becoming more troublesome. People who were attempting to settle there pleaded with the army for help, but in some cases, as Dr. Leckie has pointed out, they rejected aid if it came from black soldiers. Thus the black troops had to fight not only Indians but also the racism of those whom they were assigned to protect.[43] Troops of the Ninth Cavalry were also given the jobs of controlling cattle rustlers and highway bandits and of protecting the mails and express from San Antonio to El Paso. This was a very troublesome section of Texas, and in some cases outlaws felt that they had little to fear from black troops. They were mistaken. The records show that these troops were as efficient in this service as any other unit in the army.

In 1872 the Indians were becoming restive in New Mexico, and the Ninth Cavalry moved there. The new headquarters was at Santa Fe, and troops were scattered throughout New Mexico. The duties were about what they had been in Texas, but it was in a new field of operation, which authorities felt would benefit the soldiers. In 1885 the headquarters was changed again, this time to the Platte.[44] This was a relatively quiet sector, although there were some contests in which the black soldiers participated, such as Wounded Knee. The effort to arrest Sitting Bull brought on a clash between his braves and the army there. The Wounded Knee conflict was a slaughter for the Indians, whose weapons were greatly inferior to those of the soldiers, and Sitting Bull and many of his braves were killed.[45]

The Ninth Cavalry was among the first troops active in bringing the Sioux under control.[46] They were assisted by the Tenth Cavalry, which had been active in Indian warfare for more than two decades. For the most part, the Tenth Cavalry was made up of raw recruits.

Their situation typified that with which black soldiers on the frontier had to contend. The Tenth was headquartered at Fort Leavenworth, in the lowest part of the fort, which became flooded during rains. Many of the soldiers were on the sicklist with pneumonia and other illnesses. The commander of the post would not build walks to the black soldiers' quarters in spite of the pleading of Colonel Grierson, and the soldiers were given second-class and cast-off equipment and horses.[47]

In 1867 the headquarters of the Tenth Cavalry was moved from Fort Leavenworth to Fort Riley. Companies D, E, and I were assigned to Indian Territory, while the other companies were scattered about Kansas and Nebraska.[48] At that time, the Union Pacific Railroad was beginning to be built across the West, and the Indians were making every effort to prevent the railroad from going through their land. Along with other troops, the Tenth Cavalry was assigned the task of protecting the workers and the property of the railroad.

The next move for the headquarters was to Fort Sill, although there were companies in Kansas and Texas as well. They were at forts Dodge, Gibson, and Arbuckle, Camp Supply, and the Cheyenne Agency. In 1873 there was an attempt to move the Tenth Cavalry to Texas, but the regimental headquarters remained at Fort Sill until 1875, when it was established at Fort Concho. The companies of the Tenth Cavalry in 1873 were located as follows: Companies A, F, G, I, and L were at Fort Concho; B and E were at Fort Griffin; C and K were at Fort McKavett; H was at Fort Davis; D and M were in the field at Buffalo Springs in Indian Territory. Company D was later moved to Fort Concho, and Company M was moved to Fort Stockton.[49] During this time, the troops were very active in fighting the Indians in Texas, Kansas, New Mexico, and Indian Territory. The usual orders were given to control the Indians and to secure the property which had been taken from the settlers.[50] In Texas the Tenth Cavalry's performance was of such a high order that the regiment was praised by General Ord of the Department of Texas. He felt that these soldiers should be given some relief from their long stay on the frontier by being moved to a more favorable locality.[51] His recommendation was ignored by the secretary of war and the commander-in-chief, and the black troops were kept on the frontier.

In 1880 the Apache War, with the Indians under the command of Geronimo, broke out, and the Tenth Cavalry and most of the black troops were moved from Texas to Arizona and New Mexico to meet this new threat. The war did not end with Geronimo's surrender, for some of the Apache leaders did not agree to the peace terms and kept on fighting. The Tenth Cavalry was assigned to find these chiefs and defeat them. Even after this was accomplished, the regiment had to continue to protect settlers and to escort mail and freight across the plains.[52] Like the Ninth, the Tenth Cavalry remained on the frontier from the time it was organized until the outbreak of the Spanish-American War. It was not an easy task because of the civilian prejudice against black soldiers, but in spite of this they made good records, and their rate of desertion was among the lowest in the army.

The battles fought by black men in the military, then, were not limited to those shared by their white counterparts in uniform, and the black soldier served his country well in meeting the challenges of opposing armies, lawless men, and a rugged land. Following the Civil War, it was as members of the military that many black men first played an important part in the work of developing the West. When their period of enlistment was over, many of them stayed on in the new land and participated in various western industries. It is to these industries, and to the work done by black people in them, that we now turn.

NOTES

1. John H. Nankivell, comp. and ed., *History of the Twenty-Fifth Regiment, United States Infantry* (Fort Collins, Col., 1972), p. 6.

2. Arlen L. Fowler, *Black Infantry in the West, 1869–1891* (Westport, Conn., 1971), p. 15n.

3. William H. Leckie, *Buffalo Soldiers: A Narrative of the Negro Cavalry in the West* (Norman, 1967), p. 9.

4. Nankivell, *Twenty-Fifth Regiment*, p. 18.

5. Jesse Brown and A. M. Willard, *The Black Hills Trails: A History of the Struggle of the Pioneers in the Winning of the Black Hills*, ed. John T. Milek (Rapid City, S. D., 1924), p. 324.

6. *Denver Rocky Mountain News*, November 29, 1879.

7. Milo M. Quaife, ed., *The Border and the Buffalo* (Chicago, 1938), p. 399.

8. Leckie, *Buffalo Soldiers*, p. 9.

9. Ibid., p. 7.

10. Charles Alexander, *The Battles and Victory of Allen Allensworth* (Boston, 1914), p. 192.

11. Ibid., p. 245n.

12. Ibid., p. 253.

13. John M. Carroll, ed., *Black Military Experience in the American West* (New York, 1971), p. 350. Flipper denied this charge and said that it was a scheme to get him out of the army (Theodore Harris, ed., *Negro Frontiersman: the Western Memoirs of Henry O. Flipper, First Negro Graduate of West Point* [El Paso, 1963], p. 20).

14. Fort Robinson, Nebraska, Special Order 7 to Colonel Biddle, January 25, 1894, National Archives, Washington, D.C.

15. Carroll, *Black Military Experience,* p. 266.

16. Patricia Romero, comp. and ed., *I Too Am America* (Washington, D.C., 1968), p. 188.

17. Report of conference held on December 10, 1876, National Archives, Washington, D.C.

18. Fowler, *Black Infantry in the West,* p. 24.

19. Theodore F. Rodenbough and William L. Haskin, eds., *The Army of the United States* (New York, 1896), p. 696.

20. Fowler, *Black Infantry in the West,* p. 49.

21. Rodenbough and Haskin, *The Army of the United States,* p. 696.

22. Fowler, *Black Infantry in the West,* p. 51.

23. Poster, May 1879, National Archives, Washington, D.C.

24. Poster, May 1867, National Archives, Washington, D.C.

25. Letter from C. T. Simmons to Colonel J. D. Bingham, Quartermaster, Department of Missouri, Fort Leavenworth, February 2, 1880, National Archives, Washington, D.C.

26. Letter of E. Boundinot, printed and circulated by Benjamin Singleton, National Archives, Washington, D.C.

27. Records of the Department of War, Office of the Adjutant General, maps of public land, National Archives, Washington, D.C.

28. Department of the Interior, May 12, 1879, National Archives, Washington, D.C.

29. Report from Osage Agency, May 22, 1879, National Archives, Washington, D.C.

30. James D. Richardson, *Messages and Papers of the Presidents, 1789–1897* (Washington, D.C., 1896–99), vol. 3, p. 548.

31. Carl C. Rister, *Land Hunger: David L. Payne and the Oklahoma Boomers* (Norman, 1942), p. 7.

32. Letter from E. Hayt, Commissioner of Indian Affairs, Department of the Interior, to Joshua McLaughlin, National Archives, Washington, D.C.

33. Letter to President Rutherford B. Hayes, January 22, 1880, National Archives, Washington, D.C.

34. Copy of Resolution of December 1880, Department of War, National Archives, Washington, D.C.

35. Richardson, *Messages and Papers of the Presidents,* vol. 7, p. 598.

36. Office of Indian Affairs, Kiowa, Commanche, and Wichita Agency, Indian Territory, March 5, 1880.

37. June 22, 1880, Department of War, National Archives, Washington, D.C.

38. Adjutant General's Office, National Archives, Washington, D.C.

39. July 31, 1882, Department of War, National Archives, Washington, D.C.

40. Letter to the Assistant Adjutant General, Fort Leavenworth, Kansas, February 4, 1883.

41. Rodenbough and Haskin, *Army of the United States,* p. 285.

42. Leckie, *Buffalo Soldiers,* p. 83.

43. Rodenbough and Haskin, *Army of the United States,* p. 287.

44. Leckie, *Buffalo Soldiers,* p. 256.

45. Rodenbough and Haskin, *Army of the United States,* p. 287.

46. Leckie, *Buffalo Soldiers,* p. 15.

47. Ibid., p. 16.

48. Rodenbough and Haskin, *Army of the United States,* p. 295.

49. Report of the General, Department of Texas, 1879, National Archives, Washington, D.C.

50. Leckie, *Buffalo Soldiers,* p. 229.

51. Rodenbough and Haskin, *Army of the United States,* p. 296.

52. Leckie, *Buffalo Soldiers,* p. 258

4 • Blacks in principal western industries

The Fur Trade

The fur trade was one of the early attractions which drew men to the West. Those who participated in it had much to do with the exploration and development of this section. Fur traders traversed every section of the vast region and investigated almost every stream and located most of the mountains. Many of the fur traders were illiterate and so were unable to record in writing what they saw, but they possessed remarkable memories and reproduced in conversation the details of the area over which they had passed. These men, by helping to bring the Indians under control, were also of service to the United States Army.

It is difficult to say how many blacks worked in this industry, but many fur companies had black employees. The blacks attached to the fur trade worked in many capacities, such as cooks, personal servants, voyagers, hunters, interpreters, salaried traders, and independent trappers. Some writers believe that the black men in the fur trade filled more diversified posts on the frontier than did any other racial element.[1] To a great extent, this was due to the widespread low opinion of blacks. In most cases, the black worker was the lowest paid, and he was often asked to perform functions that whites refused. At the same time, most of the old fur traders and even the fur companies regarded blacks as quite valuable in negotiating with the Indians. Blacks supposedly had a quieting effect on the Indians and could manage them better and with less friction than could whites.[2]

For centuries, the Indians had passed over the rivers and streams in search of furs, which were put to various uses in the Indian economy. Then the white man came. Since there was a ready sale for the pelts in Europe and Asia, the French, who had entered the West before the arrival of the English, eagerly joined with the Indians in the fur trade. One of the first blacks to attract attention in the fur trade was Jean Baptiste Point Sable (de Sable), a free mulatto. Thought by some to have been born in San Domingo, he was first known as a trader as early as 1779 in Michigan City, Indiana, where he had a trading house. In 1789, because of his sympathies toward the American Revolution, he was arrested by the British but was able to secure his freedom and move to Chicago.[3] The date of Point de Sable's arrival is uncertain, but in 1794 Augustus Grignon visited Chicago and found him there, doing a prosperous business.[4]

In Chicago, de Sable sold supplies or carried on trade with French and Indian trappers and traders. He was one of the first citizens of Chicago, but in 1800 he left, selling his property to Jean Lalime of St. Joseph for 6,000 livres.[5] He then moved to Peoria where he cultivated a farm. Later he went to Missouri and, in all probability, participated in the fur trade until the end of his life.

Although the United States had owned the territory east of the Mississippi from the time it became an independent nation, it was not until after the Louisiana Purchase in 1803 that American fur companies of any significance entered the field. In 1808 the American Fur Company was organized. It was sponsored by John Jacob Astor, who thought that he could do a thriving business by trapping and trading on the Columbia River. The plan was to secure furs from the Indians and ship them to China, where there was a great demand for them. Astor attempted to send some of his men by ship to Oregon by way of Cape Horn; the rest were to go by overland method. Those who went on the ill-fated *Tonquin* had difficulty with the Indians; to prevent the vessel and her cargo from falling into hostile hands, the crew destroyed it. The overland travellers to Oregon were under the leadership of W. P. Hunt. On the trip to the mountains, Hunt met a man who proved to be a great help.

This man was a wandering black named Edward Rose. Although he played a conspicuous part in the settlement of the West, Rose was a person about whom little is known, for he left no account of his activities. It is not certain where Rose was born, but probably it was in Kentucky.[6] He is said to have committed a crime and to have had to leave the state, but the nature of the offense is not clear. Neither is it clear whether he was part Indian and black or part white. If he was born in Kentucky, it is likely that his mother was a black woman and his father a white man. He was classified as black because he had more than one-eighth black blood—the standard of measurement in many of the southern states. Hunt thought that he was one of those "anomalous" individuals on the frontier, someone without home or kin.[7]

But while Rose's origin is vague, his contribution is definite. He was one of the men who were with Ezekiel Williams when that famous trader went up the Missouri River from St. Louis in 1807.[8] In 1811 he joined Hunt's expedition up the Missouri as an interpreter after Hunt had reached fur country. Most of Hunt's men were new; only three members with the company knew the country drained by the Yellowstone River. These were Jacob Rezner, John Hoback, and Edward Robinson, all of whom had served with Andrew Henry. The only other experienced man was Edward Rose.[9] Hunt was suspicious of Rose, however, because of the latter's supposedly sinister past, and he felt that Rose was near the point of betraying the party to the Crows, with whom he had lived.[10] Rose did not complete the trip to the coast with Hunt, but precisely why he deserted the party is not certain.

When members of the Missouri Fur Company went up the Missouri River in 1812, Edward Rose was among them. The company had been up the Missouri before but had had little success.[11] Rose rendered whatever service he could. He later returned to the Crow Indians and remained with them until he joined the Rees in 1820.[12] He probably was with the Rees in 1823 when the Ashley expedition went up the Missouri. Ashley, like Hunt, suspected that Rose would prove treacherous and had hesitated to take him into his employment; however, he did employ Rose because of his knowledge of the Crow language and the languages of several other Indian tribes. Rose did not fail him, and the negotiations with the tribes were carried on through him. Ashley and his party were attacked by the Arickaras, however, not because of Rose, but because Ashley ignored the warning which Rose had given him.[13]

Shortly after the attack on Ashley's party by the Arickaras, Colonel Henry Leavenworth went up the Missouri River with a detachment of soldiers in order to find and chastise the Indians. Leavenworth, like Ashley, employed Rose as interpreter and guide, and, on the recommendation of Ashley, gave him the rank of ensign in the army.[14] Leavenworth stated that he could not find anyone who could go into the Indian village except Rose, whom he considered a brave and enterprising man who was well acquainted with the Indians.

Rose joined Jedediah Strong Smith, fur trader and explorer, and James Clyman, trapper and pioneer, on the South Pass expedition in 1823, acting in the capacity of interpreter, and went as far as the Crow country. Because he was the only one who had been in the region before, it is reasonable to assume that he may have helped direct the party toward the South Pass, although he left the company before it reached the pass. However, if he helped locate the South Pass, he gets no credit for it in the records. In the fall of 1832, Rose was killed by the Arickaras.[15]

Evaluations of the part that Edward Rose played on the fur frontier will, of course, differ among historians. The estimate of Rose given by recent writers departs in many details from the accounts given by the men who worked with him. Many of those who have written on the subject felt that Rose was not trustworthy. Nevertheless, John G. Neihardt says that, during the days of mighty men in the mountains, the names of Edward Rose, David Jackson, and Louis Vasquez were names to reckon with.[16] Alpheus Favour says that an enumeration of those persons who identified themselves with the fur trade would include most of the mountain men, especially Edward Rose and James Beckwourth, mulattoes who became chiefs of the Crow Indians and who were important figures in the fur industry.[17] All in all, documentary evidence indicates that Rose was an important figure in the early fur industry.[18]

Prominent among those who were well-known was the Bonga family. George and Stephen Bonga engaged in the fur trade in the wilds of Minnesota and Wisconsin, and they and their families influenced the history of these states. As is the case with other blacks on the fur frontier, it is difficult to ascertain whether they went west as free blacks or slaves. In the Mackinac Register, which carries the record of marriages in Mickilimacknac Parish, there is a citation dated June 24, 1794, for the marriage of Jean Bonga and Jeanne, both blacks.[19] The fur-trading Bongas may have been descendants of this early marriage. Another version is that, at an early period in the history of Minnesota, perhaps before it was organized, an army officer stationed at Mackinac or some northwestern port brought with him two black servants, one of whom was George Bonga.[20] When the officer was ordered to a new post, he left the two servants behind. They took service with the American Fur Company as traders and voyagers and later married into the Chippewa tribe. If they were servants of an army officer, they were doubtless natives of the Minnesota region and descendants of Jean Bonga, who had come to the region in the employ of an Englishman, Captain Daniel Robertson, and had remained in that service until the captain's death.[21] The origin of Jean Bonga is uncertain. Some blacks had come to the West to escape from slavery, and it is natural that they would say little about their backgrounds. George Bonga said that his father, Jean, had been with the Northwest Company and that he spoke only French.[22] He also contended that his grandfather, Pierre, had been captured at a French settlement in Missouri during the American Revolution and had been sold to an Indian trader at Mackinac. Pierre Bonga was with Alexander Henry of the Northwest Company in the valley of the Red River of the North. Dr. Kenneth W. Porter thinks that he may have been with Henry and the Northwest Company as late as 1802.[23]

During the era of the Northwest Company, members of the Bonga family were engaged in the fur industry as traders among the Ojibways. Besides the Bongas, some of the prominent traders with this tribe were Augustin Nolin, Gaulthier, Hugh McGillis, St. Germain, Brazille, Beauleau, Charles Chabouillier, William Morrison, Michel Cadotte, Roussain, and John Baptiste Corbin.[24] These early pioneers married into the tribe and left sons and daughters to perpetuate their names in the history of Wisconsin and Minnesota. The Bongas remained in business in this section as late as 1866. In that year George Bonga wrote a letter to Joel Basset, asking for help in securing licenses for his sons, James and Peter, in order to place them at Luck Lake and Red Lake, respectively. Bonga also informed Basset

that the Indians seemed "fidgety" and that this had been expected all
along. He said that he had lost all hope that the agent to the tribe,
Major Clark, could do anything about the situation because Clark
was too much under the control of the Indian traders.[25] In another
letter, written to James Whitehead, Bonga remarked that his son
James and another person had started to build a shanty at the fall of
the Prairie River. Still pursuing licenses for his sons, he asked
Whitehead "to make everything straight" with a doctor whose name
is not revealed.[26] Bonga never did obtain the licenses; however, according to some authorities, he and his family remained in the trading business for more than a century. The Reverend Joseph A. Gilfil-
lan, in the midst of his labors as a missionary, visited Luck Lake
during the 1850s and said that there were perhaps a hundred descendants of the Bongas in that area. In addition, he stated that they were
all unusually muscular, with fine physiques similar to that of George
Bonga. One member of the family was said to be so strong that he
could carry five ninety-pound sacks of flour at a time.[27]

The Bongas were highly thought of in Minnesota territory. Charles
F. Flandreau, who spent two weeks as a guest at Leech Lake, wrote
that George Bonga had become a prominent trader and a man of
wealth and that he was very popular with the citizens of Leech Lake
and always liked to relate his adventures. Flandreau described Bonga
as the blackest man he had ever seen—so black that his skin glis-
tened. But apparently Bonga recognized only two kinds of people,
Indians and white men, and he frequently spoke of himself and a
white trader, John Banfil, as the first whites who came to the fur
country of Minnesota and engaged in the fur industry.[28] There were
only a few blacks in this section of the West: most hostility between
blacks and whites was felt where the former settled in larger numbers.

One of the most famous of the blacks in the fur trade was James
Beckwourth (or Beckwith).[29] His name must be placed among the
greatest associated with the fur industry—such names as Kit Carson,
James Bridger, and Jedediah Smith. There probably is no way of
knowing who was the first white man to venture over the original
lands—from the Black Hills in the Dakotas eastward—which had
been owned by the Crow, Blackfoot, Snake, and Sioux Indians.[30]
Whoever it was, William Ashley must have followed soon after in

1823, and Beckwourth was probably with Ashley at the time. He was definitely with him in 1825.

James Beckwourth was born on April 26, 1798, at Fredericksburg, Virginia.[31] His father was said to have been an Irish overseer on a Virginia plantation; his mother, a black slave, was under his father's supervision.[32] Beckwourth's father later moved to the fork of the Missouri and the Mississippi rivers, a few miles below the city of St. Charles, Missouri. In his account, dictated to his biographer, T. D. Bonner, Beckwourth says little of his mother. Whether she went west or remained on that Virginia plantation is not known. We do know that Beckwourth spent the early years of his life working on a farm in the vicinity of St. Louis, that he was later apprenticed to a blacksmith to learn the trade, and that, although he spent several years at blacksmithing, he never learned to like it.[33]

Beckwourth later decided to travel and to do work that he did like. Joining a company of fur traders that included three other blacks, he went to New Mexico on an expedition. After reaching the Southwest, he left the party and entered the employ of Louis Vasquez, a fur trader on the frontier.[34] He later joined Ashley's party and made his first trip to the Rocky Mountains. Beckwourth soon rose to a place of prominence as a hunter, scout, and Indian fighter, and he spent much time with various parties in the fur trade.[35] Most of his actions during this period must be drawn from his book.

In 1825 Beckwourth seems to have been employed by Ashley as a wrangler, keeper of horses, and body servant. He performed these duties satisfactorily. Moreover, he seems to have performed certain other services for Ashley. When horses were needed—and this was very often—Beckwourth was depended upon to supply them. His success in doing so is perhaps the basis for the assumption among his contemporaries that he was a horse thief.[36]

Subsequently, Beckwourth joined the Crow Indians. The Crows were supposed to be the white man's friends, and it is probable that friendly relations between the Crows and Ashley's company enabled Beckwourth to join and live among them. Many accounts have been given of how he came to do this. One says that the veteran fur trader, James Greenwood, induced the Crows to adopt Beckwourth as a chief.[37] Beckwourth himself claimed that he was made a chief for bravery on the field of battle and that it was the wish of the chief of the Crows that his mantle should fall upon one as brave as Beckwourth, the mulatto fur trader.[38] This is plausible since the Indians were always ready to reward bravery. But whatever the reason, Beckwourth did become a chief of the Crows. He was well-liked by the Indians, and not only did he live among the Crows as their chief but also among the Blackfeet, and he had a wife in that tribe.[39]

When Beckwourth went to California is not known. Edwin Sabin thinks that he made his first appearance as a horse thief with Peg-Leg Smith in the 1830s, when they swept the pastures between San Juan Capistrano and the Santa Ana River clean of the best horses and escaped through the Cajon Pass to the Mojave Desert.[40] From the desert they took the Spanish Trail to Mexico. If Beckwourth did steal horses, he committed one of the worst crimes of frontier life. The penalty for horse stealing was execution, either by the courts or the Vigilance Committee. But in the 1830s the San Juan Capistrano and Santa Ana River country was settled by Mexicans, whom, like the Indians, white men considered to be of no importance. At best, little effort was made to capture and punish those who had taken Mexican horses. Colonel Isaac Williams does not accuse Beckwourth of actually stealing the horses but says that he preceded the raiding party to the ''Spanish Country'' as a spy and made it possible for Peg-Leg Smith to do the stealing.[41]

Bancroft's view is that Beckwourth was not in California as early as 1833, that he did not cross the Sierra Nevadas in that year but probably did so in some later year.[42] Certainly Beckwourth was in California in 1846 with Fremont, who took part in the California war in the Bear Flag Revolt.[43] After this excitement, he remained in California for some time and became a dispatch rider in the Sacramento area.

We find Beckwourth in Denver in 1860. Jerome C. Smiley, the historian of Denver, pictures him at this time as a well-formed, elderly man with long black hair, a complexion much like that of a Mexican, and eyes like those of an Indian.[44] This is confirmed by his portrait, which hangs in the library of the Colorado Historical Society in Denver. Smiley also says that Beckwourth was the most famous frontier fighter of his generation and that his body was scarred from wounds received in battle. As an elderly man, he was portrayed as the very embodiment of courtesy. We also find him with another wife, the daughter of a black woman. Beckwourth was then engaged in the merchandising business on the west side of Cherry Creek, where he remained several years. For a time he seems to have been very much devoted to his black wife, who was the first laundress of Denver, but, like the others, she did not hold his interest for very long. After a while he left her and returned to the mountains.[45]

One of the greatest contributions of this many-sided man was the discovery of a mountain pass through the Sierra to the Pacific Ocean. This important pass was subsequently named Beckwourth Pass and was used by gold seekers to get to mining areas and by others to go into the Sacramento Valley.[46] It was later used as a pass for the Western Pacific Railroad. Beckwourth does not appear to have been a miner, but he did profit indirectly from mining. He built a hotel and trading post in Beckwourth Valley and served those who were bound for the gold fields.[47] At the mouth of Fountain Creek, Colorado, there was a fort, known as the Pueblo, which was built by James Beckwourth or George Simpson.[48] It was built in 1842 before Beckwourth had come to California for the second time. That same year, according to Kendall, a group of trappers found Beckwourth living with a Spanish wife near the Rockies. Reese P. Kendall says of Beckwourth that he was a splendid fellow and that his children were "noble specimens in many ways."[49] Beckwourth probably married the Spanish woman in Mexico or Santa Fe, even though he was living in Indian country.

On September 25, 1866, we come across Beckwourth again on the plains at Fort C. F. Smith. A group of Indians appeared at the fort, and at first Beckwourth thought that they were friendly Crows. Instead they were hostile Sioux.[50] The Indians, well-armed with rifles and revolvers, attacked the fort, but they did not gain entrance. Later, James Bridger and Beckwourth were sent on scouting parties to visit the Crows in their villages. According to some accounts, Beckwourth, at the age of seventy, came to his death while staying with the Crows in the North Platte country of Wyoming in 1867.[51]

Beckwourth, then, has been variously characterized by students of the history of the West.[52] Some historians, such as Parkman and Bancroft, having decided that he was a villain of the worst sort, are inclined to pass over Beckwourth's own statements, but there are those who take a more moderate view. Much has been said of

Beckwourth's loyalty and trustworthiness. The statements of the men who worked and suffered with him, including Kit Carson and Lucian Maxwell, testify to the honesty of the man in the dealings that they had with him.[53] Ashley must have found him dependable: in 1825 he sent Beckwourth to St. Louis with about $75,000 worth of pelts. While it is evident that Beckwourth did not do all that his own account of himself claims, it is safe to say that he was an important figure in the fur trade and one whom many of the most enterprising men in the business knew well.

Edward Rose, the Bongas, and James Beckwourth are major figures among black men in the fur trade. While others did not leave as deep an imprint on the history of the West, the names of some have survived to testify to the activity of blacks in this industry. Three such minor figures are Peter Renne, Allen B. Light, and John Brazo.

In August 1826 Peter Renne was with a party of seventeen men who set out from Salt Lake City on a journey to California. The leader of the party was Jedediah Smith. While some members of the group went on, Smith and the rest remained at a camp near a place he called Bernardino—probably somewhere in the vicinity of the San Bernardino Mountains. Smith later moved northward but left a part of his company behind to tell the others when they arrived at Camp Bernardino to move forward to San Francisco. Among those whom he could trust with this assignment was Renne.[54] In 1827, when Smith was to start his second journey to the present states of Nevada and Utah and as far east as the southern end of Great Salt Lake, he took along Renne and nineteen other men.[55]

Renne seems to have been constantly with Smith, and, if judged by the assignments given him, Smith considered him to be one of the most reliable and trustworthy of his workers. Renne had formerly been with Ashley, who says that he sent Arthur Black, John Gather, and Peter Renne to meet Smith and to get horses which had been purchased.[56] Ashley and Smith were so closely associated in their ventures that if a man was a good worker, they would both know about him. Undoubtedly, therefore, Renne came to Smith with Ashley's recommendation.

On May 17, 1828, according to Smith's journal, Renne was not well. It is likely that the climate and the hardships of the mountain travel had not agreed with him. His sickness seems to have been of long duration, for on July 10 it was reported that he had been sick for nine weeks with a swelling in his legs.[57] In spite of his illness, the group still carried him along. He seems to have recovered; he was later reported with the company and nothing was said of his illness.[58]

On one occasion Renne had trouble with the Indians. They had previously visited Smith's camp without arms and were supposed to have been very friendly.[59] Renne apparently took berries and fish from the Indians without paying for them. They wanted his knife in return for the commodities. Renne gave an alarm and shot at the Indians, but he did not hit any of them. Much confusion in the camp ensued, and Smith reprimanded Renne for giving a false alarm.[60]

Of Allen B. Light's early life little is known, but occasional bits of information may be pieced together. George Nidever, a fur trader, says that Light deserted from some ship, perhaps the *Pilgrim,* a trading vessel from Boston, although we cannot be sure. Light was naturalized in California and became a resident of Santa Barbara.[61] The fact of his naturalization suggests that he was from another region and had recently come into California, which at that time was under Mexican law. He might have been naturalized in order to share the privileges of Mexican citizenship, which in many cases included land grants.

During the period that Light lived in California he was better known as "Black Steward." In all accounts he is referred to exclusively by that name, and he is described as very dark, quite intelligent, well-behaved, and skilled in hunting.[62] Light was a trapper and at times he worked with George Nidever. On one trip, he and Nidever went as far as Point Conception and secured twenty-one choice otter skins. The trappers had several encounters with the Indians, one of which occurred with the Northwest Indians in January 1826. At the time of the attack, Light and his companions were about a quarter of a mile from shore; he was the first to detect the Indians and give the alarm. During this and another encounter, the trappers killed several Indians.

The most profitable fur trade was in otter fur. This was largely the kind of fur trade in which Light was engaged. Governor Alvarado of California, convinced that in many cases these pelts were taken illegally, decided to appoint an agent much like a game warden, whose duty was to see that the animals were taken according to law. The appointment went to Light.[63] He was instructed to stop unlawful trapping by whatever means necessary, even force. Thus, enforcement of the regulations was assured and the animals were protected.

Allen B. Light seems to have spent several years on the Pacific Coast. After 1840, however, his actions are not recorded. It is not known whether he settled in Los Angeles or left the coast to live elsewhere. He seems to have disappeared as mysteriously as he had appeared.[64]

John Brazo's origin and his means of entering fur country are in doubt. He probably came into the country as a slave, perhaps as the slave of John Brazeau. Brazo was a full-blooded African who spoke English well, spoke French better than most Canadians, possessed good manners for an uneducated man, and was hardy and courageous.[65] He was also a fine marksman, and on several occasions Larpenture took him on hunting trips. Brazo seems to have had an understanding of both the country and the Indians, and he could sense when the latter were in the vicinity. On one occasion he alerted his party, but the Indians proved to be friendly Assiniboines.[66]

Brazo was a man with strong nerves, and he was occasionally employed to flog men who violated regulations. Once, in the midst of a Christmas celebration, it was decided that persons considered traitors merited thirty-nine lashes. The job fell to Brazo, and he performed it with such vigor that it was necessary to order him to restrain himself. In general, he had a high sense of duty and he always did his work well. When smallpox struck Fort Williams in Minnesota, many of the Indians died. Brazo was appointed to dispose of the bodies, a task he pursued with a kind of macabre gusto.[67] Brazo worked for the American Fur Company and its successors for many years and remained on the Pacific Coast until his death at the age of seventy.

The Mining Industry

Mining in the West was an enormous attraction to men from other parts of the country. Chief among the many factors which made for the rapid development of the West was the discovery of gold in 1848 at Sutter's Fort. As a consequence of this discovery, the economic and political background of the West was radically changed.

The fact that gold and silver lured persons of every class and race to the West is generally acknowledged. One writer has said, however, that although every nationality was represented in the mining population, relatively few blacks migrated to the camps.[68] J. D. Borthwick reported that in some sections of the mining country the blacks were quite numerous, but not as numerous as in the eastern states.[69] The gold and silver mines in the West were, after all, a long distance from the center of the black population. There was little work for them except in the mines or in work connected with mining. And it should be remembered that only slaves who could be depended upon to remain in slavery or who came to work in the mines for a fixed time in return for their freedom were brought to mining camps. The masters of slaves knew that a slave, if he exerted himself and took his case to the courts, could secure his freedom in California. The mining industry was nevertheless significant for blacks even though they were not a large part of its population. For free blacks the industry offered a foothold in the West; and for some slaves there was the prospect of freedom as well as riches.

The first mining in the United States was lead mining, and it was done in the upper Mississippi states. Most of the mining camps in these states developed before 1849. Lead mining precipitated brisk migration into Wisconsin, Illinois, and Missouri, but there is reason to believe that blacks did not go in large numbers to these mines because slaves could not go unless they were taken and because there was prejudice against free blacks. Some blacks, though, went despite the opposition.

The first blacks who came to the present state of Missouri were brought by Renault, who had been given a grant by the French government in 1723. On his way from France to America to take possession of his claim, he stopped at San Domingo and purchased 500 slaves to be used in the Missouri mines.[70] Early mining in Wisconsin and Illinois was largely carried on in the Galena region, one of the best-known lead-mining regions in the United States. As in Missouri, some blacks were brought into this region as a source of labor. Colonel James Johnson, for example, went to the Galena mines from his home in Kentucky and took with him a number of working men, including some black slaves.[71]

Although the lead mines attracted many people, they never had the appeal of the gold and silver mines. Some idea of the magnitude of the gold-mining movement may be gained if we observe those who gathered at a few of the earliest centers of the gold-rush migration. John Wood claimed in 1850 that there were 10,000 persons at St. Joseph, Missouri, who were preparing to go west at that time.[72] Some, he thought, were no doubt headed for Oregon, but most of them went to California. The *St. Joseph Gazette* said that there were on the road 4,300 wagons which, if they had all been in one cavalcade, would have made a column fifty miles long. In addition, on the plains there were about 200 men with pack mules, and, roughly estimated, an additional 36,000 men, women, and children.[73] There were also some who went by sea. From September 1849 to January 1, 1850, 383 ships had sailed from various Atlantic ports.[74]

Slaves were among the property which men took with them to the gold fields. A Major Sherman brought slaves to Rose Bar, California, in June 1849. In July of that year, General Thomas Jefferson Green and a group of other men brought slaves to California and staked claims for themselves and their slaves.[75] In his narrative of the gold fields of California, Daniel Woods says that the company with which he was associated had with it two black servants. These were hard-working men, and one, an athletic fellow, was called upon to do many of the chores which required great strength. He is described as a very happy person who was always singing some snappy tune. The other black servant, an old man called Allen, was the property of the president of the company; he was to be given his free papers when they left mining country.[76] On the river below the location of this company was a group which operated a company composed of white Americans, Mexicans, Indians, and blacks. Five blacks were with the Washington County Gold Mining Company from Tahlequah in the Cherokee Nation. Benjamin Hayes, who belonged to another company which reached the coast in 1850, had two blacks with him in the gold field.[77] Calloway, from Polk County, Missouri, brought with him to the gold field his slave Frank, who worked faithfully with his master for a time but later instituted a suit by which he secured his freedom.

There is one case on record of a mine which was worked entirely by slaves. It was owned by Colonel William English of Georgia and other slave-owning Georgia citizens. Located in the Nevada gold fields, this mine was known as the Old Kentucky Ridge Mine. The slaves, provided they worked faithfully while in the gold fields, were promised their freedom. However, the work was unusually difficult. The slaves were required to carry the ore in large baskets, often on their heads, as much as a half-mile to the mill. When English died, the slaves took their savings (accumulated by working at odd jobs at the mines in their spare time), purchased a burial lot, and paid for his funeral. English's nephew then took control of the property and compelled the slaves to purchase their freedom a second time.[78]

One aspect of the situation of blacks in the mining industry was revealed by the experience of Howard Barnes, a slave from Missouri. He went to California with the Boggs family, which was one of the prominent families of the state. (One of its members, Lilburn Boggs, became governor of Missouri.) While in California, Barnes worked in the mines, cooked occasionally for the miners, and traded anything that he could get. Eventually, he went into the restaurant business and sold pies for as much as one dollar each. Barnes worked to secure money to purchase his freedom on the installment plan. By the end of the Civil War he had not finished paying for his freedom, and he had the unusual distinction of being sued and forced to pay the rest of the installments as late as 1870. Finally, he moved to Jefferson City, Missouri, where he operated a successful restaurant and catering business and where he had the honor of becoming a member of the Board of Trustees of Lincoln Institute, now Lincoln University.[79]

There was much lawlessness in the mining industry, and considerable time and effort were required for the evolution of a community spirit and respect for law. Slave-holder miners who attempted to take their slaves into the mines sometimes encroached upon the claims of other miners and ignored the code of the mining country.[80] In California, some difficulty arose regarding the use of black labor in the mines. In 1850, when Colonel Thorn brought to Los Angeles a number of slaves whom he proposed to use in the mines, the white miners in some sections of the mining field were determined that the blacks should not be so engaged. Perhaps they felt that slaves working in the mines would give their masters an unfair advantage. In any case, the miners stampeded Thorn's slaves and ran them off. The owners did not even have the advantage of collecting the cost of bringing them to California.[81] The slaves thus obtained their freedom simply as a result of being chased off the mining fields.

In general, however, hostility to the use of slave miners in the northern gold fields was not as great as it was in the southern gold fields, and some important black settlements formed. One of the best-known sections in which blacks were located was Negro Bar, situated on the American River. This village, settled in 1849, was destroyed in 1850, when the Virginia Mining Company was forced to drain the river bed at that point.[82] Another important black settlement, located on a mountain some two miles below Goodyear Bar, was known as Negro Slide. Negro Tent was on the ridge between Comptonville and Goodyear. Originally the site was nothing more than a tent, but business grew to such an extent that the black proprietor erected a comfortable building for his gambling business.[83]

Some slaves made rich finds while working for their masters. One such person was Elijah Baker, who came to Downie Ravine from Georgia in the 1850s with his master, James Baker. James hired out Elijah and returned to Georgia, leaving his slave to work and care for himself. Elijah, who was about forty years old at the time, was industrious, and earned money by working for the miners. He could neither read nor write, but he was able to secure some friendly white miners to do business with him. He discovered a rich vein and shortly thereafter was in possession of a considerable amount of gold. Despite his find and the laws of California through which he could have obtained his freedom, he attempted to return to the Georgia plantation when his master directed him to do so. Elijah died before he reached the plantation, and James Baker appropriated the money that his slave had accumulated.[84]

The experiences of some blacks inspired certain writers to say that blacks in the gold field were "proverbially lucky." In 1851 a young southern planter brought his slave to Hangtown in hopes of making a rich find. The two worked and lived together as master and man, sharing equally the labors in the operation of the mine. One night the slave dreamed that he and his master had been working inside a certain cabin and had taken out a great pile of gold. He related the dream to his master, but neither paid serious attention to it. A few nights later the slave had the same dream, and this time his master took it seriously. He bought the cabin and at once began dismantling it and digging under the floor. Before they were half through, they had taken out $20,000 worth of ore.[85] In less than a month, two blacks were able to wash from their claim $80,000 in gold, whereupon they left the gold fields and returned to their homes in the eastern part of the United States.[86] In 1852 Moses Dinks, a black miner, set out from his cabin, located between Jackass Hill and Turtletown and not far from Hawkins Bar. In sight of Shaw's Flat, at the base of Table Mountain, he noticed a gleaming object protruding from the earth and, on examination, discovered that it was a large lump of gold. Not wanting to return to his cabin, Dinks decided to bury it in the earth at the spot where he found it and continue his journey. At the end of three weeks he returned and was greatly disturbed when he found a company of Italians working the ground where he had buried his treasure. Fortunately for Dinks, the Italians had missed the gold nugget by two feet.[87]

Such "proverbial luck" also held true for blacks attached to the William Downie party, which was led by Downie (usually called Major Downie) and Michael Deverney, a Scotch lad who came to California from New York in 1849. These men, along with ten black sailors, decided to desert the ship on which they were serving and go to the gold fields. They thought that there had to be large nuggets of gold in the high reaches of the mountains because those which were first found had been washed down from higher ground. The names of two of the black miners with this company are given as Charles Wilkins and Albert Callis, the latter being the cook for the outfit.[88] They began to climb the mountains in the gold region on October 5, 1849. When they reached the upper level, each man was allotted a claim. The section allotted to Callis proved unusually rich; gold could be seen in considerable quantities by simply brushing away the dirt. The company had arrived at its destination on a Sunday, however, and Callis, because of his beliefs, would not take any of the gold that day. He settled in the town of Downieville, married, had a family of some size, and supported it, following the gold rush, by barbering.

But not all blacks were lucky, or their luck did not last. One individual, known only as Dick, made a rich find. Some idea of its value can be gained from the fact that he was able to sell several shares to other miners and, working the part that he had reserved for himself, he was able to leave the mines with $100,000 in gold. Dick went to Sacramento with the intention of having "a good time." The result was that he soon gambled and drank his money away. Reduced to an infamous loafer, kicked and cuffed about, he finally cut his throat.[89]

And not all blacks who went to the mining fields worked in the mines. Some were excluded or discouraged by racial prejudice. Others felt that they could earn more by going into some other business. In 1851, for example, James Williams went from San Francisco to Sacramento on a vessel called the *Jenny Lind* and at once went to the mines. He first worked at Negro Hill but had little success there. He went into the restaurant business in Sacramento but was unsuccessful there as well. Williams left California and went to Mexico when a controversy arose with a slave holder about a boundary claim. Equally unsuccessful in Mexico, he returned to Sacramento, where he could secure work only on the wharf. He had difficulty with the white workmen and had to resort to the court to secure the right of blacks to work on the wharves of Sacramento. Williams then hired out for work in the southern mines of California where he was promised $100 per month, but he was driven out by competing white workers and did not receive any compensation. He returned to Sacramento once more and opened a junk shop but soon sold it and entered the express business, in which he remained until 1859. In that year he went into the business of furnishing supplies for miners in California and Montana.[90]

Frank Soule, John Gihon, and James Nisbet suggest that a considerable number of blacks arrived in San Francisco for the purpose of going on to the mines but instead secured work in the city. Many of them remained in San Francisco and worked in hotels and boarding houses. To serve the miners, hotels were set up almost everywhere. William H. Brewer tells of a trip that he made from the San Joaquin River to a mining field in the Tehachapi Valley where he found a hotel which served the miners and other workers. It had workers of a variety of races: the proprietor was Scottish, the cooks were Chinese, the waiters were blacks, and the stable boy was a Digger Indian.[91] Other blacks went into the restaurant business. One miner has given us an idea of the cost of a "breakfast on the hills": one box of sardines cost sixteen dollars; one pound of hard bread was two dollars;

one pound of butter, six dollars; one-half pound of cheese, three dollars; and one bottle of ale, sixteen dollars.[92] Perhaps these prices were not typical, but produce costs were high and those merchants who could secure food were able to charge exorbitant prices for it. It also cost a great deal to secure foodstuffs from the producers.

Still other blacks invested in mines and formed companies. Robert Anthony owned the first quartz mine in California, located between Yuba and Dry Cut.[93] In Brown Valley, Yerba County, the Rare Ripe Gold and Silver Mining Company was organized by blacks to mine both gold and silver. As the days of placer mining came to a close, only those who could provide equipment to enter quartz mining could hope to succeed. The old Rare Ripe Company was a corporation established to engage in quartz mining, and it possessed the kind of equipment to do an excellent job. This company offered the public 300 shares of its stock, and the editor of the *San Francisco Elevator* noted that the prospectus looked promising.[94] In 1865 the Convention of Colored Citizens of California reported that there were three mining companies; two were doing well and had good balances. Joseph Batty, an English boy who had come to America and worked as a clerk in Baltimore before going west to seek his fortune, has related his experience with a black mine owner. The owner offered Batty a partnership and was willing to allow him to share his cabin. Batty accepted the offer temporarily because he had no place to go, but he said that living with a black man revolted him. Despite his black partner's hospitality, the English boy finally left his cabin.[95]

Although important, silver mining did not have the lure of gold mining and influenced the population movement less. The method of mining silver might have been one reason why it was less attractive. Placer mining had ended and the companies had to do the work, resulting in little for the individual miner. Blacks participated in silver mining, but not as prominently as in gold mining because they had to work for an organization rather than as individuals. Those blacks listed as miners by the census reports of Nevada, Montana, and Colorado were probably silver miners. They include Benjamin Fort, a washerman who in 1870 owned a bit of real property valued at $300 and personal property valued at $600. Also in 1870, in Benton City, Chouteau County, Montana, M. D. Clark, Tom Clark, Gus Thornton, Berry and David Clark, and William Edward were working as gulch miners, and Miles Litchfield was working as a miner in Salt Lake City. In 1860 David Overton and U. L. Chaperson were employed in the mines in Carson City in Utah Territory.[96]

In 1873 F. H. Grice, a black man of Salt Lake City, wrote to the editor of the *San Francisco Elevator* that he had been at the mines most of the past season, that the prospects for blacks in Utah were excellent, and that, if all went well, money would be made the following year. The Elevator Mine had been sold for the sum of $15,000 and the company had invested in some capital prospects in the Big Cottonwood mining district. Other black-owned mines mentioned by Grice were the Rare Ripe Company and the Sweet Vengeance Mine.[97] In another issue, the *Elevator* also noted the success of Lewis Walker, an old resident of Idaho Territory; his prosperity is confirmed by his purchase of land in Portland.[98]

After the California rush, the most spectacular and romantic gold rush was that of Colorado. One of the most significant figures in the gold mines of Colorado was Clara Brown, a former slave. Born in Kentucky, she was no longer a young woman when, after years of toil, she purchased her freedom. She joined the procession of gold seekers in Gregory Gulch and cooked and washed for the miners. The returns for her work were such that she was able, within a few years, to bring to Colorado her relatives from Kentucky. Clara Brown invested some of her money in mine property and contributed a great portion of her savings to charity in Central City.[99] The *Rocky Mountain News,* in an article which appeared in 1880, said that Aunt Clara Brown, the colored woman who had a state, if not a national, reputation as a successful mine owner and philanthropist, was in camp looking over some of her properties.[100] In the 1870s she was one of the first blacks to be elected a member of the Colorado Pioneer Association, and she was buried with honors by the association in 1883.[101]

Among the blacks who came to Colorado in search of gold and silver were the members of a small party who came with other prospectors during the early years of the history of Summit County. Finding sentiment strongly against them, they banded together for self-protection and later took claims in French Gulch. The prospect proved very profitable, but they were forced from this location by large numbers of white miners who wanted that section. The black miners took claim on a hill which proved to be a very great find. The name "Nigger Hill" was given to this settlement as a badge of derision, but the attitude toward it changed when it proved profitable. The hill extended between French and Indian gulches, about eight miles from the timber line of Bald Mountain. There were many important mining properties on this mountain and many declivities which were developed as fast as capital became available.[102] In Hinsdale County as well, blacks were operating a mine, the Morning Star Mine.[103] In Walsenburg, black miners were employed to work in the mines but left for reasons unknown.[104]

Records of mining activities in Colorado contain the names of blacks such as John W. Dobbs, known as the "Uncle Tom of the Rockies." He was born a slave on a Georgia plantation and remained there until 1884. In that year he and his wife came to Walsenburg, Colorado, where he worked in the mines. Later he settled on a homestead and took timber for use in the mines.[105] And there was Edwin Sanderlin of Denver, who retired from the barbering business by 1890 and then devoted his attention to his mining and farming interests. He was one of the first blacks to come to Colorado during the Pike's Peak excitement.[106] Sanderlin was probably the best-known black in Denver because of his business ability and success as a miner. John Frazier was a black prospector who struck a rich find on Brown Mountain. His lode was called Black Prince and contained 300-ounce ore.[107]. In 1880 a correspondent of the *Rocky Mountain News* reported that a half-dozen wealthy capitalists were in Georgetown, dining, wining, and carriage-riding "Black Jim." Jim was born a slave in North Carolina, where he lived until he came to Colorado. He owned a thick vein of ore near Decatur which netted a thousand dollars to the ton. Jim was offered $100,000 for his claim, but he refused.[108]

The courtesies bestowed upon Black Jim were no doubt testimony to men's avarice. But the mining industry did influence the social life of the West, and in general whites in the mining country exhibited more tolerance of blacks than was usual in the eastern states. To say this, however, is perhaps more to criticize the East than to praise the West. If blacks in the West could gamble in the same parlors where whites played, they could not sit at the same table; and if they wished to be served a meal, they were allowed to sit at the dining table only after the whites had gone.

The Cattle Industry

The cattle industry constitutes one of the more fascinating and romantic phases of economic and social life on the western frontier. It began its great expansion following the Civil War. Soldiers who returned to the Southwest found their farms in deplorable condition, and many had to find new means of gaining a livelihood. They had learned that the price of beef was higher in the North than in Texas, but they were faced with the problem of how to get cattle to the market. Many difficulties faced both cattle and men on the long drive through mountains, forests, and over the fields of hostile farmers. In 1866 the first attempt was made to drive cattle from Texas to Sedalia, Missouri, terminus of the Missouri Pacific, but the drive was unsuccessful because of the hardships experienced.

In 1867 two new factors influenced the cattle industry. One was the decision of the Kansas Pacific Railroad Company to push its tracks out to the Great Plains so that the railroad reached Topeka and Abilene. The second, related to the first, was a young cattleman from central Illinois, Joseph G. McCoy, who saw the opportunity of making Abilene a loading point for cattle. He built pens there and sent out messengers, urging cattlemen on the plains to bring their cattle to Abilene, since the new terminus of the Kansas Pacific meant that they did not have to pass through agricultural settlements and thereby incur difficulties with farmers.

All the cattle which were driven north could not be kept on one trail; they had to graze along the way, and they had to be supplied with water. As a result, many trails were developed. As railroads pushed westward, new towns, such as Dodge City, Wichita, Newton, and Junction City, sprang up on the Kansas plains. They became competing terminal points for alternate trails. The Kansas Trail ended at Dodge City, the Goodnight-Loving went through New Mexico to Cheyenne, and the Chisholm, the most famous of all, developed alternate terminal points at Abilene and Dodge City. In order to drive cattle over the long distances north, an "outfit" had to be organized. Most outfits consisted of a foreman and from three to a dozen cowboys and cowhands, a cook, and a "remuda" man. The foreman, who was the owner or someone in whom the owner had absolute confidence, was in charge of the cattle. Cowboys differed from cowhands in that the latter did almost any kind of work which might be required on the trail or the ranch, while the former were not asked to do the more menial kinds of jobs. The cook presided over one of the more important pieces of equipment, the chuck wagon, which, with its pots, pans, and provisions, usually led the procession on the drives across the plains. The remuda men were in charge of the extra horses which had to be brought along. They had to be good wranglers, for it was their duty to attend to the saddle horses on the entire trip and remain far enough back to see that no animals were lost.

Almost every aspect of the cattle industry has been portrayed in song, story, and historical account, and the lives of cowboys, rustlers, and cattle barons, on the plains and on the long drive, have been described in detail. But the part that blacks played has not been fully recounted. While the workers on the cattle range were mainly of English, Scottish, and Irish descent, the Southwest added many hands of Mexican and a number of Indian and black extraction.[109] The black cowboy was by no means a principal figure, but he was always among those who shared the hardships of this typically American industry. Usually blacks worked as cooks, but they also served as cowhands and remuda men.[110] A few were cowboys.

There are accounts of various early settlers who employed black cowhands on their ranches during antebellum days. James H. Baker, in San Saba County, Texas, was one of these. Baker moved to Texas early enough to associate with Sam Houston and was known as a "Sam Houston man." He moved his young family and his slaves to Bastrop County in the early 1840s and began to raise cattle and horses. In time his herd increased to great proportions. Given a land grant by Houston for his years of service, he selected a spot on the San Saba River which in later years became known as Baker Valley. On his death, his sons, Jim and George Baker, took over the business and had a mixed group of cowhands consisting of blacks, whites, and Mexicans. About one-third of them were black.[111]

One group of blacks inadvertently helped create the term "mavericking." The practice took its name from the Maverick family, which set out from North Carolina for Texas in December 1837 and settled in San Antonio, where Samuel, the head of the family, practiced law. In 1845 a neighbor, in debt to Maverick in the amount of $1,200, offered to pay his debt with 400 head of cattle. Maverick did not want the cattle, but it was that or nothing, and so he reluctantly took them and put them in the custody of one of his black families (which was practically free) while he returned to San Antonio. The cattle were left to graze and fatten on the open plain. Many accounts state that the blacks were so indolent that they paid no attention to them. But the poor management of the cattle was not to be blamed wholly on the blacks, who had an interest in the enterprise but had little authority to protect the cattle from marauders. George Maverick explained that his slaves were driven off the cattle range by rustlers with threats to their lives. As a result, the cattle were neither protected nor branded. Consequently, their unbranded yearlings were claimed by anyone who wished to brand them. Thus arose the term ''mavericking'' as applied to branding and collecting unbranded cattle.[112]

By the heyday of the long drives in the 1870s and 1880s, blacks were a common sight on the trails. Nonetheless, they did encounter prejudice. There were many men in Texas who hated a black as much as they did a Yankee. Poll Allen, the leading cowboy with John Husley's outfit, was such a man. When, in 1878, Husley picked up an unidentified black who wanted to work and brought him to the Twenty-Two Ranch, Allen objected. During a drive to Kansas, he would not allow the black to eat or sleep anywhere near the rest of the outfit. Finally, Allen ran him off by shooting at him. In accordance with the custom of the region, no questions were asked.[113]

The first person killed in Dodge City was a black man known only as ''Texas.'' He was part of a crowd that had gathered to watch some local excitement. Several shots were fired over the heads of the crowd; one, however, was aimed at Texas, and it killed him instantly. The killer was not known until several years later when a white gambler called ''Denver'' began to boast that he had fired the shot that killed Texas.[114] It is not known whether he was punished for this crime or what his motive was.

Despite attitudes of this sort, friendships between blacks and whites often developed on the trail because of the individual abilities of each. One famous Texas cowboy, for example, Charles A. Siringo, had good relations with black cowhands and cowboys. In the spring of 1875, Siringo had an argument with Sam Grant, a cowboy known as a killer of blacks. Siringo was wounded in the knee by a shot from Grant's sixshooter, but his life was saved by a black cowboy named Liege who, on hearing the report of the gun, galloped out of the heavy timber and brush. Siringo also seems to have had a friendship with a black named Gabe. On a trip up the Chisholm Trail in the early spring of 1876, the two slept apart from the other cowboys and shared whatever they had, including corn which they had found and parched together.[115]

Some black cowboys became local legends. Henry Beckwith was one. A black of mixed Indian, Mexican, and Caucasian descent, he was a short, round-shouldered man with a chest much like that of a panther. Beckwith worked for Bob Ringling, who owned the s.o. brand. He had a habit of rising before daylight. For some reason he always slept in the bushes some distance from the other men. A Mexican cowboy who worked with Beckwith for eight years never saw him with bedding. The Mexican believed that he was so close to the wild animals that he needed little sleep.[116]

A well-known cowboy who grew up during the Civil War was Emanuel Organ, called Texas's greatest black cowboy of the 1870s.[117] He was born in Tennessee in 1848 and was moved to Texas in 1853 by his owner, who settled on Bushy Creek. Here Organ grew up, married, and became the father of seven boys and three girls. At first he was interested in farming but later began to ride wild horses and punch cattle—two occupations which went well together. The cattle industry in his day was a tough one, and he was away from home sometimes for months at a time, riding the Old Santa Fe, the Goodnight-Loving, and the Chisholm trails with herds of Texas cattle. To comprehend the hardships endured by the cowboy, one has simply to note that at times Organ was without water, except what he could obtain from cow tracks, and many times he slept on frozen ground with only his saddle blanket for a pillow. But he proved himself superior to these rigors. He was good at catching, taming, and training wild broncos into good cowhorses. He could not read, but he knew almost every stream between the Texas, Colorado, and Snake rivers. In the latter part of his life, he was employed to bring cattle to market for slaughtering. Organ rode horses until about six months before his death at the age of ninety.[118]

Williamson County, Texas, produced an outstanding black cowboy in Bill Pickett, one of the first to gain widespread fame for bulldogging cattle. Pickett worked for the 101 Ranch and introduced the art of bulldogging a steer from a running horse. A very small but unusually strong man, his technique in handling steers has not been surpassed. His most famous feat, which placed him in a class by himself, was to grip a steer's nose with his teeth while throwing him.[119] His feats are still the talk of those who handle cattle in that section of Texas.

Another famous black cowboy was Nat Love. He was born in Ohio, far from the cow country, and he did not arrive in Dodge City until 1869 when he started looking for a job. Love went among some cowboys and, after being forced to give a demonstration of his riding ability, got a job with the Duval Ranch, whose brand was the "Pig Pen."[120] Nicknamed "Red River Dick," Love remained with the Duval Ranch for three years and rode the Kansas Trail to Dodge City regularly until 1872. In that year he was hired by the Gallanger Company, whose immense ranch was located on the Gila River in southern Arizona. Love became one of the most trusted men in that outfit and took part in all the big roundups throughout western Texas and Arizona. He learned Spanish and was made a brand reader. Brand readers attended all roundups and cutouts to pick out cattle belonging to the home ranch. They had to be able to ascertain whether or not the brand had been altered and to supervise the branding of their ranch's cattle.

In 1876 in Deadwood, Arizona, a group of gamblers and miners collected a purse of $200 for a Fourth of July roping contest. Cowboys gathered from many miles around. Six blacks, including Love, were among them. The contest consisted of roping and saddling a mustang and riding him in the shortest time. It did not last long, for Love succeeded in nine minutes, a record that held until he left the range. From that time on, he was known as "Deadwood Dick."[121]

Nat Love had many other uncommon experiences, accounts of which fortunately have been preserved. He met Billy the Kid several times and was at the Maxwell Ranch the night the Kid was killed.[122] He also had several fights with Indians. On his first trip south from Dodge City with the Duval outfit, he engaged in a skirmish on October 4, 1876. While out rounding up stray cattle, he encountered Chief Yellow Dog's tribe, made up mainly of half-breeds with a large percentage of Negro blood. Love fought until he was overpowered by numbers, but he did not give up until he had killed many braves. He was not killed by them but was held prisoner, a fact which he attributed to the bravery that he had shown.

One of the most famous of the black cowboys was "Eighty" John Wallace, so called because he came to the western part of Texas in the dust of a herd of Clay Mann's cattle which had the number 80 branded on their sides from backbone to belly.[123] Wallace was born in 1860 in Victoria County, Texas, of slave parents and knew only cow-work, having been reared in one of the principal cattle areas of the state. When he reached the age of fifteen, he was working for wages. At seventeen he made the first long trip from Victoria through Indian country with a cattle outfit. Wallace began to work for Sam Gholson, veteran Indian fighter and cowman, but he did not remain with Gholson for long, for he soon joined the UWN outfit, owned by John Nunn. This was an important outfit that at times had more than 8,000 head of cattle on the range. Nunn, who did not allow his cowboys to sue profanity, was most fatherly toward all his workers, including the young black.[124] Wallace worked for him for sixteen months and later rejoined the Clay Mann outfit, where he remained for fourteen years. There he saw every phase of the cattle industry and almost every section of the cattle frontier.

Wallace also worked for several other cattle barons who became famous in the industry, among them Wingfield Scott, Gus O'Keefe, the Slaughter brothers, Bush and Tillar, Sug Robertson, and the Elwoods of Spade Ranch.[125] Early in the 1880s he realized that the cattle industry was changing and that the days of the open range and free grass were over. Anyone who wanted to stay in the business would have to buy land and fence it in. This Wallace did. By the depression of 1929 he owned 1,200 acres of Mitchel County land on which there was no mortgage. In fact, he did not even owe taxes.

Wallace was a member of the Texas and Southwest Cattle Raisers Association for more than thirty years. He was also a member of the pioneer organizations of his region and a financial adviser to many of the people in his county, both blacks and whites.[126] Clay Mann thought him uncanny in his ability to calculate the number of cattle in a herd. Once, when some cattlemen were speculating on how many cattle there were in a herd, Mann was asked if he would bet on its size. He replied that he would if he was allowed to consult Wallace. The latter looked at the cattle and said that the herd numbered slightly less than 5,000. The actual figure was 4,975. Mann won the bet.[127]

Wallace's fame is rivalled by that of Matthew "Bones" Hooks, who lived in the Texas Panhandle at Amarillo until his death on February 2, 1951. He came to the West with the vanguard of civilization and was a great black cowboy on the plains of Texas at the time when the open range was at its zenith.[128] By his own account, Hooks was the last of the old cowboys who rode up the Chisholm Trail from Pecos country to Dodge City.[129] Stories are still told of his exploits as a cowboy. He was known best as a breaker of horses. The most talked-of incident in his life concerned the time when Hooks broke a horse called "the Hurricane Deck" and "a thousand pounds of dynamite" because no one had been able to ride him. At the time, Hooks was working for the Santa Fe Railroad. The horse was saddled and at the depot when the train pulled into Pampa, Texas. Hooks dropped off his Pullman and, unaided, mounted the horse in an open field and rode him until the horse gave up. He then climbed back onto the train and continued his run.[130]

Noted for his homely philosophy, Hooks gave women a great deal of credit for their part in the development of the plains territory and the entire West because it was they, not the men, who demanded the settled life. For years he followed the custom of sending a White Guerdon of Honor to the family of every famous cowboy or other notable person. He took this means of honoring the men and women who helped to build the great empire on the plains. The practice began when his old cowboy friend Tom Clayton was fatally injured by a falling horse. Before Clayton died, Hooks sent white flowers to him to remind him of the range; after Clayton's death, his mother placed the flowers on his grave. In the years that followed, Hooks sent the White Guerdon of Honor to such persons as Franklin D. Roosevelt, Eleanor Roosevelt, Winston Churchill, and boxing champion Joe Louis. By 1944 he had sent 300 guerdons.[131]

Hooks regarded as cowboys only a few of the other blacks who worked on the ranges of the Southwest. We know little about these men, but Hooks gives us their names and the names of the High Plains ranches on which they worked. They include the following: Dan Sowell, "Figure 4"; Henry Mangum, "T.J.M."; Bill Freeman, "Quarter Circle Heart"; Charles Fowler and Edward Jones, "L.F.D.S."; and Brook Lee, "Diamond Trail."[132]

There are records of few black cowboys outside the Old Southwest, but certainly there were men such as William Harding Hooper, who was born in North Carolina at Mount Airy in 1869 and brought by his parents to Colorado in 1877. The family settled in Colorado Springs. When young William grew up, he was not satisfied with the city; he was more interested in the open country and outdoor life. He took a job as a cowhand on the ranch of William Gilpin where he soon earned the rating of a top cowhand.[133]

Like other cowboys and ranch employees, black cowmen were also lawless at times. Conditions in early Abilene were such that the town decided that one of the solutions was to build a prison. The first occupant of the new jail was a black who cooked for one of the Texas outfits which was camped on Mud Creek, eight or ten miles from the town. The cook and his cowhand friends were in the town amusing themselves by shooting out street lights. When the town police came along, he and his companions fled. The others escaped because they had speedy horses, but the cook was overtaken, captured, and placed in prison. He was rescued by his friends since, from their point of view, it was a disgrace for a cowhand to be in jail. The townspeople in turn tried to recapture him but were unsuccessful.[134]

In 1879 Fort Griffin, Kansas, was the supply point for cattle outfits. Each outfit camped and spent a day or so in that vicinity before moving on. One of the outfits which were there in June 1879 decided to shoot up the town. Although the sheriff was ready when the cowboys began their wild spree, all of them were able to elude him and his deputies except the black cook, who had an inferior horse. The cook was ordered to surrender, but he began to shoot instead. His horse was shot from under him but, using its body as a shield, he continued to shoot. He was shot six times, finally brought under control and arrested. When he recovered from his wounds, he escaped.[135]

One of the most romantic and picturesque figures in the Old West was Albert Williams, better known as "Speckle Nigger," a name that came from the fact that his brown face was covered with freckles. Born a slave, Williams began to work in the coal fields of West Virginia. Following that occupation for several years in various parts of the country, he finally landed in Rock Creek, Wyoming, and went to work for the Union Pacific Mining Company. He lost that job when Chinese miners were brought into service. "Specks," as he was called most of the time, went to Brown's Hole in Wyoming along with Tom Davenport, a Welsh miner. Davenport started a cattle ranch, and Specks soon learned to ride broncos and rope steers.

When he came to Brown's Hole it was just coming into its own as headquarters for the largest gang of cattle rustlers and thieves ever known in the West. Before 1900, when the place was civilized by the rifle of the famous Tom Horn, it was the hideout of some of the West's most notorious outlaws and badmen. Specks knew personally every one of the outlaws who came to Brown's Hole. For many years he operated a ferry across the Green River and looked after the desperadoes' horses while they rested between raids. His special hero among the outlaws was Butch Cassidy, whose handyman he was whenever that famous outlaw was in the Hole. Cassidy rode out one day after telling Specks that he would soon be back, but he went to South America and was killed there in 1907. Until the day of his own death, Specks believed that some day Cassidy would be back.

Specks witnessed the violent deaths of many men during his fifty years among the badmen. Often he had the sad experience of seeing the bodies of his friends floating down the river. He even saw the outlaws set up a vigilante committee and handle one of their own members. His own body was scarred from wounds he had received as an innocent bystander in raids and fights among the badmen. Once he was severely wounded by a drunken outlaw, but the outlaw's wife nursed him back to health. Specks was in Brown's Hole when the law finally came and took away the dangerous killers, and he helped to bury the victims of the dangerous rifle of Tom Horn. He saw the exodus of most of the desperadoes from the Hole.

Specks was able to survive because, although he knew a great deal about the badmen, he was wise enough to keep his mouth closed. He knew enough to hang nearly every man in Brown's Hole, but he refused to tell anything until he knew he was about to die in 1934. Then he gave the names and talked about the activities of the many outlaws who used to hide there. When he died, Specks was the last relic of the old outlaw gang.[136]

Blacks are still working as cowhands throughout various parts of the country, perhaps in greater numbers than in the days of Nat Love and ''Eighty'' John Wallace. The cattle industry has grown bigger and more persons are employed in it, but it no longer has the open range and the long drives. As homesteaders settled the land and fenced it, war broke out between the cattlemen and the sheep raisers. These contests brought the open range to an end. With the passing of the range went much of the romantic interest in the West. The cattle business still goes on, but the cattle are shipped by train and truck from the sections where they are raised. The wide-ranging, free-living cowhands of song and legend and their black companions of the old trails are no more.

Agriculture

Because they were romantic, the gold rush, the fur trade, and the cattle industry have received a good deal of attention from historians and literary writers. In comparison, agriculture has been neglected. But the agricultural settlement began long before gold was discovered, and it continued after the close of both the gold rush and the fur trade. Between the years 1830 and 1900, agriculture gave a powerful impetus to the westward movement. The demand for more and better farm land stimulated the continuing migration into the western states. Low prices of farm products in the Mississippi Valley and the difficulty of getting these commodities to market were additional factors which inspired settlement on the frontier. The land policy of the United States also contributed to the development of the West, encouraging persons of all nationalities and races to move to the frontier as farmers and farm workers. As a result, productive agriculture made the West the attractive region it is today.

Some blacks in the agricultural frontier had been carried there as slaves. Subsequently securing their freedom, they acquired land and permanently settled themselves in agriculture. Others were free blacks who were among the many Americans who were inspired to move into the West because of the prospect of obtaining free land. In both cases, however, their eligibility was questioned. On November 13, 1856, Isaiah Lawrence wrote to the Secretary of State, William L. Marcy, inquiring about conditions of settling on public land. Lawrence said that he was a citizen of the United States of African descent who desired to go to Minnesota Territory for the purpose of settling there on a section of government land. He wanted to know if there was anything in the laws or regulations of the United States or its territory which would interfere with the fulfillment of such a desire.[137] Marcy referred the letter to the Secretary of the Interior, R. M. Clelland, who wrote to Lawrence on November 18, 1856, stating that there was nothing that would prevent him from settling on public land in the territory of Minnesota and acquiring the right of preemption.[138] William J. Hardin, a politician in Denver, had the same question as Lawrence, and he wrote to G. M. Chilcott for the answer. Chilcott replied that he had been informed by the commissioner of the General Land Office that blacks had the same right to preempt or take homesteads as other citizens. Chilcott requested Hardin to give this information to those who were interested.[139]

The years that followed saw an exodus of blacks moving westward. There were several reasons for the occurrence of the exodus, which reached its peak in 1879. Basic among these was the economic factor: blacks in the South were unable to obtain the kind of land they wanted and needed. Moreover, they were disappointed with emancipation, which did not guarantee to them civil and political rights. They felt that the much-publicized free land in the region west of the Mississippi River offered relief from this discrimination. Possibly the greatest and most magnetic force in the migration of blacks to the farming frontier was a black man named Benjamin Singleton. He began the work of inducing blacks to leave the South for Kansas as early as 1869, a decade before the exodus from the South was noted by the newspapers. Singleton and Henry Adams, a co-worker, sent circulars far and wide to blacks, acquainting them with conditions and describing the good fortune of those who already had settled; they climaxed their appeal by urging the blacks to trade the South for life in Kansas. Such an extensive campaign was expensive, but Singleton paid the cost from his own funds.[140]

The number of blacks who came to Kansas and other parts of the West in search of farm land is difficult to ascertain. Henry King, who at the time was postmaster in Topeka, Kansas, and later became editor of the *St. Louis Globe Democrat,* suggested that between 15,000 and 20,000 came to Kansas alone by April 1, 1880, but this is only an estimate.[141] According to King, the migrants came from different sections of the South: 30 percent from Mississippi, 20 percent from Texas, 15 percent from Tennessee, and the other 35 percent from other states. King believed that one-third of them were supplied with teams and farm equipment and gave promise of becoming self-supporting. A third were employed as house servants, while another third lived from hand to mouth, working whenever they could.[142]

The blacks who first came to Kansas attracted no attention whatever. It was only when they arrived in large numbers that the movement excited the country. The newspapers then took notice and carried stories of the blacks' departure from parts of the South and their whereabouts in the West. Many of the papers of the Central West and other sections wrote editorials and articles concerning this movement. On April 24, 1879, for example, the editor of the *Home Journal* of Lawrence, Kansas, estimated that about five or six hundred migrants had just arrived and thirty had been placed with farmers. The editor felt that these people would be of value to the agricultural system of Kansas.[143]

But while there was some need for farm labor on the frontier, there was not sufficient demand to absorb the influx of blacks who came to Kansas at this time. Moreover, authorities in the large cities that were in the path of travel feared that many from the influx would descend upon them and become a burden, since so many of the immigrants would not be able to pay their way. Indeed, the black migrants were coming in considerable numbers to St. Louis, Kansas City, and Lawrence, and many of them were indigent. As many as 280 arrived at St. Louis at one time, but only 80 had sufficient funds to take them to Kansas City. Without jobs or money, many took to loitering on the wharf. The mayor of St. Louis hoped to stop the influx of blacks into the city by securing a regulation which would place a fine on transportation companies, ranging from $25 to $300, for bringing persons who were not able to care for themselves.[144] His position was doubtful because the railroad had no constitutional right to ask a man if he had enough money to support himself.

In many cases, impoverished blacks had to depend on charity. An indication of their condition was revealed on March 17, 1879, in Leavenworth, Kansas, when twenty-three black men and women called on the mayor and asked for aid.[145] The governor of Kansas, John P. St. John, was urged to issue a proclamation prohibiting destitute blacks from coming to Kansas. He refused, thereby saving Kansas from enacting a discriminatory regulation.[146] St. John turned his attention to doing what he could to aid the migrants in adjusting to their new home by sending letters to some of the other governors, asking for help for the needy.

The matter was one of considerable concern, and meetings were held in various parts of the country to help solve the problem and provide for suffering persons. There were several motives for helping. Colorado, for example, fearing that destitute blacks would go there and throw many laborers out of work, gave help to Kansas so that the blacks would not come to their state. The editor of the *Rocky Mountain News* is representative of this attitude; he felt that the migration was the work of capitalists who hoped to get cheap labor.[147] In time, the matter reached the United States Senate, which appointed a select committee to determine whether any political influence had been exerted upon the movement. The committee called before it some of those who had been active in the migration, including Benjamin Singleton and John W. Cromwell. Singleton claimed that he had brought 7,432 persons into the various sections of Kansas. Cromwell revealed that a national convention had been held in Nashville and that representatives from South Carolina, Georgia, Alabama, and other southern states had participated. The convention had been called, he said, to discuss the status of blacks in the South. The question of migration was discussed, but there was nothing like unanimity reached on that point. George F. Marlow had been sent to Kansas by the Black Labor Union of Alabama for the purpose of reporting to the convention on the conditions in that part of the West. He reported that the land was fertile, winters were short, the climate was mild, and the population was sparse. Marlow's report also showed that there were churches and schools in every community, and that produce brought good prices. Land was within the reach of every man; prices ranged from two to ten dollars per acre. This information was made available to the public for the first time in the testimony given before the committee.

In its majority statement, the committee reported that much of the evidence given was largely hearsay and could not be admitted in a court of justice. It denied that there was outrage or violence against blacks in the South and charged that they had left because of the aid given them by immigrant aid societies in Washington, Indianapolis, and Topeka, although the societies denied this. The committee accused the Republicans of sending agents who urged blacks to leave the South. In short, the majority report held that the exodus had begun many years before it attracted national attention and that it had been organized by the blacks themselves. The minority report also asserted that the blacks did not intend to return to the South. This contention was based on the fact that when an offer was made to pay the blacks' expenses for return, only 300 out of 31,000 took advantage of it. The minority report insisted that investigation had failed to reveal that there was no demand for the migrants' services and that they were wards of the community.[148]

The other side of the question—the influence on the South—was also important. As early as July 1879, Senator B. K. Bruce had information from the South that the exodus had carried away more than 10,000 black laborers.[149] Southerners tried, both through legal methods and intimidation, to prevent blacks from leaving. There were also efforts to induce blacks who had left to return. They were offered good positions and payment of their expenses back to the South. One such case is revealed by C. A. Stitch of Garnett, Kansas, who was asked by a company in St. Louis to locate a black man named Salmon Butler. On behalf of the company, Stitch offered to pay Butler's way back to the South. Butler replied that he was certain that a mistake had been made regarding his return. He had never had a home in the South, and he had seen no possibility of getting a home until he went to Kansas. He could not let slip his first opportunity to have a home in a place where he could enjoy liberty. While he thanked those who made the offer, Butler related in some detail the experiences he had had in the South and said that he could not consent to make his home there again.[150] Others shared his view. Many who went to the West wrote to their friends, relating how successful they had been in getting farms and homes. The conditions in the South were such that these people were happy to get out of that section, and they were willing to try almost anything. The opportunity to better their lot was one of the reasons why the migrants were willing to endure the hardships of the frontier.

One result of the black exodus was the establishment of the black agricultural towns which were founded in several states. The first of these agricultural colonies was organized by a leader of the exodus, Benjamin Singleton. He felt that the salvation of blacks lay in obtaining and cultivating land. He established a colony in the Cherokee settlement near Baxter Springs, Kansas, always spoken of as the "Singleton Colony." The Cherokee settlement influenced the organization of other colonies, such as the one begun at Lexington, Kentucky, in 1877 for the purpose of founding a settlement on government lands in Kansas. The fee charged for membership (at Lexington) was five dollars, which entitled the member to the vacant lot of his choice.[151]

The best-known of these colonies was Nicodemus, which was settled along the Kansas Pacific Railroad in Graham County. A correspondent for the *Chicago Tribune* visited this black colony and described what he saw. The colony, scattered over an area about twelve miles long and six miles wide, was located in Graham County, about thirty-five miles northeast of Wakeeny and about one hundred and twenty miles from Kansas City. It had a population of seven hundred. The timber along the Salmon River furnished fuel and wood for constructing huts. A feeling prevailed among the settlers that no better place in Kansas could have been selected for the colony. The correspondent also reported that to the best of his knowledge, this colony was the only black colony to survive, and he attributed its success to its leaders, who possessed ability and common sense.[152]

In 1877 the people of Nicodemus, limited to a few teams of horses or oxen, put under cultivation all the land they could. During the first year an average of about six acres per person was under cultivation. Some had small plots while others had as much as twenty acres.[153] From a small beginning, this Kansas colony progressed so that by 1879 it was a prosperous community and had a post office, stores, hotels, and a land office. Like other villages in Graham County, it aspired to become the county seat.[154]

In 1879 the citizens of Nicodemus passed a series of resolutions in which they thanked the people of Kansas and other states for their help to the colony and requested that no further charitable assistance be extended them. As explained by the authorities in the colony, the reason for this request was that some among them would use charity as a means to avoid working. Charity would also bring into the community many destitute, undesirable persons.[155] The people of Nicodemus believed in work. They also believed in self-support. After four years, the colony form of life was dissolved and every individual worked for himself, with women working alongside men in the fields.

Nicodemus continued to grow, and as late as 1910 it was a thriving farm community. In that year the town's first farmers' institute was held for the purpose of improving the agriculture of the community.[156] According to a *Chicago Tribune* reporter, the success of Nicodemus had some influence on other agricultural towns which developed on the frontier in later years. Ironically, some of the population of Nicodemus was drawn off to these.

Several other agricultural colonies were established in Kansas. In 1878 a town was organized about twenty-five miles from Dodge City and about the same distance from Spearville on the Atchison, Topeka, and Santa Fe Railroad. This colony consisted of 107 families, most of whom came from Harrodsburg and Lexington, Kentucky. During the first year they suffered as the settlers in Nicodemus had when they began. They planted vegetables, and in a short time they were not only self-supporting but also able to care for all who came into their settlement.[157] P. T. Moore established a colony in Hodgeman County, northeast of the present site of Jetmore, but it never flourished. A colony established in 1881 by Daniel Victor, a Quaker, thrived until it was destroyed by the flood waters of the Verdigris River and the Big Hill Creek. This colony differed from the others because its members experimented with cotton and proved that it could grow in Kansas.[158] This knowledge was important to agricultural interests in the West.

Some people who went to Kansas to settle did not find what they desired there; consequently, they moved to adjoining states, especially Indian Territory, Oklahoma Territory, and Texas. The black towns in Oklahoma differed from those in Texas. Blacks in Oklahoma enjoyed more freedom than did blacks in Texas where they were denied the franchise. The Oklahoma towns were founded in the knowledge that even greater freedom for blacks was possible. They were organized exclusively to provide further political expression and economic requirements for blacks. The Texas towns, most of which consisted of fewer than 100 persons, were rather the consequence of the tendency of people of like condition to associate with one another. In this respect, these towns did not differ essentially from the black sections of the larger cities. And in most of them some whites lived, unlike an Oklahoma town such as Boley. Developing less out of conscious effort and more as the accidental result of people thrown together by circumstance, the Texas towns exhibited less vitality and potential. They never became as large and as important as black towns became in other states.

The towns in Oklahoma which have attracted the most attention were Taft, Langston, and Boley. Taft was one of the early all-black

towns inhabited by a number of free black men and women who settled near the confluence of the Arkansas and Verdigris rivers, about
six miles from Muskogee. Many of the people who settled this town
had come west with the Creeks. After the Civil War, the United
States required the Creeks to free their slaves; the latter became citizens and as such were allowed to inherit land because they were on
the Creek rolls.[159] Black freemen settled in Taft soon after the Civil
War. The original town occupied sixteen acres purchased from D. H.
Twine, a prominent black man for whom the town was first named.
By 1904 a post office was established for Twine, and the first postmaster, James Patrick, was appointed July 18, 1904.[160] The name of
the town was changed from Twine to Taft in honor of President William Howard Taft.

Among the state facilities for black citizens established in Taft
were the Blind and Orphan Home, authorized in 1909, the State
Training Institute for black girls, and the state hospital for the insane.
In 1933 these three institutions, owning land amounting to 400 acres,
were consolidated under one administration.[161] Taft has only small
stores, but it is so close to Muskogee that many of its needs are
supplied from that source. Despite the changes which have occurred
in Oklahoma, this all-black town has continued and the state institutions have remained there.

Langston was organized in 1882 by a black lawyer from Fort
Smith, Arkansas. It is not certain whether the purpose was to organize an all-black town or a black state. In any case, little was accomplished at first. The situation improved when E. P. McCabe,
who had served as state auditor of Kansas from January 1883 to
January 1887, moved to Oklahoma and became interested in the welfare of his fellow citizens. He developed the town and named it in
honor of John M. Langston, the well-known black antislavery
worker, educator, and Virginia politician. The population at one time
reached more than 2,000 persons, many of whom had been attracted
by the enthusiasm and flattery of McCabe. When many of those who
had gone there had spent most of their funds and could not find
employment, the population decreased. The situation worsened when
McCabe was elected deputy auditor for Oklahoma and moved to the
state capital. Without his enthusiastic effort, the town languished.
Were it not for Langston University, the town of Langston might

have disappeared. The university, the state's contribution to black higher education, was established in 1897. It was supported by the state legislature and was granted funds by the Morrill Act, the Smith-Hughes Act, and the national government.[162]

Taft and Langston were directly influenced by the Kansas exodus; while Boley got some of its population from this source, its origin was different. Boley was established by W. H. Boley, president of the Fort Smith and Western Railroad Townsite Company. It was a railroad town situated in Okfuskee County, where many blacks had been given land grants. The railroad offered employment to many of those who settled in Boley. In 1903 Booker T. Washington visited the town. He said that it was the youngest, the most interesting, and the most successful of the all-black towns in the United States.[163] Boley had two banks, two cotton mills, a black newspaper, a hotel, and a college, the Creek Seminole College and Agricultural Institute.[164] The first post office was authorized and the first postmaster appointed on July 7, 1903.[165] There were enough merchants in various lines to care for the needs of the citizens. Those who lived in Boley were for the most part descendants of black persons who had moved west from the southern states to find a better life. One of its outstanding mayors was R. T. Ringo, who was born a slave in Kentucky and who did much toward the development of the town. In the beginning, cotton competed with the railroad in furnishing employment to the citizens of Boley. Cotton is no longer the important crop it once was, however, and for this reason the development of Boley was limited.

One of the Texas agricultural towns was Douglasville, founded in 1853 by John Douglas, who later built a log cabin which was still standing in 1940.[166] This was a village where many slave owners left their slaves before the Civil War. Many of their descendants stayed on as sharecroppers and renters. Douglasville remained a farming community, although many left the farms and found employment in the saw mills which were busy producing lumber. Not more than half of the people in the town were black, and it can be classed as a black town only because of its founder and the blacks who settled around him and in the area which the town serves.

Neylandville, Texas, on the other hand, was an all-black town. It was founded by a farmer and one-time slave, Jim Bingham, and named in honor of Bingham's master.[167] The railroad reached Neylandville in 1886, but the population remained very small and very few of the facilities which most black towns offered were available.

Kendleton, Texas, began when a land grant was sold to freed blacks after the close of the Civil War. It was an all-black town consisting primarily of a grocery store around which a few families settled. Kendleton was in every sense a farm village.[168]

Of the thousands of blacks who participated in western agriculture, a few achieved extraordinary success. One was Junius G. Groves of Edwardsville, Kansas, widely referred to as the "Potato King." Groves was born in 1859 in Green County, Kentucky. Like many blacks in the South at that time, he attended school only two or three months each year, but by his own efforts he was able to acquire some education. Groves migrated to Kansas in 1879, the year that the black exodus was attracting national attention, and reached Edwardsville with ninety cents in his pocket. Upon his arrival, he was employed on a farm for forty cents a day. Later he was given ninety-five cents a day and nine acres of land to farm on shares. He was so successful that the following year he was given twenty-five acres to cultivate. He married and his wife worked side by side with him. After several years they were able to buy a farm.

By the turn of the century, Groves owned 320 acres of land in the rich Kaw Valley. He was now consistently spoken of as the Potato King because of the very great acreage yield of his potatoes. He was able to produce 396 bushels an acre while farmers around him were producing as little as 25 bushels. Groves attributed his success to the careful preparation of the soil, the cutting of the potatoes by hand, and the frequent working of them.[169]

Groves grew products other than potatoes, and in 1900 he sold at good prices a carload of onions, three carloads of corn, 20,000 heads of cabbage, 35 tons of hay, and small quantities of parsnips, carrots, and sorghum cane. As a leader in the marketing of his own and other farmers' produce, in 1900 he became the secretary of the Potato Growers Association; in that year, he owned 320 acres of land valued at $48,000. Groves lived in a fourteen-room house which cost $5,000; his barn was worth $1,500. His workers lived in six other houses on his property which ranged in value from $200 to $1,200.[170] Groves continued to improve his land holdings so that by

1909 he had increased his farm to 600 acres. One year later, he owned a farm of 2,100 acres which was reputed to be one of the finest in Kansas. The improvements on the farm kept pace with the increase in the land holdings. Groves erected a house with 22 rooms at a cost of $18,000; it was considered one of the finest farmhouses in the state.[171] Junius G. Groves was known not only in Kansas and nearby states but also throughout the nation because of the extensive publicity given his agricultural achievements.

It was customary to call a man a potato king if he raised the largest crop of potatoes in his state or, in some cases, his county. The potato king of Kansas in 1893 was H. P. Irving, who lived about a mile from Larring. His farm, like that of Groves, was in the Kaw Valley, where almost any farm product would grow. In that year he planted potatoes in 500 acres of land. The yield on his land was 150 bushels per acre, which came to 75,000 bushels of potatoes for this one farmer.[172]

Henry C. Bachman was another prosperous black farmer in Kansas. He was born and reared in Lincoln County, Kentucky. During the Civil War he entered the army and fought for his freedom. When the war ended, he returned to Lincoln County, leased land, and began farming, which he subsequently abandoned to engage in the grocery business in Atchison, Kansas. After ten years Bachman sold his grocery and returned to his first vocation. He bought 100 acres in Walnut Township, Kansas, and continued to acquire land until his farm consisted of 500 acres.[173]

In 1900 Robert Keith was probably the wealthiest black farmer in Shawnee County, Kansas. He had been born in Columbus, Georgia, later had moved to Ohio, where he remained until 1884, and had then moved to Kansas. In Ohio, Keith owned 200 acres of farm land and was active in civic affairs, serving as trustee of Butler Township and as a member of the school board. He continued the same type of life in Kansas and engaged very successfully in truck-farming near Topeka.[174] His brother, Green Keith, was one of the most successful farmers in Douglas County, thus acquiring considerable wealth. He was highly esteemed by his fellow citizens. When he died, the City Commission ordered the flag on the City Hall flown at half-mast. The editor of the *Emporia Gazette* noted that this was in respect for his honesty and leadership.[175]

Other successful black farmers in Kansas include Monroe

Tompkins, who owned an eighty-acre farm in Jefferson County, three miles from Oskaloosa. He served in the Union Army, but after separation from the service he went to Kansas and worked as a farm hand. In time, he was able to secure his own farm and become one of the most successful farmers in eastern Kansas.[176] Robert N. and William T. Turner were among the most prosperous market-garden farmers in Shawnee County. Starting with an eighty-acre farm north of Topeka, they used the 1889 profits from it to buy another farm in 1900. The Turners gave all their time to market gardening, from which they always derived two crops each year.[177] They were noted for their unfailing energy and industry, and it was not unusual for them to arise at three in the morning and arrive in Topeka with a load of produce before most farmers were out of bed. Another prominent black of Kansas, Major John Brown, owned a hundred-acre farm north of Topeka, just three miles from the State Capitol Building. As the result of a homestead, Brown secured the 360 acres in Wabaunsee County on which he began his farming career.[178] He gained fame for his specialty, the cultivation of Irish and sweet potatoes. Within two miles of Oskaloosa, in Jefferson County, George W. Jones owned and lived on a farm of 320 acres. He had been born in slavery and had gone to Kansas with his parents after the Civil War. He operated his farm with very modern equipment.[179]

Some of the most successful farmers in Kansas were blacks who entered the state without a dollar but, because of their industry and frugality, were able to accumulate small fortunes. They were especially successful in the counties of Wyandotte, Shawnee, Douglas, Jefferson, and Leavenworth.[180] But not all prominent black farmers were in Kansas. One of the first blacks to attract attention on the farming frontier was George Washington Bush of Oregon Territory. Bush was born on September 4, 1781, and although it has been claimed that he was born elsewhere, Pennsylvania seems the most likely place of his birth.[181] He moved a great deal, first from Pennsylvania to Cumberland County, Tennessee, with a man named Montgomery. Bush lived there until he was eighteen, and then he went to Illinois where he engaged in stock raising. He was next a soldier with Jackson at New Orleans in the War of 1812. The record shows him later as a farmer in southeast Missouri. In 1816 he was continuing his agricultural operations in Platte County in northern Missouri. During that period he prospered, saved his money, and gave evidence of the industry and economy that characterized his activities in later years.

In 1844, at the age of sixty-three, Bush and his family joined the Gilliam train going from Kentucky to Oregon. He furnished from his own stores resources and teams to take several of his neighbors on the journey.[182] Before Bush and the company with whom he was associated reached Oregon, the provisional government of Oregon passed an act which made it illegal for blacks and mulattoes to reside there. The company thought that it would be well for Bush to remain at Dalles, a town on the eastern frontier of Oregon, since he and his family were the only blacks in the group. During that winter Bush occupied himself by caring for his stock and that of the others.[183] In the spring of 1845 he joined the rest of the party at Washougal and travelled with his family down the Columbia River by the Pack Trail. He remained at Washougal until the fall of that year, when he moved to an unbroken wilderness in Thurston County. This later became Washington Territory, and Bush lived there until his death in 1863.

Bush settled under what was known as a donation land claim of 640 acres located five miles south of Olympia on the Des Chutes River.[184] The Donation Land Law provided for a generous grant of land to settlers if they made the settlement before December 17, 1855. Bush soon found, however, that according to the law he could not claim the land because he had more than one-half black blood. He was thus a squatter in this new country. The action against Bush was of more than passing concern to Michael T. Simmons, who was a member of the Oregon legislature. Simmons and Bush were good friends. Bush had given Simmons assistance on the journey across the plains and had furnished him funds in the new territory. Reputedly, Bush had put up $3,000 (brought west in the false bottom of his wagon) to assume a silent partnership in a mill which Simmons erected in 1846 at Tumwater.[185] At Simmons's urging, the Oregon legislature requested that Congress remove without delay the disability against Bush. Congress did so, conferring on Bush the right to hold a donation claim.[186]

The first winter on Puget Sound was a very difficult one for the Bush family and others. The British hoped to gain control of the territory to the north of the Columbia River in the event that hardships forced the Americans to move south. Accordingly, they forbade Dr. Tolmie, agent of the Hudson's Bay Company at Nisqually, to sell anything to the Americans.[187] Bush and his family had come to the new land with sufficient food for their own use, but many of their neighbors were not so fortunate. Bush divided his food with them— an act of genuine mercy, for there was danger of severe suffering for Bush's own family. They had, as the principal items of their diet, clams, oysters, salmon, and game, together with a little wheat and dried peas remaining from their original store. They also learned to eat and relish the roots of ferns, which they used as green vegetables. Despite the adversity, Bush began farming and soon prospered.

The migration into Washington country grew larger year by year, thereby increasing the demand for food, especially farm products, and driving prices up sharply. Food was out of the reach of those migrants with large families and those who had used most of their resources to cross the plains. Because of his skill as a farmer, Bush had large supplies of food, and although he would not sell a pound to anyone who wanted it for speculation, he did supply seed for planting and food for those in need. He accepted no money; the only condition that he placed upon those who obtained supplies from him was that they would return them when they were able. In this way, Bush divided a great deal of his crop, worth thousands of dollars, with those in need of help.[188]

When migrants first moved to Puget Sound, Washington was wild and undeveloped country, and the Indians were a constant threat. They killed two Americans who had moved into the territory. Bush is said to have had some difficulty with the Indians, and for a time he moved his family to Fort Tumwater.[189] After a while he and the other settlers, eager to return to Bush Prairie, built a fort on the Bush farm for protection in the event of Indian attack.[190] The fort was partially enclosed by fourteen-foot logs set upright in trenches, thereby making it bullet-proof.

In the early days, some of those who went to Washington found Bush there and testified to his importance. One was Mrs. Elmira Whitaker, a white woman, whose family erected its log cabin and lived for some time across from the Bush home.[191] Another migrant who came into the vicinity of Puget Sound was John Roger James, who arrived with his father in 1850. He found Bush doing well at Bush Prairie. Bush sold the elder James a small grist mill and seven head of sheep. This helped James and his son to get a foothold in the new country.[192] Such generosity explains why Bush endeared himself to the people of Washington. A leader in Puget Sound, he was constantly experimenting with grain and with animals to improve their yield. In 1856 he introduced the first mower and reaper into Washington Territory.[193]

After the death of George Washington Bush, the farm was managed by William O. Bush, one of the sons who had crossed the plains with the elder Bush in 1844. William O. Bush was a pioneer in the operation of an agricultural experiment station, and his work was of great value in advertising the resources of Thurston County and the Pacific Northwest. Among other things, he planted 200 different species of wheat in separate rows and tested them in order to improve the wheat which was grown on his own farm.[194] Developing the farm into a model homestead, he exhibited wheat from the farm at world fairs in Philadelphia, Chicago, and Buffalo, and won first prize at all of them.[195] Bush continued to live on his father's farm for many years and was there when Ezra Meeker wrote his *Reminiscences,* nearly sixty years after his father had braved the wilds of Washington country. The fact that William O. Bush was a member of the first legislature of the state of Washington is an indication of the high esteem in which he was held in that state. He is spoken of in the legislative record as an influential member. In 1906 he died on his farm, much beloved by the people of the community.

The Bush property then passed to Lewis Bush, born in Oregon Territory, who was the last member of the original Bush family. In 1914, as an old man, he had the distinction of being the only man living on an original family donation land claim west of the Coastal Range in the state of Washington. In every other case, the original owners had parted with their claims, but the Bush property had been inherited by members of the family in an unbroken line.[196]

Another prosperous black farmer in the Northwest was George Washington. He was born in Frederick County, Virginia, on August 15, 1817. His mother was an Englishwoman and his father was a slave. Young George was adopted by James Cochran, who moved first into Delaware County, Ohio, and then into Missouri. It was there that Washington grew into manhood. He was energetic and entered several kinds of business. When he and a partner began a saw-mill operation fifteen miles from St. Joseph, he discovered that he had no legal status in the state of Missouri. Cochran secured a petition, signed by several of his friends, in which he asked the Missouri legislature to grant his adopted son the rights of a citizen because he was a free man of color and the son of a white woman. The state passed a special act which gave Washington all the rights and privileges except that of holding office.[197] Washington had difficulties in Illinois when he attempted to open a distillery. He found that it was illegal for any person of color to manufacture, handle, or sell spirits or malt liquors. This, together with other problems, made him decide to go to Oregon.

In March 1850, Washington and his foster parents left for Oregon and reached that territory in 118 days. He settled the Cochrans at Cowlitz Landing, a trading post of the Hudson Bay Company. Then he looked for a place that he could cultivate. He found such a location on the Chehalis River, and in 1852 he staked out a squatter's claim on which he built a one-room cabin. During the first year he cleared twelve acres and sowed wheat, oats, and vegetables.

This section was attractive to the new settlers. Since blacks could not legally own property in Oregon, the only way Washington could keep his farm was to turn it over to Cochran, who filed for the claim. Cochran, in turn, deeded it to Washington after he had lived there for four years. Washington paid Cochran $3,200 for 640 acres, and for many years thereafter he was a successful farmer in the Chehalis Valley.

Such were the major industries in which blacks in the West were employed. The fur trade was an early vehicle for travel to unsettled regions. When its time was done, many of those who had been active in the trade remained in the West and entered other occupations. The mining industry had its spectacular aspect: it saw thousands of people rush to the West—especially to California—inspired by the dream of sudden wealth. For blacks there was the prospect of freedom as well as gold. Some slaves were granted their freedom in return for work, while others escaped and were able to settle as free people. The early years of the cattle industry have held a special place in America's imagination. Largely ignored, however, has been the extent to which black people participated in this field. Although less romantic than the fur, mining, and cattle industries, agriculture is of great significance in the history of black people in the West. As slaves in the South, most blacks had done agricultural work. It was natural that they should continue to do that which they knew. Following the Civil

War, therefore, many blacks were drawn to the West by the offer of farm land there.

But it must be emphasized that these were the *major* industries. The western opportunity was nothing if not diversified, as the following chapter will show.

NOTES

1. James R. Harvey, "The Negro in Colorado," unpublished M.A. thesis (University of Denver, 1941).

2. John C. Ewers, ed., *Adventures of Zenas Leonard, Fur Trader* (Norman, 1959), p. 139.

3. Reuben Gold Thwaites, ed., "The British Regime in Wisconsin—1760–1800," *Wisconsin State Historical Society Collections* 18 (1908), p. 384n; Milo M. Quaife, ed., *John Askin Papers* (Detroit, 1928), vol. 1: *Chicago and the Old Northwest, 1673–1835*, p. 138. Quaife makes no speculation as to de Sable's origins.

4. Augustin Grignon, "Seventy-Two Years' Recollections of Wisconsin," *Wisconsin State Historical Society Collections* 3 (1857; rpt. 1904), p. 292.

5. French money, originally the value of a pound of silver.

6. Frank Triplett, *Conquering the Wilderness* (Chicago, 1883), p. 383.

7. Washington Irving, *Astoria,* ed. Edgeley W. Todd (Norman, 1964), p. 214.

8. Clarence Vandiveer, *The Fur-Trade and Early Western Exploration* (Cleveland, 1929), p. 179. Hiram M. Chittenden, *American Fur Trade of the Far West* (New York, 1935), vol. 1, p. 676, thinks that it was 1807 or 1809.

9. Chittenden, *American Fur Trade,* vol. 1, p. 586.

10. Washington Irving, *Adventures of Captain Bonneville, U.S.A.,* ed. Edgeley W. Todd (Norman, 1961), p. 166.

11. John C. Luttig, *Journal of a Fur Trading Expedition on the Upper Missouri, 1812–1813,* ed. Stella M. Drumm (St. Louis, 1920), p. 157.

12. John G. Neihardt, *The Splendid Wayfaring* (New York, 1920), p. 43.

13. Triplett, *Conquering the Wilderness,* p. 383.

14. Chittenden, *American Fur Trade,* vol. 1, p. 677.

15. Letter from John F. A. Sanford to William Clark, St. Louis, July 26, 1833, National Archives, Records of the Bureau of Indian Affairs, Letters Received, Mandan File, as cited in Dale Morgan, *The West of William S. Ashley, 1822–1838* (Denver, 1964), p. 263.

16. Neihardt, *The Splendid Wayfaring,* p. 82.

17. Alpheus Favour, *Old Bill Williams, Mountain Man* (Chapel Hill, 1936), p. 100.

18. See Charles L. Camp, ed., *James Clyman, American Frontiersman, 1792–1881* (San Francisco, 1928), p. 38.

19. Reuben Gold Thwaites, ed., "The Mackinac Register of Marriages—1725–1821," *Wisconsin State Historical Society Collections* 18 (1908), p. 497: "June 25, 1794, I, the undersigned priest and apostolic Missionary, received the mutual consent of Jean Bonga and Jeanne, the former a negro and the latter a negress, both free, and I gave them the nuptial Benediction in the presence of the following witnesses to wit: Messr. Jean Nicolas Marchesseaux, Hamelin, the elder, Francois Souligny, Charles Chandonnet, some of whom signed; the others, being unable to write, made their usual marks. Le Dru, apostolic Missionary." Le Dru seems to have been the first American priest in Mackinac.

20. Charles E. Flandrau, "Reminiscences of Minnesota during the Territorial Period," *Minnesota Historical Society Collections* 9 (1898–1900), p. 199.

21. Kenneth W. Porter, "Relations between Negroes and Indians within the Present Limits of the United States," *Journal of Negro History* 17 (July 1932), p. 360.

22. Ibid.

23. William W. Warren, "History of the Ojibways, Based upon Traditions and Oral Statements," *Minnesota Historical Society Collections* 5 (1885), p. 488.

24. Ibid.

25. "Letters of George Bonga," *Journal of Negro History* 12 (January 1927), p. 41 (letter dated August 27, 1866).

26. Ibid., p. 42 (Bonga to Whitehead, September 13, 1866).

27. Maude L. Lindquist and James W. Clark, *Early Days and Ways in the Old Northwest* (New York, 1937), p. 48.

28. Flandrau, "Reminiscences of Minnesota," p. 199.

29. Evidence shows that his name was Beckwith and it was so signed with Ashley. Later the name was signed Beckwourth, and this spelling will be used throughout this narrative.

30. Edwin Sabin, *Kit Carson Days* (New York, 1935), p. 75.

31. Moses Meeker, "Early History of Lead Region of Wisconsin," *Wisconsin State Historical Society Collections* 6 (1872; rpt. 1908), p. 280n.

32. Hubert Bancroft, "History of Nevada, Colorado, and Wyoming, 1840–1888," *Works of Hubert Howe Bancroft* (San Francisco, 1890), vol. 25, 352.

33. Meeker, "Lead Region of Wisconsin," pp. 280–281n. Bancroft says that he went west in 1817 ("History of Nevada, Colorado, and Wyoming," p. 352); Chittenden claims that he went first with Ashley in 1824 *(American Fur Trade*, vol. 1, p. 679).

34. Jerome C. Smiley, ed., *History of Denver, with Outlines of the Earlier History of the Rocky Mountain Country* (Denver, 1901), p. 160. This is not confirmed by Chittenden.

35. Vandiveer, *Fur Trade*, p. 261. There are several authorities who put little credence in Beckwourth's story. Francis Parkman says that Jim

Beckwourth was "a ruffian of the worst stamp; bloody and treacherous, without honor or honesty" *(Oregon Trail,* p. 133). Hubert Bancroft says that no dependence can be put in Beckwourth's account *(History of California,* [San Francisco, 1884], vol. 2, p. 713). Dr. Le Roy Hafen of the Colorado Historical Society says that the historian is forced to turn to Beckwourth's *Life and Adventures* for data ("The Last Years of James P. Beckwourth," *Colorado Magazine* 5 [August 1928], p. 134).

36. Favour, *Old Bill Williams,* p. 98.

37. Sabin, *Kit Carson Days,* p. 206.

38. James P. Beckwourth, *Life and Adventures of James P. Beckwourth,* written from his dictation by T. D. Bonner (New York, 1856), p. 175.

39. Alonzo Delano, *Across the Plains and Among the Diggings* (1854; rpt., New York, 1936), p. 143.

40. Horace J. Bell, *Reminiscences of a Ranger, or Early Times in Southern California* (Los Angeles, 1881), p. 289.

41. Ibid., p. 290.

42. Bancroft, *History of California,* vol. 2, p. 713; vol. 4, p. 453.

43. Harry L. Wells, "Beckwourth's Ride," *Pony Express Courier* 2 (October 1935), p. 16.

44. In Smiley, *History of Denver,* p. 160.

45. Ibid.

46. George W. James, *Heroes of California* (Boston, 1910), p. 110.

47. Bancroft, *History of California,* vol. 2, p. 714.

48. Randall Parrish, *The Great Plains: the Romance of Western American Exploration, Warfare, and Settlement, 1527–1893* (Chicago, 1907), p. 95.

49. Reese P. Kendall, *Pacific Trail Camp-Fires* (Chicago, 1901), p. 341.

50. Grace R. Hebard and E. A. Brininstool, *The Bozeman Trail* (Cleveland, 1922), vol. 2, p. 143.

51. Sabin, *Kit Carson Days,* p. 121.

52. Parkman felt that the standard rules of judging character fail in Beckwourth's case, for Beckwourth was capable both of stabbing a man in his sleep and performing the most desperate acts of daring *(Oregon Trail,* p. 133). That Beckwourth's behavior and acts were approved by those with whom he associated is indicated, according to Chittenden, by the fact that the American Fur Company paid him a salary of $800 per year, which, at that time, was a good salary and indicated a good standing with the company *(American Fur Trade,* vol. 1, p. 681).

53. Vandiveer, *Fur Trade,* p. 261.

54. Dale L. Morgan, *Jedediah Smith and the Opening of the West* (Indianapolis, 1953), p. 194.

55. Neihardt, *Splendid Wayfaring,* p. 261.

56. Harrison Dale, *The Ashley-Smith Explorations and Discovery of a Central Route to the Pacific* (Glendale, Ca., 1941), p. 223.

57. Morgan, *Jedediah Smith,* p. 267.

58. Ibid., p. 270; Neihardt, *Splendid Wayfaring,* p. 267.

59. Dale, *Ashley-Smith Explorations,* p. 252.

60. Ibid.

61. William H. Ellison, ed., *Life and Adventures of George Nidever, 1802–83* (Berkeley, Ca., 1937), p. 108.

62. Ibid., p. 39.

63. Bancroft, *History of California,* vol. 4, p. 713.

64. In another incident, Black Steward was the principal actor in a contest with a bear. On one of the trapping excursions, he and his associates went hunting for animals for the mess, and in the course of the hunt they became separated. Black Steward wounded a deer, dismounted, and started to crawl up to the deer in order to kill it. In passing through a clump of bushes he was attacked by a bear. It all happened so quickly that he had no time to defend himself before he was knocked down. He was a powerful man, and he grappled with the bear. During the contest he received many severe bites, and his coat was torn to bits. He and the bear rolled over and over until they fell down a steep hill, at which time he was able to free himself and kill the bear (Ellison, *Life and Adventures of George Nidever,* p. 62). This same affair is related in Alfred Robinson's "Recollections of Early Years in California," *Recollections of Alfred Robinson,* vol. 1, Bancroft Library, University of California, Berkeley.

65. Charles Larpenteur, *Forty Years a Fur Trader on the Upper Missouri* (New York, 1899), p. 121.

66. Ibid., p. 154.

67. Ibid., p. 134.

68. Harold B. Briggs, *Frontiers of the Northwest* (New York, 1940), p. 74.

69. J. D. Borthwick, *The Gold Hunters* (New York, 1917), p. 162.

70. William F. Switzler, *Switzler's Illustrated History of Missouri, from 1541 to 1877* (St. Louis, 1879), p. 143.

71. Reuben Gold Thwaites, "Notes on Early Lead Mining in the Fever (or Galena) River Region," *Wisconsin State Historical Society Collections* 13 (1895), p. 290.

72. John Wood, *Journal* (Columbus, 1871), p. 7.

73. *San Francisco Pacific News,* August 25, 1849.

74. Ibid., March 31, 1850.

75. Edwin Sherman, *Biographical Material* (Bancroft Library).

76. Daniel B. Woods, *Sixteen Months at the Gold Diggings* (New York, 1851), p. 155.

77. Benjamin Hayes, *Pioneer Notes from the Diaries of Judge Benjamin Hayes,* 1849, 1875 (Los Angeles, 1929), p. 136.

78. *San Francisco Chronicle,* October 11, 1903.

79. W. Sherman Savage, "Workers of Lincoln University" (unpublished manuscript), Lincoln University, Jefferson City, Missouri.

80. *California History Nuggets,* vol. 3, p. 92.

81. J. Albert Wilson, *History of Los Angeles County, California* (1880; rpt., Berkeley, 1959), p. 70.

82. Carl I. Wheat, ed., " 'California's Bantam Cock': the Journals of Charles E. De Long, 1854–1863," *California Historical Society Quarterly* 10 (September 1931), p. 293.

83. Ibid. 8, p. 211.

84. John Bidwell, *Echoes of the Past about California,* ed. Milo M. Quaife (Chicago, 1928), p. 260.

85. J. D. Borthwick, *Three Years in California* (London, 1857), p. 161.

86. Delano, *Across the Plains,* p. 174.

87. Edna B. Buckbee, *The Saga of Old Tuolumne* (New York, 1935), p. 329.

88. Theodore H. Hittell, *History of California* (San Francisco, 1897, vol. 3, p. 92.

89. Ibid., vol. 3, p. 118.

90. James Williams, *Life and Adventures of James Williams a Fugitive Slave* (San Francisco, 1873), pp. 28ff.

91. Frank Soule, John Gihon, and James Nisbet, *The Annals of San Francisco* (Palo Alto: Lewis Osborne, 1966), p. 412. William H. Brewer, *Up and Down California in 1860–1864* (New Haven, 1930), p. 395.

92. Edward G. Buffum, *Six Months in the Gold Mines* (London, 1850), p. 81.

93. Delilah L. Beasley, *Negro Trail Blazers of California* (Los Angeles, 1919), p. 105.

94. *San Francisco Elevator,* April 10, 1865 (this was a black paper, published in San Francisco).

95. Joseph Batty, *Over the Wilds to California,* ed. John Simpson (Leeds, 1867), p. 44.

96. U.S. Census report, 1870.

97. *San Francisco Elevator,* December 14, 1872.

98. Ibid., December 20, 1873.

99. James H. Baker and LeRoy R. Hafen, eds., *History of Colorado* (Denver, 1927), vol. 3, p. 1095.

100. *Denver Rocky Mountain News,* September 19, 1880.

101. Harvey, "The Negro in Colorado," p. 20.

102. *Denver Rocky Mountain News,* May 2, 1880.

103. Ibid., September 8, 1885.

104. Ibid., May 22, 1885.

105. Harvey, "The Negro in Colorado."

106. Ibid.

107. *Denver Rocky Mountain News,* July 3, 1884.

108. Ibid., September 28, 1880.

109. Philip A. Rollins, *The Cowboy* (New York, 1922), p. 22.

110. John M. Hunter, comp. and ed., *The Trail Drivers of Texas,* 2nd ed. (Nashville, 1925), p. 231; Robert J. Lauderdale and John M. Doak, *Life on the Range and on the Trail,* ed. Lela N. Pirtle (San Antonio, 1936), p. 14.

111. H. Bailey Carroll, "Texas Collection," *Southwestern Historical Quarterly* 48 (July 1944), p. 100.

112. Mary A. Maverick, *Memoirs of Mary A. Maverick,* ed. Rena Maverick Green (San Antonio, 1921), p. 123.

113. W. J. Elliot, *The Spurs* (Dallas, 1909), p. 208.

114. Floyd B. Streeter, *Prairie Trails and Cow Towns: The Opening of the Old West* (Boston, 1936), p. 157.

115. Charles A. Siringo, *Lone Star Cowboy* (Santa Fe, N.M., 1919), pp. 30, 48.

116. James F. Dobie, *The Longhorns* (Boston, 1941), p. 324.

117. Letter from H. Bailey Carroll, Secretary, Texas State Historical Association, to author, July 27, 1944.

118. Information furnished to author by John Organ, Georgetown, Texas. The material was dictated by Emanuel Organ before his death.

119. John M. Hendrix, "Tribute to Negro Cowmen," *Cattlemen,* February 1936.

120. Nat Love, *Life and Adventures* (Los Angeles, 1907), p. 41.

121. Ibid., p. 91.

122. Ibid., p. 120.

123. John H. Herman, "Black Cowboys Are Real," *Crisis* 47, p. 301.

124. MS furnished by Mrs. Wallace Fowler, who was working on the biography of her father. Mrs. Fowler's unfinished manuscript was completed by her sister, Hattey Wallace Branch, under the title, *The Story of 80 John.*

125. Hendrix, "Tribute to Negro Cowmen."

126. Herman, "Black Cowboys Are Real."

127. MS by Mrs. Fowler.

128. Letter, Hooks to the author, October 18, 1944; letter, L. F. Sheffy to the author, August 10, 1944.

129. *Amarillo Press,* September 14, 1941.

130. Ibid., September 8, 1944.

131. Ibid., September 7, 1941.

132. Ibid., September 28, 1944.

133. Harvey, "The Negro in Colorado," p. 22.

134. Stuart O. Henry, *Conquering Our Great American Plains* (New York, 1930), p. 126; Wayne Gard, *The Chisholm Trail* (Norman, 1954), p. 168.

135. *Pony Express Courier* 3 (November 1936), p. 15.

136. Ibid.

137. Letter of November 13, 1856, Records of the Secretary of the Interior, National Archives, Washington, D.C.

138. Department of the Interior, Land and Railroad Division, National Archives, Washington, D.C.

139. Harvey, "The Negro in Colorado," p. 25.

140. United States, Forty-Sixth Congress, Second Session, Select Committee Minority Report (1880).

141. Isaac O. Pickering, "The Administration of John P. St. John," *Kansas State Historical Society Collections* 9 (1905–06), p. 386n.

142. Everett N. Dick, *The Sod House Frontier, 1854–1890* (New York, 1937), p. 197 (quoting Henry King in *Scribner's Magazine,* April 1, 1880).

143. *St. Louis Globe,* April 24, 1879.

144. Ibid., April 30, 1879.

145. *Leavenworth Times,* March 7, 1879.

146. Pickering, "Administration of John P. St. John," p. 387. Kansas

was the state to which the majority of the migrants went, but other states were to receive some of them.

147. *Denver Rocky Mountain News,* June 3, 1879.

148. United States, Senate Special Committee on Exodus, Forty-Sixth Congress, Second Session (1880). Members of the committee were senators D. W. Vorhees (chairman), Z. B. Vance, George H. Pendleton, William Windom, and Henry Blair.

149. *Rocky Mountain Sentinel* (Santa Fe, N. M.), July 10, 1879.

150. *Garnett* [Kansas] *Plaindealer,* April 16, 1880. He said he had been forced to see his friend killed and could say or do nothing about it, for he expected every minute to suffer the same fate.

151. Nell Blyth Waldron, "Colonization in Kansas from 1861–1890" (dissertation, Northwestern University, 1923).

152. *Lawrence Western Home Journal,* May 1, 1879.

153. Ibid.

154. Ibid., May 6, 1879.

155. Ibid. The town of Nicodemus was named in honor of a noted slave who was said to have come to America on the second slave ship and who became an outstanding figure after he purchased his freedom (Dick, *Sod House Frontier,* p. 197).

156. Material on the exodus of blacks into Kansas, Clipping Files, Kansas State Historical Library, Topeka.

157. *Topeka Daily Commonwealth,* May 17, 1879.

158. William F. Zornow, *Kansas: A History of the Jayhawk State* (Norman, 1957), pp. 186–187.

159. *Oklahoma: A Guide to the Sooner State* (Norman: University of Oklahoma Press, 1945), p. 237.

160. George H. Shirk, "First Post Offices Within the Boundaries of Oklahoma," *Chronicles of Oklahoma* 26 (Summer 1948), p. 229.

161. *Oklahoma: A Guide,* p. 237.

162. Ibid., p. 255.

163. William L. Katz, *The Black West* (Garden City, N.Y., 1971), p. 313.

164. Ibid., p. 315.

165. Grant Foreman, "Early Post Offices of Oklahoma," *Chronicles of Oklahoma* 6 (September 1928), p. 295.

166. *Texas: A Guide to the Lone Star State* (New York: Hasting House Publishers, 1940), p. 378.

167. W. P. Webb and H. Bailey Carroll, eds., *The Handbook of Texas* (Austin, 1952), vol. 2, p. 278.

168. Ibid., vol. 1, p. 946.

169. B. T. Washington, "The New Potato King," *Outlook* 77 (May 14, 1904), p. 115.

170. Material on blacks in Kansas, Clipping Files, Kansas State Library, Topeka.

171. *Kansas City* (Missouri) *Star,* May 17, 1910.

172. *Afro-American Advocate* (Coffeyville, Kansas), August 11, 1893.

173. Sheffield Ingalls, *History of Atchison County, Kansas* (Lawrence, 1916), p. 337.

174. Material on blacks in Kansas, Clipping Files, Kansas State Library,

175. *Emporia Gazette,* September 8, 1915.

176. Material on blacks, Clipping Files, Kansas State Library, Topeka.

177. Ibid.

178. Ibid.

179. Ibid.

180. Ibid.

181. Bush Family Bible; John E. Ayer, "George Bush, the Voyageur," *Washington Historical Quarterly* 7 (1916), p. 42.

182. Ayer, "George Bush," p. 41.

183. Francis Henry, "George Bush," *Transactions of the Oregon Pioneer Association,* Fifteenth Annual Reunion (Portland, Ore., 1887), p. 68.

184. Georgiana Blankenship, comp. and ed., *Early History of Thurston County, Washington* (Olympia, 1914), p. 320.

185. George Washington Bush owned the first mower and reaper in the Puget Sound area, according to Leslie M. Scott, "Soil Repair Lessons in Willamette Valley," *Oregon Historical Society Quarterly* 18 (March 1917), p. 66.

186. *Territorial Papers of Washington Territory,* vol. 1, March 17, 1885, National Archives, Washington, D.C.

187. Blankenship, *Early History of Thurston County,* p. 321. However, according to Murray Morgan, in a letter to the author: "The statement that Tolmie was forbidden to sell food to the Americans appears from the records to be a flat error, though it was widely believed by the pioneers. The records of Fort Nisqually show sales of food stuffs (wheat, coffee, and even meat) to the Americans. Further, there are letters from Douglas, the acting factor at Fort Vancouver, to Tolmie at Nisqually, telling him to sell to the Americans at the standard price and even to extend them credit (with a $25 limit). Tolmie was also told to buy shingles from the Americans and hire them if they offered bodily labor. The source of most of their trouble was . . . the unusual severity of the winter. Usually winters are open in this part of the country but that winter there was snow on the ground for six weeks and temperatures below freezing. This would have made game hard to track and would have prevented the Indians from supplying the white settlers with much food."

188. Ezra Meeker, *Pioneer Reminiscences of Puget Sound* (Seattle, 1905), p. 82.

189. Blankenship, *Early History of Thurston County,* p. 322. Murray Morgan said that Bush had little trouble with the Indians; he and Simmons were Indian agents. There was little hostility toward the settlements of the Des Chutes.

190. Ibid. This was not much of a fort. Murray Morgan says that it was just a big cabin in which the party lived during this troubled period.

191. "Mrs. Elmira Whitaker, Thurston County," *Told by the Pioneers* 3 (1938), p. 151.

192. "Autobiography of John Roger James, Thurston County," *Told by the Pioneers* 2 (1937), p. 79.

193. Leslie M. Scott, "Soil Repair Lessons in Willamette Valley," p. 68.

194. Ayer, "George Bush, the Voyageur," p. 45.

195. Blankenship, *Early History of Thurston County,* p. 324.

196. Ibid., p. 320.

197. *Laws of Missouri, 1842–1843* (Jefferson City, Mo.), p. 207.

5 • Black businesses, professions, and occupations

So far we have examined the role of the black in the major occupations in the West: the fur trade, mining, cattle, and farming. But blacks worked in myriad other capacities as well. Some were in the employ of others, while some were independent businessmen. Some gained a sparse or moderate livelihood; others amassed considerable wealth and were powerful and influential figures in the history of the West. We cannot cover here all the ways in which blacks worked in the West, but we shall suggest something of the variety of that work, as well as the degree of prominence achieved in some cases by blacks who took part in the shaping of the West.

In 1900 more than 1,500 blacks were employed in the western states as barbers.[1] Whether their patrons were exclusively white or whether they worked among blacks as well is not documented, but we do know that there was some opposition to the entrance of blacks into the trade, largely from foreign-born competitors who were settling on the western frontier at the same time. We know as well a number of details concerning individual barbers.

Peter Biggs, for example, was one of the first black barbers in the West, and he was the first American to open a barber shop in Los Angeles. Biggs had gone to California with his master, Reuben Middleton, but did not long remain a slave. Once a freeman, he established a barber shop and charged one dollar for hair cuts and fifty cents for shaves.[2] In 1855 Judge Benjamin Hayes, who had known Biggs in Liberty, Missouri, when the latter had been the slave of Middleton, came to Los Angeles and was taken to Biggs. Horace Bell, who also saw Biggs in Los Angeles, said that he was quite a figure in the town and that he had had a monopoly on the barbering trade until the arrival of a French barber who knew more of the "fine art" of barbering. As a result of this qualitative competition, Biggs suffered a reduction in his business. Trying to recapture part of his lost patronage by reducing his prices, he inserted an advertisement in the *Los Angeles Star,* offering hair cuts for fifty cents, shampooing for fifty cents, and shaves for twenty-five cents. Biggs also offered his personal service in many other ways—cleaning, polishing, drayage, washing and ironing, running errands, blacking boots, and waiting and tending parties.[3] The life of this picturesque character was cut short when he was killed by a Mexican.[4]

Other black barbers in California include Byron Rowan, who settled in the San Bernardino Valley about the time of the Mormon migration. As late as 1887 he owned and operated the Pioneer Barber Shop on Third Street between c and d streets in the city of San Bernardino.[5] John Lloyd, George Woods, James D. Brown, and George Carter were other black barbers. Carter's property was valued at $10,000, which suggests that it was possible for a black barber to achieve affluence in this trade. By 1900, 170 blacks, or about 1-½ percent of the state's black population, were barbers in California.

Nevada reported a few black barbers who seem to have built up good businesses. J. W. Whitfield and G. Cailif were successful barbers in Elko County. Whitfield is listed as owning $1,000 worth of real property and $500 worth of personal property, figures which are not as impressive as that for Carter but which show nonetheless some measure of success. John W. Price, who went to Nevada from Maryland, was listed as a barber in Virginia City. In 1900, although there were only 134 blacks in Nevada, seven were listed as barbers—about 5 percent of the state's black population.

In 1870 both Utah and Colorado also had small populations, yet there were a few black barbers, such as James Valentine in Salt Lake City, Paul Lancaster in Ogden, and Jim Bell and Edward Sanderlin in Denver.[6] Bell was the first black barber in the city of Denver. He did not own a shop, but he worked in a shop which catered exclusively to white patronage. Robert Sum was the first black to own and operate a shop in Denver. It was located in the Oxford Hotel from 1892 to 1900.[7]

There were black barbers in Wisconsin and Minnesota as early as 1850. Minnesota had two black barbers—Titus Patrick and John Williams—in Columbia County. In Wisconsin, Jared Gray, Henry Cook, and John Bellows were barbers in Milwaukee County; there were two barbers in Kenosha City—George Day and George Cripup; and William Henry Talbot worked as a barber in Rock County.[8] Minnesota had a black population of 259 in 1860, and it had at least one black barber, J. F. Anderson, who was at work in Winona City. He seems to have attained a modest prosperity: his real estate possessions were valued at $800 and his personal property at $400. That barbering apparently offered gainful employment to blacks in these states as well as others is shown by the 1900 census report that there were 273 black barbers in a black population of 7,492.[9]

The census shows as well that there were 654 black barbers in Iowa, Washington, Nebraska, Kansas, and Dakota Territory. J. P. Williams worked at his trade in Clayton County, Iowa, and Nathaniel Matthews and Jeremiah Crump were at work in Douglas County, Nebraska, in 1860.[10] In 1879 the first Directory of Bismarck revealed that several black barbers worked in W. H. Comer's shop, which was located on Main Street. Among them were B. H. Smith, H. E. Taylor, and George Brown.[11] Harvey Mitchell was a prosperous barber in Sioux Falls. He had worked in other states before coming to the Dakotas.[12] In Kansas, John Fleming was an unusual and prosperous barber. He went to Horton in about 1870 and for more than thirty years was the town's barber. When he died, the business establishments of the town closed as a tribute to him. In addition, the mayor issued a proclamation which called to the attention of the city the worth of one of its praiseworthy citizens.[13]

As might be expected, the restaurant and hotel business in the West increased with the growing population. The gold rush in particular was an important factor in the growth of these industries. By 1900 seventy hotels were scattered over the West. At least one black hotel or rooming house existed in all of the states except Nevada, North Dakota, South Dakota, Arizona, Wisconsin, and Idaho. These hotels were in the section of the city where the largest black population resided, indicating that most of their business was transacted entirely with blacks.[14] The restaurant business was in many cases a part of the hotel and boarding-house business. In 1900 there were 200 restaurants in the West. The largest number, forty-six, were in Kansas, while in Iowa and California there were some twenty such establishments. A. J. Jones built the first hotel owned by blacks in Los Angeles. It was located on San Pedro Street in the section which was then called Wilmington. Jones's specialty, hot biscuits, built for him a large patronage.[15] A similar type of establishment was operated as early as 1860 in Corinne City, Box Elder County, Utah. These establishments were a source of employment for many; in the hotels and restaurants in this area, more than 5,000 persons were required as cooks, waiters, porters, and janitors.

Most of the restaurants and boarding houses were rather ephemeral, but the one run by Henry Clay Wilson was an exception. Wilson was born a slave in Tennessee but at an early age was brought by his family to Arkansas. Henry's father was restless, and the family moved on to Kansas while Henry was still a small boy. There the elder Wilson erected a building and operated a thriving restaurant business which he called the "Holiday House" in honor of his friend, Cyrus K. Holiday, the leading spirit in the organization and development of the Atchison, Topeka, and Santa Fe Railroad. This business enabled Henry Wilson to serve almost every Santa Fe train which passed through Topeka. Because of his success at the Holiday House, Wilson is credited with being important in the founding of the Harvey House System.[16] This system furnished meals for the trains at a time when all trains stopped to feed the passengers. The Harvey Houses constituted one of the great restaurant systems, quite similar to the Howard Johnson restaurants of today.

Blacks were employed on the frontier in the building trades as early as the 1850s. In 1850, in Sacramento County, California, William Hunter was listed as a carpenter. Isaiah Bell was so listed in Tucson, Arizona, in 1860. Shawshone Rich was in that trade in Washoe County, Nevada. He owned a small piece of property valued at $500.[17] The opposition to black carpenters must have been severe, however, for in 1900 there were fewer than 100 blacks listed in that occupation.[18] In the Rocky Mountain Basin and in the Plateau and

Pacific states there were almost 200 blacks engaged in the mason trade, both brick and stone. Some blacks were general contractors in the building trades; for example, John A. Barber was a contractor and builder in California. He was born in Nantucket, Massachusetts, and went to California in the great migration between the years 1848 and 1853.[19] All in all, according to the 1900 census, the various phases of the building trades provided employment for about 500 blacks.

Figures for blacks who were employed in the saloon business are not available. A conservative estimate is about 100. One who attracted attention in this business was John William Stuart. In 1860 he was employed in Los Angeles in a saloon on Los Angeles Street, north of First Street. Using his homestead rights, Stuart took a grant which is now within the limits of the present city and opened a saloon of his own. He prospered, for the location increased in value with the growth of the city.[20] In 1870 Moses Jackson was engaged in the saloon business in Virginia City, Nevada. He reportedly owned real estate valued at $1,000. John Johnson, a saloon owner of Dakota County, Minnesota, was reported as owning property in 1860 valued at $500. William McAndrews owned a saloon in Clinton County, Iowa, and reportedly owned real estate valued at $5,000 and personal property valued at $800.[21] So at least a few blacks who went into this business for themselves were able to accumulate some property.

Before 1900 more than 200 blacks were employed as grooms and hostlers. In the West many communities held fairs which featured horse races. Oney Fred Sweet, a reporter and lecturer for the Redpath Chautauqua in Iowa, thought that the races brought picturesque characters who arrived before the opening of the fair and spent their time grooming the horses for the track. To him they were different from ordinary people because of their bright-colored dress and their superior attitude toward the local people. Some blacks seemed peculiar to many in the small towns because of their droll expressions and their constant singing of spirituals and other songs while at work.[22]

One of the outstanding sportsmen of the West was E. J. "Lucky" Baldwin who built the Santa Anita Race Track at Arcadia, California, at which he employed several blacks. On one of his trips east, Baldwin heard about a young black, John Wesley Fisher, who was to have considerable influence on the development of specially designed shoes for race horses. Born a slave, Fisher was freed at the age of eight and later became an apprentice in a blacksmith shop, where he showed exceptional artistry. It was said that he could curve shoes for race-horses like no other. He insisted that horse-shoeing was a work of art and could make or ruin a race horse. Baldwin demanded a demonstration. Accordingly, Fisher had the stable boy run a horse before and after he changed the shoes. Because of the specially designed shoes, the horse cut a second from his best time. Baldwin was convinced and gave Fisher lifetime employment at Santa Anita. A year after hiring him, Baldwin sent Fisher south to bring out a carload of field hands and horse handlers to work at the Rancho Santa Anita. Some of the descendants of those blacks still live in Monrovia, California.

Regarding the Santa Anita Race Track and its development, Fisher said that he and Baldwin developed not only their own horses but also their own jockeys. Baldwin brought in Freddy Welch and Isaac Murphy to train their jockeys. Murphy, a black, was among the greatest jockeys of all time. He trained horses and men in the West and several times won the famous Kentucky Derby as well as many other important races.[23]

Some blacks found employment in the livery-stable business. In 1900 there were about a dozen stables owned and operated in the West by blacks. One prominent black in this area was George Washington Dennis. He migrated to California in 1849 and went first to the gold fields but was unsuccessful there. Dennis then opened a livery stable in San Francisco, at Sansome and Washington streets. He later took James Brown into the business and went into the coal and wood business on Broadway near Montgomery. Dennis completed some real estate transactions, joined in a partnership with Mifflin Gibbs, and bought a group of lots on Montgomery Street between Jackson and Pacific streets for $18,000. In six months he sold them for a profit. Another successful black in the livery stable business was Robert Owen, who owned a stable in Los Angeles on San Pedro Street. After his death the business was continued by his son, Charles, who moved the stable to First and Main streets, where he operated them the rest of his life. On his death the business passed to his two sons, Robert C. and Henry L. Owen, who moved it to Spring Street on the property of Biddy Mason. Over a period of three generations, the Owen family, through its livery stable business, real estate, and government contracts, became one of the best-known and wealthiest black families in America.[24]

Another occupation for blacks was "going to sea." The first blacks came to the Pacific Coast on ships and worked as sailors or as common laborers. This occupation offered some employment until the turn of the century, when there were only a few blacks so employed—fewer than 100 in all capacities. Some worked as longshoremen and some worked on ships sailing regularly to other sections of the country. Edward Allen was one of the blacks who worked on steamships. On July 6, 1851, a report was sent to the Pacific Coast by civil authorities in Philadelphia to apprehend Allen. The report labelled him a thief and a thoroughgoing criminal. He was employed as first steward on a steamer bound for San Francisco and was described as a large, powerful man with a light brown complexion.[25] In 1848 Frisbie Hood and a black cook whose name is not given worked as steward and cook on the *Izaak Walton*. The government had chartered a steamer, *Anita,* for sending supplies to the troops stationed on the Pacific Coast.[26] Hood and the cook remained with the *Izaak Walton* until August 1851, when they deserted and were hired by the *Anita* when it was out at sea.[27] Other blacks listed by the census of 1870 as workers on steamers were John Sanders, Henry Brown, and someone known simply as "Andy."[28]

Blacks also worked in various capacities on lake boats. An account is given by a Danish visitor, Robert Watts, who went to the West in the 1870s on the steamship *Savannah,* which sailed from St. Paul to Prairie du Chien, Wisconsin, and Red Wing, Minnesota. The Dane was impressed by the number of blacks who were employed to load and unload the sacks of flour and to handle the engines. He also noted the songs that they sang, especially "My Old Kentucky Home."[29] The number of blacks who worked on the lake boats was small, however, because even as late as 1900 only a few blacks lived in the states which touched the lakes.

Although blacksmithing was of great importance in the West, only a few blacks were employed in that occupation during the period of the westward movement. Among them, Henderson Boon conducted with much success a shop in Pasadena, California, for more than a quarter of a century. After his death the business was continued by his wife and son.[30] In 1850 Ben Peters of Sacramento was listed as a blacksmith with personal property worth $1,000. In the same year Manuel Marsey worked as a blacksmith for John Porter of Corinne, Utah.[31] In 1900 there were sixty-nine blacksmiths in the Rocky Mountain section and the Plateau and Pacific areas.

The professions were represented by only a few blacks. This is not surprising since they required long periods of training in special schools. Blacks had enough difficulty gaining entrance to the common schools, let alone specialized institutions. Thus as late as 1900 there were in the western states fewer than 100 blacks in the professions of medicine, dentistry, and teaching. Dr. John S. Outlaw was a pioneer physician in Los Angeles. In 1884 he went to Los Angeles from Washington, D.C., where he had begun his practice after graduating from Howard University Medical School.[32] Dr. M. A. Majors was another early black physician in Los Angeles. He acquired his training in Texas and moved to Los Angeles in 1888. As late as 1900 the census report lists no black dentists in the West. In 1901 Dr. Alva C. Garrott began his practice in Los Angeles.[33] Although a few teachers were employed in the schools for blacks in California and Nevada, they were never firmly established in this region. In 1900 only five blacks were employed as teachers. More entered the professions, however, when blacks were prohibited from attending public schools.

Similarly, few blacks were engaged in the arts. A few, such as Emma and Louise Hyers, Sarah Miles Taylor, and William Blake, did gain some prominence in the field of classical music. The Hyers sisters made their debut jointly at the Metropolitan Theater in Sacramento in 1867. Both were highly commended.[34] To encourage the study of classical music among blacks of the West and to foster music appreciation among blacks, the Pacific Musical Association was established in 1877.[35] The weekly meetings of this organization contributed tremendously to blacks' interest in classical music.

One profession in which blacks did engage in some numbers was the ministry. Black churches were numerous, and there was a corresponding need for many black ministers. More than 600 blacks were engaged in the ministry in the West. The majority of them were in those areas having large concentrations of the black population. Kansas, for example, had more than 200 ministers of all faiths, whereas South Dakota had only two clergymen, New Mexico had two, and Utah had only one.

Some of the black ministers were well-trained, as was revealed in 1870 by the *Olympia Daily Pacific Tribune*. In that year a black applied for a license to preach in the Presbyterian church. He was

given an examination which included Hebrew, Greek, Italian, and all
the books required of Presbyterian theological students. The content
of the sermon which he delivered as part of the examination was
good, and his manner of delivery was convincing and eloquent. The
editor of the *Tribune* noted that, although his deformed body prejudiced
the Presbytery against him, he was granted his license.[36]

One of the pioneer blacks in the ministry in the West was the Reverend Barney Fletcher, who was well-known in northern California.
Born a slave, he purchased his own freedom and his wife's on the
installment plan for $2,000. He raised the money by selling New
York papers on the Sacramento river boats. Fletcher was later or-
dained a minister in the African Methodist Episcopal church, in
which he preached for many years. He ranked high in Masonic cir-
cles, and he organized a Black Woman's Beneficial Society which
was still in existence as late as 1884. Fletcher was also the first black
to serve on a United States jury in northern California.[37]

Blacks understandably took pride in those among them who
achieved stature and wealth. At each convention of black citizens in
California, the property value for blacks in each county of the state
was reported, as well as how each person was employed. In 1857,
only seven years after statehood, blacks in the various counties of
California owned property in the following amounts: San Francisco,
$450,000; Nevada, $260,000; Mariposa, $75,000; Shasta, $76,000;
Butte, $96,000; Yerba, $94,000; Siskiyou, $65,000; Sierra, $65,000;
Tuolumne, $90,000; Plumas, $20,000; Santa Clara, $21,000; El-
dorado, $250,000; Sacramento, $84,703; Amador, $50,000;
Alameda, $50,900; San Joaquin, $80,000; Napa, $30,000; and
Sonoma, $5,000. Increasing profits in both agriculture and industry
added to these figures. In Napa County, for example, the reported
value of property owned by blacks increased from $30,000 in 1857
to $51,000 in 1865.

By 1865 the property owned by blacks in San Francisco and other
counties in the state had increased considerably. In San Francisco
County alone, blacks owned four tobacco factories, two soap factories, one tallow processing plant, two salvage stores, and two laun-
dries. There were also two black real estate agents and two news
editors of black newspapers.

The black newspaper deserves special attention because it was not
only a form of business enterprise but also a means for the black man
to record his achievements and to protest the injustices done him.

The first black newspaper in the West appeared in California. Like any other business, the papers had to have financial support, which initially could be given only by blacks in California, since it had the largest black population among the western states. In San Francisco, the *Mirror of the Times* began its publication in 1855 and continued to operate until 1862. It was succeeded by the *Pacific Appeal* and the *Elevator*. In the eastern states, as on the Pacific Coast, the *Pacific Appeal* was considered a reliable index of what the black was accomplishing on the West Coast. Philip A. Bell, one of the early black editors, was connected with the *Pacific Appeal* and wrote its sober editorials.[38] In 1865 Bell began the *Elevator*, which was known as a journal of progress devoted to science, art, literature, and drama. He managed to keep this paper in operation until the time of his death in 1889. How long it continued after that is not known; copies in the Bancroft Library bear dates up to 1898.

Besides the California papers, about a dozen others appeared in other sections of the West. In 1883 the *Rising Sun* appeared in Des Moines, Iowa, and in 1888 three papers were born: the *American Citizen* in Topeka, Kansas; the *Afro-American Sentinel* in Omaha, Nebraska; and the *Afro-American Independent* in St. Paul, Minnesota. The following year two more began operations: the *Progress* in Omaha and the *Statesman* in Denver. After this, black papers were established with greater frequency. The year 1891 saw the beginning of the *Avalanche* in Des Moines, the *Northwestern Recorder* in Milwaukee, Wisconsin, and the *Enterpriser* in Omaha. In 1894 two papers, the *Seattle Republican* and the *Colorado Statesman,* made their appearances.

Black newspapers tended to be quite transitory. Most of them did not continue in operation for several reasons. One factor was the smallness of the black population, resulting in inadequate financial support. Another factor which operated against them was their method of getting news, for they did not have the advantage of membership in the news-gathering agencies. Consequently, most of their news concerned the achievements of the black, together with church and social news. Black papers still follow that general pattern and, in that role, render the greatest service to those who wish to study the black in the United States.

One of the first of the prominent black businessmen in the West was William Alexander Leidesdorff.[39] He went to California in 1841 and established himself as a merchant in Yerba Buena, later known as San Francisco. Leidesdorff developed a considerable trade with the ships which came to Yerba Buena and with the many merchants and ranchers in northern California. In 1844 he began the building of a warehouse at the foot of California Street on the beach of San Francisco Bay. The structure was completed in 1845; it gave him room to deal in many kinds of merchandise for which he found a ready market. A sign of Leidesdorff's prosperity was the fact that he owned the largest private house in Yerba Buena.[40]

Another manifestation of his business acumen was his provision of quick transportation from Yerba Buena to Sacramento, especially from Sutter's Fort, which was situated on the Sacramento River near where the present city of Sacramento now stands. Leidesdorff dreamed of furnishing twenty-four-hour express service from New Helvetia, as Sutter's Fort was then called, and San Francisco.[41] He had planned to supply this service by steamship. He purchased from Sitka, Russia, a vessel which had been built by an American firm for the Russian-American Company and which had been used exclusively for the pleasure of Russian officials. Leidesdorff fitted the vessel to carry rapid trade between the two points and, on its maiden voyage, invited his friends to make the trip to New Helvetia.[42] The trip proved disappointing. Instead of the anticipated twenty-four hours, it took six days because the ship was slow and very small, measuring only thirty-seven feet in length, nine feet in width, and three-and-a-half feet below deck. These dimensions also made the vessel top-heavy, and soon after the first trip it sank in San Francisco Bay. Thus Leidesdorff's efforts to provide rapid transportation on the Sacramento River came to an end. But despite the failure of this venture, he was the first to use a steamboat on San Francisco Bay, and his effort demonstrated that steam transportation was possible under more favorable conditions.

Leidesdorff's land holding was extensive, though he did not live to see it developed. He followed the lead of some other American citizens who came to California while it was under Mexican control and became a Mexican citizen in order to take advantage of certain privileges which were not open to American citizens. Later, the Mexican government granted him eight leagues of land, the equivalent of 35,000 acres. It was located in Sacramento Valley on the left bank of the American River, called Rio del Rancho Americano.[43]

Leidesdorff was certain that his land was rich in gold, but he had not been able to develop it. James Forbes, claiming that he possessed great knowledge in mining, wrote Leidesdorff on May 15, 1848, offering his services in mining the land. Leidesdorff could not avail himself of Forbes's offer, however, for he died from typhus three days later, on May 18, while still a young man of only thirty-eight.[44] He left no will, an omission that resulted in confusion for several individuals and for the state of California because of the large amount of money involved. Actually, at the time of his death, Leidesdorff was $60,000 in debt, but in that year of 1848 gold was discovered at Sutter's Fort. Suddenly the value of his property skyrocketed, and the debts became trivial in comparison.[45]

The United States consul, Thomas Larkin, wrote a letter to Leidesdorff's clerk, saying that he thought that he, as consul, was the only person who could settle the estate. Leidesdorff had served as subconsul to Larkin, and whether Larkin had forgotten that Leidesdorff was a Mexican citizen or whether he had been misled by Leidesdorff's enthusiasm for the American cause is not clear. Certainly Larkin ought to have known of Leidesdorff's citizenship and should have realized that he could not dispose of the property. Larkin made it plain that he personally did not want the job (he and Leidesdorff had quarrelled) and that he hoped that a clerk could transact the business, but, he pointed out, in the likely event that he himself would have to settle the estate, he would have to move to San Francisco, and he would want to stay at Leidesdorff's house. He also wanted a room for his clerk.[46] On May 23 Larkin wrote to W.D.M. Howard, a San Francisco merchant and friend of Leidesdorff, to inform him that he had moved to San Francisco for the purpose of administering Leidesdorff's estate.[47] When Larkin began to examine the records, he found that Leidesdorff was a Mexican citizen and knew that he could not administer the property. The job of settling the estate passed to Howard, who was appointed by the alcalde of Mexico to take over as administrator of the property. His bond was set at $50,000, and two bondsmen were to serve as security for him. Howard took over Leidesdorff's palatial home and began the work of settling accounts. He remained until 1849, when the property was taken over by Captain J. Folsom.

The wealth left by Leidesdorff had aroused a great deal of interest among many persons, including Folsom. A native of New Hampshire, he graduated from West Point, where he then took a position as instructor. Later he was sent to San Francisco as a member of the Quartermaster Corps. He was in charge of the Quartermaster Depot in San Francisco when he heard that Leidesdorff had died without a will and had left no relatives in the United States. When Folsom saw the land increasing in value, he slipped away to New York and from there to Saint Croix Island where he paid Marie Ann Sparks, Leidesdorff's mother, $50,000, thereby buying out her interest in the estate.[48] It was easy to give so little for so much property because Marie Ann Sparks had no knowledge of the true value of the property. When she did learn something of its value, she protested to Folsom, who paid her another $25,000, making a total of $75,000 for a deed to the property which was now valued at $1,500,000.[49]

Folsom, however, was not to enjoy his newly acquired property without a fight. The state made an attempt to get control of the property because Leidesdorff had died without making a will. Through the attorney general, the state contended that Marie Ann Sparks had never been in the United States, was not an American citizen, and could not inherit California land. This was significant, for if she could not inherit the property, it would pass to the state and Folsom could not purchase it from her. The case was first tried in the Circuit Court of the Fourth Judicial District of San Francisco County, where the state's contention was not upheld. An appeal was carried to the California State Supreme Court by the attorney general, who argued the illegality of Marie Ann Sparks's inheritance of the property. The chief justice, Hugh C. Murray, who delivered the decision of the Court, felt that, because of the value of the property involved and the complicated diplomatic entanglements, this case had excited more public attention than any case which had come before the Court up to that time. He ruled that Marie Ann Sparks could inherit the property even though she was not a citizen of the United States. This confirmed the decision of the San Francisco court.[50] Supported by the highest court in the state, there was little to disturb Folsom's claim.

In 1856, however, Leopold Unger appeared at the County Recorder's Office and recorded a deed that constituted a new claim against the property. This deed, executed in Germany, with the seal of a court in Cologne, was purported to have been made by H. M.

Leidesdorff, residing in Bonn, H. C. Leidesdorff of Mulhard, and J. D. Leidesdorff of Bremen.[51] Allegedly, their relatives had conveyed all their property to William Alexander Leidesdorff, who had recently died in San Francisco. The claim was weak, however, for there were many records to show how William Leidesdorff had obtained his property. Nevertheless, these would-be heirs left it to Unger to see what he could secure at his own expense and risk. His feeble contention that William Leidesdorff was not the son of Marie Ann Sparks convinced no one, and the claim failed.

Even so, Folsom was not to enjoy for long the property for which he had fought so hard. He died at the age of thirty-eight. Once again the property had to be settled, this time by being sold off without contention.[52]

Another figure who became notable in the history of California was Mary Ellen Pleasant, whose relationship with Thomas Bell brought her into contact with the economic and political life of San Francisco. So many versions of her birthplace exist that her actual birthplace is uncertain.[53] In the story that she reported to Sam Davis, editor of the *San Francisco Pandex of the Press,* she was born in Philadelphia on August 19, 1814, at Nine Barley Street. The story continues that her father was a native Kanka on the Sandwich Islands and her mother was a full-blooded black woman from Louisiana. Mary was sent to Boston to obtain an education. Instead she was given hard work. Later she came into contact with Boston abolitionists and in this connection met Alexander Smith, a Cuban merchant, and was taken to the West Indies to live on a Cuban plantation.

After the death of Smith, Mary Ellen was offered $500 a month as a cook, but she refused. She married John Pleasant, who had been an overseer on the Smith farm and had probably been of some assistance in looking after her financial interests. The couple liquidated the property and moved to California in 1848 or 1849.[54] Mary Ellen operated a restaurant in San Francisco, invested her money in real estate, and also made loans at 10 percent a month. According to the many accounts appearing in the San Francisco papers, she handled large sums of money, and the rumor went around that she furnished John Brown with funds for his raid in Virginia.[55] She gave up the restaurant, went to Canada, and returned to San Francisco where she entered the employment of Thomas Bell as manager of his household. She exerted a mysterious influence over Bell and was able to extract from him, without security, any amount of money she desired. On one occasion she sent Bell's wife Theresa to Leandro, a small town in California, telling Bell that his wife had gone to New York. She then asked him for $25,000 to forward to New York. Ten days later she asked for $25,000 more which she said was necessary because Theresa had lost her money.[56]

Despite her reputation as a woman of means, Mary Ellen Pleasant was found to be not as wealthy as was popularly thought. Disclosure of her will at the time of her death showed that she did own a back lot in the Bell Block on Sutter Street near Octavia valued between $35,000 and $40,000 and interest in a law suit over jewels valued at $150,000.[57] Much litigation, lasting more than a quarter of a century, developed over her property.

One of the most progressive blacks in the West who exerted some influence on the economic development of San Francisco was Mifflin Wister Gibbs, a free black who went to California from Pennsylvania.[58] After some difficulty in adjusting to life in the West, he saved his earnings and eventually entered the clothing business with an already established firm in San Francisco. A year later he entered into a partnership with Peter Lester. The new firm was known as Lester and Gibbs, importers of fine boots and shoes. Operating out of their store, the Boot Emporium, at 636 Clay Street, they shipped their products all over California and into parts of Oregon.[59]

In 1858 there was much concern about the citizenship of blacks in California, and Gibbs was one of the leaders in that civic contest. Also during this time, gold was discovered in the Fraser River in the Hudson's Bay Company territory, a section which was later organized as the colony of British Columbia. This discovery caused a rush of gold seekers, speculators, and miners to that region. Gibbs went too, for it offered him an opportunity to leave California and its restrictions on blacks and to continue in business in a section of North America where there were no restrictions. He took with him a supply of miner's outfits, flour, blankets, picks, and shovels, which he was able to sell at a handsome profit.[60] At Victoria, Canada, he established the first merchandise general store other than the Hudson's Bay Company, and he invested his profits in real estate which paid off in huge returns. Gibbs bought a lot with a small house on it for $3,000, which was to be paid in six months, made $200 worth of improvements, and rented it for $500 a month. He also invested in the coal industry. In 1867 he built a railroad for Queen Charlotte coal mine to Skidgate Harbor, became superintendent of the railroad, and helped develop coal mining in the Pacific Northwest.[61] In 1869 Gibbs returned to the United States. Having studied law in Canada, he entered Oberlin College and graduated from the Law Department. Subsequently, he held various offices of importance with the United States government.

Some successful blacks, such as Biddy Mason, who acquired her wealth in the real estate business, and Clara Brown, who amassed a fortune in mining property, have already been discussed in other contexts. We have observed, too, that George Washington was a successful farmer in Washington. He was also the founder of Centralia, Washington. When the Northern Pacific was built, it crossed his land. In 1872 he thought of his farm as an excellent place to develop a little town where neighbors could live and form a cooperative community. Many who heard of the plan thought that it was foolish; they were sure no town could develop in such an isolated area. Washington, however, realized the significance of the fact that his farm lay midway between Kalama and Tacoma. He filed a plan of his proposed city, called Centerville, in the Chihalis courthouse in 1875 and offered 170-foot by 140-foot lots for ten dollars each. Washington would not speculate, but everything his hands touched turned to money. He built hundreds of boxlike houses for $300 each and rented them for six and seven dollars a month. From these transactions he amassed a small fortune.[62]

Through the variety of his own successes, George Washington illustrates the opportunity open to blacks in the West. We have seen that black men and women who went west entered many businesses and occupations. In some endeavors, such as barbering, they were relatively numerous. In others, such as real estate, they were few, but the degree of success attained by a handful of individuals such as William A. Leidesdorff and Mifflin W. Gibbs compensated for the small number of persons involved. All in all, the work done by blacks in the West before 1900 is of more than passing interest in the consideration of the region's development.

NOTES

1. U.S. Census Report, *Negroes in the United States* (U.S. Census Office, Washington, D.C., 1900)

2. John S. McGroarty, *Los Angeles from the Mountains to the Sea* (New York, 1921), vol. 1, p. 201.

3. Horace Bell, *Reminiscences of a Ranger, or Early Times in Southern California* (Los Angeles, 1881), p. 94.

4. Ibid., p. 27. There were others who held that he was not killed but left after his business failed.

5. U.S. Census Report of 1870 (Government Printing Office, Washington, D.C.).

6. Ibid.

7. James R. Harvey, "The Negro in Colorado," unpublished M.A. thesis (University of Denver, 1941), p. 79.

8. Census Report, Wisconsin, 1850 (Robert Armstrong, printer, Washington, D.C.).

9. Census Report, *Negroes in the United States*, 1900.

10. Census Report, Nebraska, 1860 (Government Printing Office, Washington, D.C.).

11. *Jewell's First Annual Directory of Bismarck, Dakota Territory.*

12. *Kansas City* [Missouri] *Call,* August 19, 1941 (a reprint of a tribute given by the Sioux Falls daily paper).

13. *Atchison Globe,* August 21, 1914.

14. Census Report of 1900.

15. Delilah Beasley, *Negro Trail Blazers of California* (Los Angeles, 1919), p. 136.

16. *Topeka Daily Capital,* May 30, 1937. This system was kept by the Santa Fe until only a few years ago, when speed became a factor in transportation and the Santa Fe made a greater use of dining cars.

17. U.S. Census Office, *7th Census, 1850* (Globe Office, Washington, D.C., 1851).

18. U.S. Census Office, *11th Census, 1890* (Government Printing Office, Washington, D.C., 1890). No separate records of blacks were kept prior to that time. Mifflin W. Gibbs in his *Shadow and Light* (Washington, D.C., 1902, p. 48) says that he was forced out because of hostility.

19. Beasley, *Negro Trail Blazers,* p. 124.

20. Federal Writers Project, "History of the Negro of Los Angeles County," unpublished manuscript, 1936, Sacramento State Library, California.

21. Oney F. Sweet, "An Iowa County Seat," *Iowa Journal of History and Politics* 38 (October 1940), p. 383.

22. W. Sherman Savage, "The Negro in the Westward Movement," *Journal of Negro History* 25 (October 1940), p. 538.

23. Carl B. Glasscock, *Lucky Baldwin: the Story of an Unconventional Success* (Indianapolis, 1933), p. 238.

24. Beasley, *Negro Trail Blazers,* p. 110. The family suffered reverses during the depression in 1929 and has largely lost its influence in the life of Los Angeles.

25. Mary F. Williams, ed., "Papers of the San Francisco Committee of Vigilance of 1851," *Academy of Pacific Coast History Publications* 4 (1919), p. 201.

26. William R. Grimshaw, *Narrative of Life and Events in California During Flush Times, Particularly in the Years 1848–1850,* manuscript in Bancroft Library, University of California, Berkeley, p. 15.

27. Ibid., p. 4.

28. Census of Washington Territory, 1870, U.S. Census Office, *9th Census, 1870* (Government Printing Office, Washington, D.C., 1872).

29. Jacob Hodnefield, trans. and ed., "Minnesota as Seen by Travelers: a Danish Visitor of the Seventies," *Minnesota History* 10 (September 1929), p. 417.

30. Beasley, *Negro Trail Blazers,* p. 132.

31. U.S. Census Office, *7th Census, 1850* (Globe Office, Washington, D.C., 1851).

32. *Los Angeles Times,* February 12, 1909.

33. Beasley, *Negro Trail Blazers,* p. 246.

34. *San Francisco Chronicle,* April 22, 1867.

35. Beasley, *Negro Trail Blazers,* p. 207.

36. *Olympia Daily Pacific Tribune,* June 2, 1870.

37. *San Francisco Daily Alta Californian,* November 4, 1884.

38. Irvine G. Penn, *The Africo-American Press and Its Editors* (Springfield, Mass., 1891), p. 95.

39. Leidesdorff was born on Saint Croix Island in the Danish West Indies. His father was a Dane, his mother a mulatto. The relationship of his mother and his father was extralegal. The laws of Denmark, however, allowed the father to legalize the son, as is shown by the court records of Saint Croix bearing the date of July 18, 1837, which of course put the son in line to inherit his father's property. There are several versions of the place of his birth. Hubert Bancroft says that his mother was a mulatto *(History of California* [San Francisco, 1887], vol. 4, p. 711). See also Robert O'Brien, *This is San Francisco* (New York, 1948), p. 60; Rockwell Hunt, *California Firsts* (San Francisco, 1957), p. 207.

40. Heinrich A. Lienhard, *Pioneer at Sutter's Fort, 1846–1850,* trans. and ed. by Marguerite E. Wilbur (Los Angeles, 1941), p. 69, note 5.

41. Felix Riesenberg, *Golden Gate: the Story of San Francisco Harbor* (New York, 1940), p. 84.

42. George McKinstry, "Documents of the History of California," undated letter to I. C. Calmoney, Bancroft Library.

43. Zoeth S. Eldredge, *The Beginning of San Francisco* (New York, 1912), vol. 1, p. 527.

44. Papers of William A. Leidesdorff (1848), Bancroft Library.

45. William H. Davis, *Seventy-Five Years in California* (San Francisco, 1967), p. 225.

46. Papers of Thomas Larkin, vol. 7, p. 272, May 22, 1848, Bancroft Library.

47. Ibid., letter of May 23, 1848, to W. D. M. Howard, Bancroft Library.

48. Papers of Joseph Folsom (1848), Bancroft Library, Marie Ann Sparks probably had not heard from her son for some time, for Leidesdorff never spoke of his family. Of the many Leidesdorff letters, none is from Marie Ann Sparks. It was said in New Orleans, when Leidesdorff was a clerk in a mercantile establishment, that he became engaged to a young woman, but the marriage was never consummated because he revealed to her that he had black blood. He left New Orleans, went to New York, and then to the Pacific Coast.

49. Frank Soule, John H. Gihon, and James Nisbet, *Annals of San Francisco* (New York, 1855), p. 754.

50. *Reports of Cases Determined in the Supreme Court of the State of California*, San Francisco, 1851–1934 (St. Paul, Minn.: West Publishing Company), vol. 5, p. 379. The Court at the time was composed of three justices, and the decision was two to one. Justice Heindenfelt concurred with the chief justice; Justice David Terry dissented.

51. *San Francisco Daily California Chronicle*, January 4, 1856. The editor of the *Chronicle* said that he did not want to take sides, but that all information seemed to indicate that Folsom's title was valid and that Leidesdorff was the son of Marie Ann Sparks. This was the general opinion in San Francisco and perhaps did much to aid Folsom in keeping the property.

52. Documents in California Historical Society Library, in Charles Tunill Collection.

53. Nine Barley Street. The story goes on to say that all agree that she went to Boston and that no one denies that she was married to Alexander Smith, a Cuban merchant. The name is spelled variously, but in this account I shall use the form "Pleasant."

54. *San Francisco Evening Post*, June 12, 1904.

55. Augusta (Maine) *Comfort*, November 1903. Article by Sam Davis, who wrote a letter to *Pandex of the Press*. He said that Mary Ellen gave John Brown $30,000. Boyd B. Stutler said in a letter to the author dated July 25, 1944, that no such amounts were involved, but that she was in Chatham and bought four lots there, the deeds for which were in the possession of Dr. Stutler.

56. *San Francisco Chronicle*, July 9, 1899.

57. Ibid., January 12, 1904. The litigation arose over diamonds and other jewels in a safe deposit box in the Donahue Kelly Bank which were appraised at more than $100,000. Mary Ellen Pleasant claimed that they belonged to her and were deposited in her name and that she had been accustomed to let them out to persons who wanted to wear them at functions.

58. See Chapter Six, pp. 000, 000.

59. Mifflin Gibbs, *Shadow and Light* (Washington, D.C., 1902), p. 45.

60. Ibid., p. 62.

61. Beasley, *Negro Trail Blazers*, p. 113.

62. Herndon Smith, comp., *Centralia, the First Fifty Years, 1845–1900* (Centralia, Wash., 1942), p. 214. Washington lost confidence in banks and buried his money around his house. He died without revealing the money's location, and it is believed to be still buried.

6 • The fight for civil rights

Blacks who went west before the Civil War faced certain civil restrictions which became more oppressive after the passage of the Fugitive Slave Law. Among these were the denial of the right of suffrage, the denial of the right to testify in the courts against anyone except blacks, and the denial of the right to attend public schools. Some of these restrictions were in operation in various states for some time after the Civil War.

Blacks in California had been denied their political rights from the time they first entered the state. One form of discrimination was a poll tax, and some blacks showed their opposition to the tax by refusing to pay it. When the San Francisco shoe firm of Lester and Gibbs refused to pay the tax, the city tax collector seized twenty-five or thirty dollars worth of the firm's property to cover the amount of the tax. The seized goods were then offered for sale to the highest bidder. But at the sale friends of Lester and Gibbs explained why the goods were being sold at auction, and when the auctioneer called for bidders, none appeared. The shoes were then returned to the owners.[1]

Determined to let the public know about the provisions of the poll tax act, Gibbs wrote a protest which appeared in the city's press. He stated that during a residence of seven years in California he, along with hundreds of other blacks, paid city, state, and county taxes on real estate and merchandise. His firm had also paid taxes on licenses to carry on businesses and every other special tax which had been levied from time to time for the support of the government. Now, however, he and other blacks objected to the poll tax. Gibbs could not understand why a white man in California could refuse to pay each and every tax for the support of a government under which he enjoyed every privilege, from robbing a black man to being governor of the state. He felt that it was a flagrant misuse of legal power to compel blacks to pay a special tax for the enjoyment of a special privilege and then break their heads if they attempted to exercise that privilege. Such a protest was not so much against the poll tax as it was for the black American in California who thought that every resident who had the privilege of becoming a full citizen should pay the tax. This point of view was not held at that time in many parts of the country; rather, it was generally felt that the poll tax should not be a prerequisite for voting and that there should be no qualifications to exercise the right of suffrage.

The blacks in California were determined to secure the civil rights to which they felt entitled. They published a protest in one of the San Francisco papers in which they argued that the state might confiscate their property, but if there was no redress and the great state of California continued annually to rob black citizens, they would never willingly pay the poll tax of three dollars as long as they remained disfranchised, oath-denied, and outlawed Americans.[2] Councils and conventions were held, and during the years 1854–1857, resolutions calling for the civil rights of blacks were formulated, discussed, and sent to the state legislature, where, in some cases, they were introduced as bills by friends.[3] A committee comprised of Jonas P. Townsend, William H. Newby, Mifflin W. Gibbs, G. W. Dennis, and James Brown formed a company and founded the weekly newspaper, *Mirror of the Times*. The paper advocated the cause of equal rights for all Americans, but it was established primarily to call the blacks to civic action. It also stimulated the convention movement.

The third convention of colored citizens of the state convened in Sacramento on December 9–12, 1856, and became a permanent organization. President W. H. Hall gave the keynote address in which he listed the wrongs that had fallen upon blacks who had moved into the state from other sections of the country. The business committee later reported to the convention and presented a set of resolutions for adoption. It was resolved that they would continue to remind their white fellow citizens of California that they were forcing the same wrongs on the blacks that had caused the American colonies to rebel against Great Britain and to appeal to arms. The committee wanted to point out the inconsistency of those who controlled the government of California. The second resolution reported that the laws of California which disfranchised blacks on the grounds of color were a blot upon the state, had no precedent in the annals of the world, and were unworthy of and a disgrace to the enlightened and progressive spirit of the American people. This statement was not wholly true, but hyperbole is understandable in the light of the issues. Another resolution pointed out that black citizens claimed as theirs the rights enjoyed by any other American citizen. Members of the convention felt that by their industry, integrity, and intelligence, the black citizens of California compared favorably with any class of men in the state and that they were deserving of better treatment than they were receiving.[4]

The bill to exclude blacks from California had been introduced in the state legislature on April 23, 1857. Sponsors of the bill feared that it would not pass because of a letter sent to the legislature by persons in the state giving accounts of acts of hostility against blacks. Such acts might arouse sympathy for the black cause. The editor of the *San Francisco Daily Evening Bulletin* felt that blacks ought to be given the right to testify as witnesses before a court or else be excluded from the state. This was a logical deduction. If blacks were not to be slaves for whom someone else was responsible and if at the same time they were denied all the rights which were theirs under the civil law, then they should be excluded from the state.[5]

Blacks were concerned about this law because it denied them human rights and because its passage would deny them authority to protect their property, estimated at $5,000,000.[6] Some blacks regarded the bill with a kind of grim satisfaction. One insisted that he was proud that blacks had progressed despite opposition and especially that those who comprised the population of California were not a selected group but just ordinary citizens. He was willing that the bill should pass, for in that case the blacks of the state would have no rights whatever.[7] Others began to prepare themselves for the bill's passage. On April 15, 1858, a meeting was held in San Francisco to consider the expediency of blacks' moving from the state in the event that the law passed. A group hoped that a place of permanent settlement might be founded either in Central America or Canada where they could reasonably expect to escape indignities because of race. The majority favored Central America, but San Francisco organizations sent committees to Canada and elsewhere to ascertain the kind of treatment they might receive if they migrated there. The committee which was sent to Vancouver reported that it had been favorably received by the governor and that it was much impressed by the treatment accorded it.[8] Letters were also written to other communities concerning the possibilities of black settlement. The contents of one reply became known as the result of a dispute between the committee and the *Sacramento Daily Union*. When the letter, from an official in New Granada, was not made available to the newspaper, the editor complained.[9] A committee member, C. A. Rogers, replied that the letter was the property of the Executive Committee of the Organization of Black Citizens and must be presented to them prior to publication. Rogers was certain that the letter contained no treason, but even if it did, the state of California, from which blacks had received so little, was in no danger. He insisted that he did not wish to treat friends discourteously, but the exploitation of the black race demanded that they should keep their own counsel.[10] Since the letter was publicly discussed, it was necessary to know its contents. In it, the New Granada official spoke with some authority about public opinion in his country on the question of race and assured the committee that color made no difference. The one thing that did count was ability.[11] He assured the committee that there were many blacks who held offices of importance in New Granada at that time.

While the possibilities of moving to New Granada were being discussed in meetings, some blacks were making definite preparations to leave the country. About the middle of April 1858, a meeting was convened at Zion African Methodist Episcopal church on Pacific Street to ascertain how many people were going to leave California. It was established that sixty-five were to leave on the steamer *Commodore* a day or so later. This group had decided in favor of Vancouver because, when the decision had been made, the New Granada offer had not yet been received. A farewell address was delivered by

Mifflin W. Gibbs, and the *San Francisco Chronicle* wished them much success.[12] This was a pioneering experiment, and if it was successful, others were to go to Mexico and New Granada. Whichever place they might choose, they had decided to leave California. Meanwhile, the committee was to continue its explorations into the possibilities of settling outside the United States. On May 6, at a meeting at Zion A.M.E. church, a committee reported that the immigrants had been received by the governor of Vancouver, who assured them that they would be treated as other citizens were treated.[13]

At that same meeting, the blacks decided that, since they were leaving their country as well as the state of California, they ought to explain the reasons for their departure. Therefore they passed resolutions which clearly set forth their motives. The preamble said that blacks were fully convinced that the aim, spirit, and policy of the mother country was to oppress, degrade, and outrage them. They were determined to find asylum in the lands of strangers in order to escape the oppression, prejudice, and relentless persecutions that had pursued them in their mother country for more than two centuries. The black citizens added that a delegation had been sent to Vancouver Island, a place which in their darkest hour appeared as the prospect of a bright future. The delegation had reported on general conditions there and on the character of social and political privileges as well as living prospects and resources. In Vancouver, blacks were permitted to use the ballot and to work in the same way as other citizens. "This mission," the preamble stated, "was in the highest degree creditable; the delegation had fulfilled its assignment and had rendered the most flattering accounts."

The first resolution stipulated that the committee would find a place outside the United States where blacks would be treated as human beings. The second resolution stated that the committee did not believe that there was any country on earth which had greater resources for human happiness than the British possessions of Vancouver Island and New Caledonia. In the third resolution they spoke of what they intended to do in the British Empire. In migrating there, their principal and continued aim would be to promote intelligent Christianity and industry. They advised blacks who migrated to this asylum for oppressed black Americans to invest capital in the land where they had elected to live. Another resolution said that in leaving the friendships, early associations, and thousands of ties which bound them to the place of their present nationality, they were actuated by no transitory excitement but were fully aware of the significance of their action. Their hearts, they said, were filled with gratitude to the Great Ruler of the Universe, who had provided this refuge for them. They pledged themselves to the cause and to an effort to redeem their race from the yoke of American oppression. The blacks were advised to avoid those social distinctions of race separation which blacks were compelled to make in the United States. Associations and meetings exclusively for blacks were not to be established in the new land. Everything was to be done on a broad platform without regard to race. The last of these resolutions proclaimed that the black would cast his lot, after the toil and hardship which had wrung from him sweat and tears for centuries, in a land where bleeding humanity found a balm, where philanthropy was crowned with royalty and slavery had laid aside its weapons, and where black Americans were unshackled. In the lair of the lion, the blacks would repose from the horrors of the past under the genial influence of the Queen of the Isles.

Attached to the preamble and the resolutions was a statement which avowed that blacks were pleased to pledge their allegiance to the country in which they were able to aspire to the highest state of social enjoyment and responsibility to which intelligence, morality, religion, industry, and wealth entitled them.[14]

After these resolutions and the farewell meetings, some of the blacks left the city of San Francisco and, as one writer put it, "shook the dust of California from their feet."[15] The number of those who migrated is not definitely known. In this first departing group was the celebrated Archy, who had attracted so much attention in the news of northern California.

Fortunately, those blacks who left California in order to secure civil rights reached Canada at the time of the gold rush in the Frasier River Valley and were absorbed in the great crowd of eager adventurers who hurried to the latest Eldorado.[16] This stroke of good fortune financially established many of the first blacks who went to Canada.[17] Those who went first bought land, the value of which was increased by the influx of gold seekers. All were able to find employment at once; thus the migrants were saved the period of adjustment through which most colonists have to pass.

Of the blacks who went to Vancouver, fifty very soon applied for citizenship, which they received. The gold rush in the Frasier River Valley, however, brought American prejudice in its wake and abridged the privileges which the blacks expected to enjoy. Some whites from the United States who had been attracted to these gold fields objected to the equal treatment of blacks. Joe Levett refused to serve blacks in his saloon, and the matter was brought before Judge Pelerton, who decided that, although a bartender must serve blacks, he could charge them as much as two dollars and fifty cents per drink.[18] Another difficulty arose over the admission of blacks into theaters. One of the most significant incidents was the objection raised against blacks who attended the same church with whites. In this case, an appeal was made to the bishop of the Episcopal church to prevent the exclusion of blacks. The bishop was opposed to discrimination; as a result, many white parishioners stayed away from the church. One of the ministers who refused to exclude blacks was deserted by whites, who attended another church. The bishop was transferred from Canada, and some of the blacks who were members of the Episcopal church left Canada for other parts of the world.[19] Others left for different reasons. One authority wrote that if there were 800 blacks in Vancouver in 1858 as a result of the migration from California, that number had decreased by 1865.[20] There were at that time 300 blacks who were living in Victoria, and perhaps 100 more were scattered in the farming country around the city.[21] It is likely that many left Victoria after the gold rush fever subsided.

All California blacks did not leave the state because of the harsh treatment of their race. The proposed law which they feared so much was not passed by the legislature. In the fall of 1862, a meeting held in San Francisco took notice of other things and expressed the attitude of blacks toward the Civil War. A set of resolutions was passed, including one which stated that blacks deplored the calamities which had come upon the nation. Black citizens made it known that they were willing to forget the past and to hope for the future. They also insisted that the kind of justice meted out to the poor and oppressed was among the fundamental concerns necessary for the perpetuation of a republican form of government. Another resolution spoke of sick and wounded black soldiers and suggested that this was no time to withhold their effort or to refrain from contributing toward the welfare of these unfortunates.[22]

The blacks in California called other conventions in order to keep before themselves their pressing problems and to find the means to solve them. In 1863 the African Methodist Episcopal church convened one such convention on the welfare of blacks.[23] Another meeting was convened at the same church on October 25, 1865. The last of these conventions was held in San Francisco on October 6, 1880. The purpose of this convention, like that of its predecessors, was to consider the social condition of the black race throughout the state and the nation. Delegates came from all parts of the state.[24] The convention urged parents to send their children to the nearest public school and went on record as favoring the immigration of agricultural and mechanical laborers from the southern states. It insisted also that blacks support the Republican party because the convention believed that only the Republicans favored civil rights for blacks.[25]

After the Civil War, black citizens of California continued their interest in black citizens' status not only within the state but throughout the nation. A national convention was called in Washington, D.C., for the purpose of discussing black suffrage and other national problems which pertained to the welfare of the race. The blacks of California elected delegates in a meeting presided over by D. L. Jackson, which was held at the Salem Baptist church.[26] Another black citizens' meeting was held at the African Methodist Episcopal church in order to elect representatives to the National Black Convention. Basil Campbell Zola was chosen, and in an address he promised to serve his constituency faithfully.

Another phase of civil rights of concern to the black citizens of the West was the right to give testimony in their own defense and against those who mistreated them. It had long been the custom of the southern states to exclude black men from the right to testify in the courts. Many of those in the population of the West had come from the South, had brought southern customs, and in many cases had enacted laws in keeping with those customs and had inserted restrictions in the state constitutions. California specifically prevented black citizens from giving testimony except when it concerned other black men. The law prevented all blacks, mulattoes, Indians, and Chinese from testifying against whites in the courts of the state of California. The Japanese were not excluded because they had not come to the Pacific Coast in large enough numbers to be considered in the exclusion bill. Had enough of them been in the state, there is little doubt that they also would have been excluded by this law, which continued in force for thirteen years.[27]

The same problem appeared in some of the other states and territories. In 1861, when Nevada was being considered for statehood, a section excluding all but white men from offering evidence in the courts of that territory was added to its organic law. James W. Nye, then governor of the territory, wrote to W. H. Seward his opposition to Section Thirteen of the Territorial Act. He said that he could not approve it because it provided that no black, mulatto, Indian, or Chinese could be permitted to give evidence in favor of or against a white person. Section Thirteen further stated that any person who had one-eighth Indian blood was to be considered an Indian. He thought that a person who had one-eighth black blood was not in fact a mulatto and that the intention of the section was contrary to the democratic principle. It was calculated, he thought, to restrict improperly the privilege of testifying and that it was inconsistent with the National Civil Practice Act. In that act, persons who had more than one-half Indian blood or more than one-eighth Negro blood could not testify.[28]

In 1856 a convention of blacks on the Pacific Coast passed a set of resolutions which were to be presented to the state legislature. The right of testimony, according to one resolution, was valuable as the right of self-defense and no generous foe would deny it to an enemy. The convention made provisions which advanced the reform of the law which denied this right to blacks by creating a contingent fund to be controlled by a committee having discretionary powers. Such action enabled the committee to continue action for the improvement of the black man's lot. At the same time, it provided for an Executive Committee with full power to carry out such measures as it might deem necessary.

It was believed that the only hope to better the situation of blacks was the common school and the common law, but the black man was denied full use of both. Blacks at the California State Convention asked for the repeal by the legislature of the third and fourth para-

graphs of an act which had been passed on April 29, 1851, entitled
"An Act Concerning Crimes and Punishment" (first passed on April
16, 1850). The measure related to blacks and mulattoes and disqual-
ified them as competent witnesses in cases related to white men. The
convention felt that the law of evidence in judicial investigation
should be identified with the laws of the human mind and that every
force and circumstance which could throw light upon the subject
under investigation should be heard and judged according to its relative weight and value. It was thought also that past experience had
shown in many ways that the establishment of artificial standards of
credibility which depended upon tests such as race, color, or country
was both unwise and unjust. These served only to obstruct the investigation of truth. The establishment of these barriers could only de-
fraud and exclude classes which had to subject their lives and property to outrage and injustice from the more favored class. The
California State Convention concluded by saying that the only true
tests of credibility in a witness were his intelligence, integrity, and
disinterestedness. It was made plain that, as a race, blacks were willing to be subject to these tests but felt that they should not be subject to any others.[29] The California State Convention petitioned the
legislature to alter the state constitution by adding to the first section
of Article Two that nothing in the constitution should be construed as
preventing the legislature from permitting black men to have the
rights of suffrage and the right to testify. It was felt that the prosperity of both the national government and the state legislature depended
upon the addition of such a section.

    The editor of the *San Francisco Chronicle* insisted that a more vil-
lainous and disgraceful law never stood on the statute books of a
civilized country than that code of California which prevented persons having one-eighth or more black blood from testifying in proceedings in which a white person was a party, and that the law had
as its objective the withholding of all rights. It arose, he felt, from a
senseless and bigoted prejudice, an evil fault of society which grew
out of the soil of slavery. Such a law had been enacted at the instiga-
tion of the low desire of some to pander to a bad public sentiment
which could not be defended upon any ground. The refusal by the
legislature to repeal it was even more reprehensible because it arose
from a moral cowardice which was unworthy of an independent legis-

lature. California was settled by representatives from every race, and immigrants from every land and every island of every ocean were thrown together. This act worked not only a great hardship upon those excluded, but it was also a most serious hindrance to the cause of justice where whites were concerned. The editor illustrated his point by giving an example of a gentleman who had a faithful servant. The servant had been a family slave whom the master would trust with his life and his property. If a white thief should break into his house and murder his wife or child and rob his place and the black servant should be the only one to see it, the master could not bring the culprit to justice. The editor ended his attack upon the law by insisting that it was a disgrace upon the statute books and existed only because of a small group of politicians from the South who would cut off their noses to spite their faces.[30] The refusal of testimony from blacks and Chinese allowed white men to rob the members of these races, who could do little about it because they could not give evidence against offenders.[31] If the papers are an indication of the feeling of the people, a majority of them were against the law as it then stood.

The law was so flagrant in its application that in some cases judges made exceptions to it. Judge Blake of a San Francisco court ruled that the law against the testimony of black witnesses was not applicable when such testimony injured other parties.[32] By judicial interpretation, this action of a judge gave the relief which the legislature had not given. However, this view was not held by the California Supreme Court in 1860 when the case of *The People v. Howard* came before it. The defendant was convicted of larceny for the theft of a gold watch which belonged to a person of more than half black blood. The principle here was that a mulatto was incompetent to testify even though he was the injured person. The decision in this case was rendered by Chief Justice Stephen Field, who held that the laws of the state of California did not permit a black to testify against a white man, even when the black was the injured party.

This was in conformity with the decision which that court had rendered in the case of *The People v. Hall* in 1854. The appellant, a free white citizen, had been convicted of murder on the testimony of a Chinese witness, and the question was raised of the admissibility of evidence from such a witness. Hall appealed the case to the California Supreme Court, which ruled that the legislature meant to exclude Indians, Chinese, and blacks. The case was thus reversed, and a new trial was ordered.[33] Thus, whether a person was guilty or not did not depend upon the evidence but rather upon the color of the witness's skin.

It was easy for the legislature to make such a law, but it was difficult to enforce it and at the same time render justice to injured blacks and other racial elements. The question of excluding evidence came before the legislature in 1858, when several members were in favor of a repeal. In arguing for the bill, J. W. Owens insisted that gentlemen who were opposed to the measure were growing uneasy; they realized that keeping such a measure on the statute books was giving protection to lawless whites. In one California county, a man had been injured in a barber shop, and his assailant was allowed to go free because the only person who saw the assault was the black barber, one of the most intelligent and worthy men in the town. The legislator then argued that such an act was a blot upon the state and should be removed. This argument did not go unchallenged, for Representative Wilcox of that body asked Owens if he thought that the best man in Santa Clara County was a black. Owens then stated that the man was superior in intelligence and acquisition to more than one-third of the members of the House of Representatives in California.[34]

The right of blacks to serve on a jury was of some concern also. The convention of 1856 had insisted that it would continue to fight for civil rights, one of which was jury service. The first instance of a black's serving on a jury in California occurred in Sacramento in 1850. A man was found dead on a city street, and in order to find the cause of his death, the coroner summoned a jury of black men. The jury was unable to determine conclusively the cause of death, but it believed that the man had died from natural causes. Only three members of the jury could sign their names.[35] There had been no definite policy on black citizens and their service on a jury before the state constitution was put into operation. The law prohibiting blacks from participating in the courts by giving testimony against whites and serving on juries came after the Civil War.

In 1870 the case of *Owen O'Hara v. Breuner* came before Justice Lynch in Sacramento. The plaintiff sought damages from Breuner for running him down with a wagon on April 21, 1870, at the corner of Eighth and N streets. O'Hara demanded a jury trial, and the constable, Taylor, as a joke, secured a panel of twelve citizens, both black and white. When the black jurors were examined, all but two were eliminated as not being taxpayers, and the whites begged off. The plaintiff withdrew his case when he understood that other black men were to be selected.[36] This was an effort, on a jocular level, to get black men on a jury, but it did not materialize.

In May of that same year, black men did serve on a jury. In the city of Sacramento a black man named Daniel Sullinger was arrested, cause unknown, on a warrant sworn out by a Chinese citizen. The defense lawyer asked for and received a jury trial and postponement. The officer whose duty it was to select the twenty men for jury duty selected twenty black men. Some of them did not appear; they felt that they would not have to serve if they stayed away. But the court had a different view and sent the sheriff with a warrant for them. They were brought before the court, examined, and nine were qualified. Counsel agreed to go on with the case with these nine men rather than select others. Those constituting the jury were A. L. Jackson, foreman, Jacob Foster, Peter Hickman, Benjamin Turner, John Matox, Albert Burkhart, C. H. Valentine, Samuel Myers, and Henry Johnson. This was the first all-black jury in Sacramento, if not the first in the state. They found the defendant guilty and recommended him to the mercy of the court.[37]

In 1872 six black members were chosen for jury duty in the United States Circuit Court in San Francisco. This was the first time that black men had been selected for jury duty in a federal court. This action, it was asserted, indicated that black men were gradually being considered for jury duty.[38] In 1874 a black man was drawn for a San Francisco grand jury, but he was rejected because he was not a taxpayer.

The question of jury duty faced black men in other western states as well. It was perhaps not as noticeable as in California, nor were blacks in the other states sufficiently organized to insist upon jury duty as a matter of civil rights. The question of excluding black men from jury duty came before the courts of Nebraska in the case of *Brittle v. the People*. In 1875 Brittle was indicted for burglary. When the case came up in the lower court, the jury panel contained the name of a black man, Howard W. Crossly. He was qualified, but he was challenged on the ground that he was black. The court overruled the challenge, and the jury found Brittle guilty. Brittle then appealed the case on the ground that the court was in error. In his plea he stated that Crossly had been allowed to sit as one of the jurors who returned a verdict of guilty and that prior to the admission of Nebraska into the Union, only white male citizens were allowed to sit on a jury. When the case came before it, the Nebraska Supreme Court's decision pointed out that Congress had declared that the act of admitting Nebraska as a state of the Union could not take effect except upon the fundamental condition that within the state there should be no denial of the election franchise or of any other right to any person by reason of race or color. Nebraska had accepted that condition. Continuing, the court held that the right to sit on a jury was a fundamental right which went with citizenship, sustained the decision of the district court, and found Brittle guilty as charged.[39]

Another way in which blacks were restricted in their civil rights involved the use of common carriers. On May 3, 1863, a black woman was forcibly ejected from a car on the street railroad at the corner of Union and Powell streets in San Francisco. She refused to get out on the request of the conductor, who claimed to have strict orders from the company to refuse passage to blacks. The woman threatened to prosecute the conductor for assault and battery. She became violent, and the conductor called upon the driver for assistance.[40] A scuffle ensued, resulting in broken car windows and much confusion.[41] In a similar incident, William Bacon brought a case against the North Beach Railroad Company, claiming that he had been forcibly ejected from a car. To the great surprise of those who followed the case, Judge Sawyer of the Circuit Court of San Francisco ruled that a black could get redress for the humiliation he had suffered and awarded Bacon $3,100 damages. Charlotte Brown brought another such case against the Omnibus Railroad Company. Judge Pratt decided in favor of the right of blacks to ride in the cars. The judge held that the case was a simple one, for the company was, by the law of the state, a common carrier of passengers. Its duty was to carry all who applied. Although there were some exceptions, such as a passenger who applied at the wrong place or was shockingly filthy or had a contagious disease or refused to pay the ordinary fare, color was not one of the barriers legitimately embraced among causes which justified objections to the general rule. The company had a right to make rules for the conduct of its business but not to declare void the duties which were imposed upon it by law. The right of the passenger was superior to the rules of the company and could not be affected by them, nor would any question of profit or loss by carrying blacks affect the right of the person to be carried. The judge showed no inclination to lend the weight of the court to perpetuate a "relic of barbarism." The editor of the *Sacramento Daily Union* felt that the arguments were lucid, and the decision coincided with the sentiment of the people.[42]

One citizen, calling himself a Virginian, wrote in the *San Francisco Bulletin* that he was not an abolitionist, nor did he approve of President Lincoln's Emancipation Proclamation, but he did think that in a state pretending to be free, black men should be allowed a few more privileges than they enjoyed in a slave state. He was surprised that such an outrage as the ejection of women from cars for no other reason than that they were black should occur. He felt that no harm could be done by letting black men and women ride in the cars.[43]

Mary Ellen Pleasant did much to aid in the fight of black citizens against their exclusion from carriers. She attempted to ride, was ejected, sued, and was awarded damages of $700. Thereupon the case was carried to the California Supreme Court in 1868. The verdict was then reversed, for the court argued that there had been no malice or injury.[44] Even so, black citizens had won. The very fact that a black person could take a case of this nature as far as the California Supreme Court meant that his plea for civil rights was not being ignored, and at least insofar as common carriers were concerned, discrimination ceased.

Less decisive was the question involving the right of the black person to sit where he pleased in theaters. This was an issue over which the blacks in San Francisco fought most vigorously. The court ruled that a proprietor had the right to enforce such policy as would be most conducive to the prosperity of his business.[45] This was a different view from that handed down in the matter of common carriers, but common carriers and privately owned theaters were two different matters. To this day, there is uncertainty as to how far the courts may go in the regulation of discriminatory policies of the theatrical industries.

A case of discrimination at McGuire's New Theater in Sacramento, which came under the civil rights law in 1876, attracted considerable attention when it reached the United States Circuit Court. A large gathering of both blacks and whites filled the courtroom. White public opinion was so inflamed that most observers were certain that the decision would be in favor of the theater manager, as indeed it was.[46] A similar case occurred in Nebraska. On May 3, 1888, George Messanger, the owner of a barber shop in Lincoln, refused to shave Arthur Warwick, a black man. Since Warwick was refused because of his color, the case came under the civil rights law. Warwick sued in the district court and obtained a verdict in his favor. The case was carried to the Nebraska Supreme Court, which reversed the lower court's decision because the petition was faulty. It was not proved that Warwick was a citizen of Nebraska or any other state.[47]

The black man's struggle for civil rights has been a continual one. Much has been achieved, although full equality remains in the future. While various eastern and southern restrictions were carried into the West, that region, of all sections of the country, has afforded the black the greatest freedom. All in all, the spirit of democracy has been most evident in the West, especially as manifested ultimately in the black man's right to vote and his opportunity to make himself heard in a fair and open court.

NOTES

1. Mifflin W. Gibbs, *Shadow and Light,* privately printed (Washington, D.C., 1902), pp. 37ff.

2. *San Francisco Daily Bulletin,* May 7, 1857. Also discussed in Gibbs, *Shadow and Light.*

3. Gibbs, *Shadow and Light,* p. 48.

4. *Proceedings of Second Convention of Colored People* (San Francisco, 1856), p. 3.

5. *San Francisco Daily Evening Bulletin,* April 24, 1857.

6. Ibid.

7. *San Francisco Daily Evening Bulletin,* April 5, 1858.

8. Ibid., May 7, 1858.

9. *Sacramento Daily Union,* July 22, 1858.

10. Ibid.

11. Ibid., July 21, 1828, letter from President of Senate of New Granada.

12. *San Francisco Daily Evening Chronicle,* April 21, 1858.

13. F. W. Howay, "The Negro Immigration into Vancouver Island in 1858," *British Columbia Historical Quarterly* 3 (April 1939), p. 111.

14. *Sacramento Daily Union,* May 14, 1858.

15. Howay, "Negro Immigration," p. 113. The number was estimated at 800; see Edgar Fawcett, *Some Reminiscences of Old Victoria* (Toronto, 1912), p. 215. Those who went to Canada had prospects of doing well, for they could obtain public land for as little as twenty shillings per acre and only one-fourth of that to be paid down, the rest in installments in four years at interest of 5 percent. Then, as another inducement, they were not asked to pay taxes while they were buying land, and they were promised by the governor of the province the elective franchise, the right to sit on juries, and indeed, all of the rights of citizens after they had been there three months. These were the privileges to which they had aspired in California. See *Sacramento Daily Union,* May 9, 1858.

16. Howay, "Negro Immigration," p. 113.

17. Matthew MacFie, *Vancouver Island and British Columbia* (London, 1865), p. 388.

18. Fawcett, *Some Reminiscences,* p. 218.

19. Richard Mayne, *Four Years in British Columbia and Vancouver Island* (London, 1862), p. 351. The details of the stay of these California blacks in Canada cannot be treated here.

20. Fawcett, *Some Reminiscences,* p. 215.

21. MacFie, *Vancouver Island and British Columbia,* p. 388.

22. *Sacramento Daily Union,* October 6, 1862.

23. *Journal of the Proceedings of A.M.E. Church Convention* (San Francisco, 1863).

24. *Sacramento Record–Union,* September 22, 1880.

25. Ibid.

26. Ibid., November 19, 1873.

27. Hittell, *History of California* (San Francisco: Pacific Press Publishing House and Occidental Publishing Company, 1897), vol. 4, p. 341.

28. *Territorial Papers of Nevada,* vol. 1, letter dated December 21, 1861, National Archives, Washington, D.C.

29. *Proceedings of the Convention of Colored People* (1856). Copy in Bancroft Library, University of California.

30. *San Francisco Chronicle,* February 3, 1858.

31. Ibid., December 21, 1856.

32. *Sacramento Daily Union,* August 18, 1858.

33. Helen T. Catteral, ed., *Judicial Cases Concerning American Slavery and Negroes* (Washington, D.C., 1926–37), vol. 4, p. 332.

34. *Sacramento Daily Union,* March 6, 1868.

35. *San Francisco Pacific News,* October 25, 1850.

36. *Sacramento Daily Union,* May 10, 1870.

37. Ibid., May 26, 1858.

38. Ibid., February 13, 1872.

39. *Brittle v. People, Reports of Cases Determined in the Supreme Court of the State of Nebraska* (Chicago: Callaghan and Company, 1873), vol. 2, p. 199.

40. *Sacramento Daily Union,* May 4, 1863.

41. Ibid., November 19, 1863.

42. Ibid., October 5, 1864.

43. Delilah L. Beasley, *Negro Trail Blazers of California,* privately printed (Los Angeles, 1919), p. 65.

44. "Pleasant vs. North Beach and M.R.R. Company," *Reports of Cases Determined in the Supreme Court of the State of California* (St. Paul, Minn.: West Publishing Company, 1864), vol. 34, p. 587.

45. *Denver Rocky Mountain News,* August 20, 1866.

46. *Sacramento Record-Union,* January 19, 1876.

47. *Northwestern Reporter,* (St. Paul, Minn.: West Publishing Company, 1910), vol. 91, p. 638.

7 • Politics

Sporadic instances of blacks who voted or attempted to vote occurred before the Civil War, but it was not until after the war that they were generally considered to be voters in the West. And at that, black men in the West during the period under consideration were too few to influence greatly the outcome of elections. Nevertheless, the political parties were concerned about the part blacks might play in the future, and they did make some effort to control black men's political behavior.

Before the Civil War, blacks could exert little political influence because the political parties sponsored legislation to prohibit them from voting. Still, they continued to make efforts to register and to participate in elections in California and other western states. The experience of a black man known as "Old Gabe" was shared by many others. He applied to Harry Dixon, clerk of the Fresno County Court, for registration to vote. Dixon refused him, saying that he was discharging his duty as he saw and understood it. The clerk acknowledged that some other clerks had registered blacks, but he thought that they were thereby violating their oath of office, and he would not follow their error.[1] Gabe in turn swore vengeance, declaring that he would spend every cent he had in the world in order to register. When Los Angeles clerks denied black men the right to register, some of the latter must have resorted to the courts, seeking the writ of mandamus in order to compel the registrars to register them. Black citizens declared their intention of appealing to the District Federal Court; failing there, they would appeal to the United States Supreme Court.[2] After the passage of the Fifteenth Amendment, the issue came up again. In some cases, black men were registered in some of the districts of California, but their numbers were exceedingly small. A list of the voters of Redlands, Lugonia, Crofton, and other places in San Bernardino County, published in 1888, contained the name of only one black man, Israel Beale.[3]

In the first decade after the Civil War, the question of whether blacks should vote and participate in party affairs came before party conventions and state legislatures. Black men themselves were less concerned about such issues as the tariff, the Bland-Allison law, or the free coinage of silver at a ratio of sixteen to one than about whether the parties were concerned with their welfare. At this time, blacks in the West were members chiefly of the Republican party, for they felt that it had given them their freedom. But they were not strict party men when their rights of citizenship were involved, and in many cases they were conscious of the value of voting for candidates who would help establish their political freedom. In due time, political organizations such as the Equal Rights League of Oakland, California were established to organize blacks so that when they gained suffrage, their votes could be cast solidly for those candidates who would be helpful in securing their political rights.

In some places, despite political restrictions, black men were put up as candidates for office. In Downieville, California, in 1865, John Black of Howland Flat was put forward by the Democratic party for the office of constable for Table Rock township. Public office at the hands of the Democratic party cast Black on the horns of a dilemma. If he accepted office, he would be a hero to his supporters, and he would be in a position to do his cause a tremendous amount of good. At the same time, he feared the possibility of being regarded as a traitor to the best interests of the bulk of his Republican black neighbors. The editor of the *Sacramento Daily Union* felt that the selection of Black was a marvel of Democratic discernment and congratulated the party on his acquisition into their ranks.[4] But despite such enthusiasm and party backing, Black probably lost, although a record of the outcome of the election has not survived. In San Francisco, William Leidesdorff was more successful. He did not regard himself as a black and probably was not so considered by many others; therefore, it was possible for him to have considerable influence in local government. Together with W. D. M. Howard, Robert Parker, and E. P. James, Leidesdorff sat on the first council to administer the affairs of the growing city of San Francisco. So impressive was his performance that the City Council appointed him to the School Board, and in this capacity he became the moving spirit in the organization and operation of San Francisco's first public school. Moving from one sphere of activity into a larger and more responsible service, he found himself in 1847 in the position of treasurer of San Francisco.[5]

There were few blacks in Washington, and they participated in politics as citizens without reference to color. An example is William O. Bush, the son of George Washington Bush. On the death of the elder Bush, he took over the operation of the Bush claim and was very well liked. As a manifestation of the high esteem in which he was held, he was frequently consulted on many civic and state matters. Bush was elected to the first legislature of Washington (1889–1890) and was a very active and influential member.[6]

The political activity of blacks in Montana, Wyoming, Nevada, Idaho, and the Dakotas was limited for the most part simply to casting their votes with one or the other party. However, it was different in Colorado, Kansas, Oklahoma, and Iowa where blacks took a more active part in politics and, in some cases, made an attempt to use their votes against their enemies. Black citizens in Denver had a dynamic leader, William J. Harden, who founded political clubs before blacks won suffrage rights.[7] The leaders of these clubs, which were educational in purpose, hoped that their members would be voting in state and national elections. Harden, a courageous political leader, delivered several public addresses on the issues of the day in the interest of the Republican party. He challenged a "Bullwhacker" named Casim to a public debate, but no notice of it appeared in the press.[8] In 1866 there was a mining convention to which delegates appointed by state governors were sent. All such appointments were considered political appointments, and in Colorado they were strictly so. Many of the party faithfuls thought that the governor, a Republican, would appoint Harden to appease black voters, who had been making their presence felt in the party program. Instead, the appointment went to James M. Cavanaugh.[9]

Harden was ever vigilant and continually reminded the political organization of the importance of the black vote. He sent a telegram to Colorado's congressman, Evans, in which he called attention to the welfare of black citizens. Evans claimed that the telegram from Harden made several false accusations, one of them being that blacks had voted before 1864. Evans also said that he could not be responsible for what happened in Colorado's Republican party, and he accused Harden of being used by a group of politicians for their own advantage.[10] This was the usual response: to blame someone else for the activity of black men.

In 1874 Colorado sought admission to statehood. This became a question which affected the political status of black men and women, who feared that if the state was admitted at that time, the Republican party would not insist on granting civil rights to them. They sent a petition, signed by 130 citizens of Denver, to Congress against the admission of Colorado as a state. How much influence this petition had on the admission of the territory to statehood is questionable, but it does reflect the interest of blacks in the matter.[11] The *Daily Rocky Mountain News* claimed that Senator Sumner was responsible for linking the black question with the territory's admission to statehood and thought that Harden had been brought in as an ally of Sumner and the Republicans.[12] The truth of this accusation is not ascertainable, but it is evident that Harden was very active in the politics of Denver and the state of Colorado.

Black politicians were also active in the state of Kansas, and they perhaps played a larger part and held more important positions there than in any other state west of the Mississippi. Their political significance is largely explained by the number of blacks in Kansas. Population statistics reveal a dramatic growth rate: in 1860 the state had a black population of only 620 persons; by 1870 it had increased to 17,108, and by 1880 it was 43,107. During the last two decades of the nineteenth century, Kansas had the largest black population of any of the western states. These changes in the black population were due mainly to the exodus inspired by Pap Singleton, although blacks had been moving to Kansas before the exodus, as the population changes from 1860 to 1870 reveal.

In Kansas, the black's potential as a voter was realized early. In 1880 blacks took exception to an editorial entitled "Black Loafers" which appeared in the *Daily Rocky Mountain News*. Writing of blacks in Kansas, the editor called them loafers from the South who were trying to Africanize Kansas politics. Blacks who were former slaves, he felt, were not in a position to determine which way to vote, and the Republican Party would control their vote. The Republicans had nominated a black candidate, a mere politician, which was well enough, the editor thought, but if the party had been serious it would have nominated a black candidate who was a better man. The editorial ended with the statement that the *News* would not crawl in the dirt to get votes. The black voters responded by warning the editor of the *News* that he and the Republican party need not expect to catch the black vote in the fall election with honeyed words because these voters would remember that they had been called loafers.[13]

Kansas black voters sought to influence by their votes not only party action but also some of the major political offices of the state. One of the most important was that of state auditor. In 1882 Ephraim McCabe, of Graham County, was an aspirant for the office. Graham is the county in which Nicodemus is located and the county in which the majority of black migrants to Kansas settled in 1879. In the party convention of that year, McCabe's name was put forward for nomination, but he was able to secure only 169 votes on the second ballot, an increase over the first ballot but not enough for nomination. The friends of Governor St. John, who had taken such an active part in adjusting the migrants to their new life in Kansas, moved an adjournment to prevent the nomination of the black candidate. During the recess, the governor's friends canvassed in order to defeat McCabe, but those delegates in favor of the black candidate acquired enough votes for his nomination. McCabe was unable to win the support of the governor, but even without it he won elections in both 1882 and 1884.[14] He served successfully until he moved to Oklahoma. where he took an active part in the politics of that territory.[15]

While the black population in Kansas was large in relation to that in other states, it was but a fraction of the white population, and black aspirants to major state offices could not expect success as a result of the black vote alone. A case in point is Blanche K. Bruce,

Jr., principal of Sumner School, a black school in Leavenworth, and nephew of the United States senator from Mississippi, B. K. Bruce. In 1892 Bruce was nominated to run for the office of state auditor on the Republican ticket.[16] Despite his acknowledged ability and qualifications for the office, he was not supported by the party and went no further than the nomination. Even with party support, Bruce was not fated to win. In 1894 he again was nominated for state auditor and received more votes than anyone on the Republican state ticket, but the Democrats swept the country.[17] After this election, Bruce did not remain active in politics but instead returned to his school position in Leavenworth. There he tutored aspirants to the military academies, teaching more than 1800 future officers of the United States Army. Another candidate for state auditor was Major John Brown, a prosperous farmer in Shawnee County who ran for the office in 1900. He too was unsuccessful.

In an article in the magazine *Agora,* George W. Cross said that black candidates were put on the ticket only to secure the vote. Once on the ticket, he felt, no further attention was paid to them. He thought that blacks ought to vote but should not allow themselves to be exploited.[18] Cross's view was not strictly accurate, however, since a number of black candidates did achieve political prominence. Robert Keith, a resident of Topeka and reputed to be one of the richest black men in Kansas, served for several years as a member of the Shawnee County Republican Committee.[19] Isaac Bradley was elected justice of the peace in 1891 and held the office until 1899. In 1894 he was given a temporary appointment to the position of second assistant attorney general, which he occupied for three months.[20] He was made first assistant attorney general of Kansas and served in this capacity from 1894 to 1898. In 1900 he had the honor of serving as presidential elector. Another lawyer, John Waller, had come to Kansas in 1878 and settled in Topeka before the black migration reached its peak. Early in his Kansas residence, he developed an interest in politics and became active in the Republican Party. Waller was placed at the head of the Republican electoral ticket in 1888; he carried all the counties in the state except two, thus becoming the first black man in the country to be elected to such distinction by any party.[21] Soon after the election he was appointed deputy county attorney of Shawnee County and held that office until he was appointed by President Harrison, with the endorsement of the Kansas congressional delegation, to the responsible position of consul to Madagascar.[22] Perhaps Waller's greatest political work for the Republican party was through the publication of the *Western Recorder,* which as early as 1883 endorsed John A. Logan for president and John M. Langston, a black man, for vice-president. Along with his cousin, Anthony Morton, Waller also established the *American Citizen,* an active political paper which supported John Sherman of Ohio in March of 1888.[23] With Republican support, G. W. Jones was elected attorney for Graham County in 1892. He was later named presidential elector. William Sayers also served several successive terms as attorney for Graham County. Paul Jones, a lawyer in Kansas City, Missouri, moved across the line into Wyandotte County, Kansas, where he engaged in the practice of law and politics. Later he was rewarded with an appointment at the state capital, where he served four years in the office of the auditor. Jones also published until 1927 a magazine called the *Paul Jones Monthly.*[24]

Not all voters in Kansas were Republicans, although most of them held office under that party. When the Populist party was organized in Kansas, some blacks gave it more than passing interest because they felt that they would not get a square deal in the Republican party, and neither could they vote the Democratic ticket. The managers of the Populist party were quick to grasp the situation and made an effort to organize this discontented element of the population. A club called the Afro-American League was organized in Topeka for the purpose of securing votes and support for the Populist cause. The officers of this new political organization were Colonel James Beck, Topeka, president; C. L. Walker, Fort Scott, vice-president; G. L. Hudson, Ottawa, secretary; and W. H. Hazelridge, Leavenworth, treasurer. Committees were appointed in the various districts to enroll black members and black voters.[25] A black candidate from Kansas City ran on the ticket, but he was defeated by about 1,000 votes because most of the black voters remained with the Republicans. One editor thought that the effort of the Populist party to elevate blacks caused its failure at the polls.[26] Paul H. Gidden added that the public mind in Kansas was not at that time educated to the point of giving the black man the franchise. He thought that the people of Kansas were willing to recognize black men as Christians but could not tol-

erate them in political authority. The question constantly confronted
the regular parties, and one writer felt that there was not much future
for third parties as long as the black question had to be fought over
and over again.[27]

The role that blacks in Kansas played in politics was almost dupli-
cated in Iowa. They were not elected to state offices, but they did
take part in the politics of the state, a fact that whites had foreseen
with some apprehension. In the early history of Iowa, a committee at
its constitutional convention was appointed to determine whether free
blacks would be allowed to enter, for while there was sympathy for
the black man's condition, there was also fear of his political potential.[28] Blacks entered Iowa in considerable numbers while the river
industry was at its peak and the railroads through Iowa were being
built. Most of them settled in Davenport, Clinton, Dubuque, and
Burlington. Later, Burlington became a railroad center and blacks
went there to obtain employment in that and other industries.[29]

Black citizens of Iowa became interested in politics and began
their participation in political life. In 1888 a meeting of the black
Republicans of Des Moines was held for the purpose of considering
the nomination of C. H. Claggett, a constable of Des Moines, for the
office of police judge. He was defeated, but he received the second
highest number of votes.[30] In Buxton, where black laborers had gone
in considerable numbers to work in the coal mines as strike breakers,
they became permanent citizens. Buxton was not an organized city,
yet there were 5,000 or 6,000 persons in the community when it
flourished most.[31] About half of those engaged in the coal-mining
industry were black, and they held local political offices such as justice of the peace, constable, and other minor positions.[32] The political activities in this town did not last long, however; when the coal
failed, the influence of the black voters also diminished.

The first political convention of black voters in Iowa was held in
Mahaska County. The convention threatened to bolt the Republican
party if its members were not allowed to participate in party activities. In 1885 the vote in Mahaska County was 1,200, and since
the blacks numbered 500, their vote was very important.[33] A meeting
of blacks was held in Washington for the purpose of dealing with
questions of black welfare. Delegates were present from Tipton, Iowa
City, Washington, Davenport, and Muscatine.[34] A resolution passed

on behalf of the black citizens of Iowa thanked the Republican party for its noble effort in behalf of manhood suffrage at the November election, by which enfranchisement had been achieved by a majority of 25,000.[35] While the convention was called for other purposes, it was a political meeting in that it dealt with political matters. It was one of the first of its kind in the state.

Until 1900 the political effort of blacks in Iowa was largely centered around the life of one man, Alexander Clark, a native of Washington County, Pennsylvania, who in 1842 moved first to Ohio and then to Muscatine, Iowa. Clark participated in the political conventions and exerted considerable influence. In the convention of 1869, convened by blacks in Des Moines, he was selected as the delegate to represent Iowa at the national convention of black citizens. There was no doubt that his oratory impressed the convention in Washington; he was selected to wait on President Grant and Vice-President Colfax and to tender the congratulations of the black people of the United States on their election.[36] The Washington convention was called ostensibly to find ways and means to improve conditions, and it was also a means of dramatizing the civic needs of the black people.

This same year, 1869, Clark was a delegate to the Iowa Republican Convention. He was elected vice-president of that body and took an active part in its deliberations. The following year he was a delegate to the state convention and served as a member of the Resolutions Committee. As he had done at other conventions, he gave an address marked by force and conviction. It was said that in public speaking Clark was second only to the great black abolitionist orator, Frederick Douglass. In every election to 1890, he stumped the state of Iowa and the southern states in the interest of the Republican party. It was in this service that he acquired the title of "Orator of the West."[37]

Clark continued his activity in state politics, and by 1872 he had appeared on the national scene. In that year he was appointed a delegate-at-large by the Iowa convention to the National Republican Convention. In 1876 he was appointed an alternate to the National Republican Convention held in Cincinnati, Ohio. Earlier, in 1873, President Grant had appointed him consul to Aux Cayes, Haiti. Although he was not a poor man and had good investments in timber and mining property, he declined this appointment because of the meager salary. In 1890 President Harrison appointed him to the diplomatic post of minister resident and consul general to Liberia. He accepted this honor, assumed the office on November 25, 1890, and served until his death in June 1891.[38] Alexander Clark was one of the important figures in the Republican party for more than a quarter of a century. His career marked the height of the activity of blacks in the politics of Iowa before 1900.

Blacks played little or no part in the political life of the other western states. There were so few blacks in any given community that their influence was negligible. However, they attempted to vote throughout this period, and as the years have passed, they have continued to fight for their political rights. Thus it was that, during the period under consideration, the political stature of the black man varied in proportion to the size of the black population in the various states of the West. Where the population was relatively large, his activity in politics was correspondingly vigorous. Where the population was sparse, he was more or less politically impotent.

But although the black vote could not greatly influence most elections, party leaders sensed its future potential, and thoughtful black people themselves recognized that only through political power could they make whites listen to their plea for other civil freedoms, whether the right to serve on a jury or to ride on public transportation. At the same time, blacks recognized that one of those freedoms, the freedom to obtain an education, had a reciprocal effect on their political effectiveness. Only as intelligent and informed voters could black people hope to use political power to better their condition. The next chapter examines the education of blacks in the West.

NOTES

1. *Fresno Exposition,* November 13, 1865.

2. *Sacramento Daily Union,* May 3, 1870.

3. *Citrograph* (Redlands, Ca.), September 22, 1888.

4. *Sacramento Daily Union,* November 13, 1865.

5. *Hutchins California Magazine,* vol. 3, p. 543.

6. John Ayer, "George Bush, the Voyageur," *Washington Historical Quarterly* 7 (1916), p. 45.

7. *Denver Rocky Mountain News,* September 5, 1865.

8. Ibid., November 4, 1865.

9. Ibid., February 7, 1866.

10. Ibid.

11. *Territorial Papers of Colorado,* vol. 1, April 22, 1874, National Archives, Washington, D.C.

12. Frank Hall, *History of Colorado* (Chicago, 1889), vol. 1, p. 376.

13. *Daily Rocky Mountain News* (Denver), April 26, 1880.

14. *Topeka Daily Commonwealth,* August 11, 1882.

15. He acted as an agent in bringing blacks into Oklahoma and did much to point out to them the value of the land and the ease with which they could secure it. This proved to be the source of his political strength in that state. In the first legislative assembly which met and founded a temporary organization, E. P. McCabe was made a temporary secretary. He was a very active citizen in Oklahoma both in politics and in business.

16. *Afro-American Advocate,* (Coffeyville, Kan.), March 4, 1892.

17. *Who's Who in Colored America,* 4th ed. (1933–1937).

18. *Agora,* vol. 3 (October 1893).

19. *Afro-American Advocate,* March 4, 1892.

20. *Who's Who in Colored America.*

21. Irvine Garland Penn, *The Afro-American Press and Its Editors* (Springfield, Mass.: Wiley and Company, 1891), p. 190.

22. Roy Garvin, "Benjamin, or 'Pap,' Singleton and His Followers," *Journal of Negro History* 33 (January 1948), p. 19.

23. Penn, *Afro-American Press,* p. 192.

24. Garvin, "Benjamin Singleton," pp. 19–20.

25. Ibid.

26. Paul H. Giddens, "News from Kansas in 1870," *Kansas Historical Quarterly* 7 (May 1938), p. 180; editor of *Morning Herald,* November 16, 1870.

27. Frederick E. Haynes, *Third Party Movements Since the Civil War* (Iowa City: Iowa State Historical Society, 1916), p. 22.

28. Francis N. Thorpe, "The Political Value of State Constitutional History," *Iowa Journal of History and Politics* 1 (January 1903), p. 25.

29. Leola N. Bergmann, "The Negro in Iowa," *Iowa Journal of History and Politics* 46 (January 1948), p. 38.

30. Ibid., p. 46.

31. *Iowa City Register and Leader,* February 20, 1910.

32. Jacob A. Swisher, "The Rise and Fall of Buxton," *Palimpsest* 26 (June 1945), p. 181.

33. *Western Appeal,* July 4, 1885.

34. Bergmann, "The Negro in Iowa," p. 52.

35. Ibid.

36. Ibid.

37. Ibid., p. 53.

38. Ibid.

8 • Education

The pioneers who moved west had first to provide for themselves such necessities as food, shelter, and clothing. But they felt as well the need for cultural and spiritual content in their lives. From the beginning, education was an important concern. Black citizens especially emphasized education, for it had been denied them in the slave states. The struggle by black men and women to acquire an education in the western states is a crucial area in the civil rights contest. Without adequate education, black citizens could not hope to work effectively for improvement in social, political, and economic conditions.

In California, the school law of 1851, formulated one year after the state came into the Union, provided for the apportionment of the school fund among the several towns, cities, and villages in proportion to the number of children between the ages of five and eighteen who resided in the designated political divisions.[1] Apparently this law referred to all school-age children, regardless of color, and so would include Mexicans, Indians, Orientals, and blacks, as well as whites. In 1855 Section Eighteen of an act passed by the legislature provided for the counting of white children. This would seem to indicate that all others were to be excluded from this date forward. In 1854 the first school for black children in California had been set up in the St. Cyprian African Methodist Episcopal Church at the corner of Jackson and Vincent streets in San Francisco, and J. J. Moore taught the twenty-three pupils enrolled there.[2]

Despite the enumeration of white children, the black children had not actually been excluded by law. There was, however, a lack of uniformity in handling the admission of black children to the public schools in California. The *San Francisco Daily Globe* reported in an editorial that the Board of Education of San Francisco was still undecided as to what course to pursue with reference to the exclusion of black children from the public schools. Several solutions were proposed, including separate schools, allowing black children to attend school with white children, and giving part of the school fund to them. Some members thought that provision should be made for a black girl who had already been admitted to the San Francisco high school. The other students in the high school opposed the girl's presence and petitioned the board. The editor of the *Globe* asked whether the abolitionist members and the superintendent wanted to defeat the law by keeping the girl in school. He thought that this would offend the community and warned the board that her continued presence would not be tolerated. He pointed out that the citizens were rightfully indignant and concluded that blacks should be excluded from all schools except those especially established for them.[3]

The wishes of the editor and a large segment of the community were fulfilled when the black girl was excluded from the school. Thomas Starr King, a Unitarian clergyman who was active in community affairs, was one of those who felt that the separation of the races was correct. He said that the reason why England had been successful as a colonizing nation was that it had kept the races separated. California must not, he warned, allow a mongrel race to inhabit its valleys and mountains. And if black men had to live in California, King felt, they ought to be educated separately.[4] Like most southerners, A. J. Moulder, a southern-born gentleman and then state superintendent of public instruction, shared King's view. In his report to the legislature in January 1859, Moulder insisted that he was aware that in several communities of the state an effort had been made to introduce black pupils into the schools on an equal basis with white children. He strongly resisted such efforts and instructed school officials who had asked for information on this subject that the schools of California were intended for whites alone. The superintendent reasoned that if the framers of the Constitution had intended that inferior races should be educated side by side with whites, they would have included them in the census of 1851.[5] Since he had no authority to punish those who did not comply with his desire, he asked the legislature to confer upon him authority to withhold public money from those districts which admitted the restricted races to their schools. The legislature did not honor his request and continued the policy already in operation.

In 1866 the school law was revised. It then prohibited all school-age children of African, "Mongolian," or Indian descent from admission to schools set up for whites unless they were living under the care of white persons. If ten parents or guardians of nonwhite children made application to the district board, the board was forced to provide for their children by establishing a school for them. The law provided also that if nonwhite children in any district could not be provided for in any other way, they might be admitted to the schools for white children, provided that a majority of the parents of the children attending the school did not make a protest in writing. It is not clear what would have happened if the whites had protested.

This law was interpreted very liberally, and in some districts non-white children were admitted to the regular public school. In 1870 the law was changed again to read that the education of Indian children and children of African descent should be provided for in separate schools. Upon written application of the parents or guardians of at least ten children to any board of trustees or board of education, a separate school was to be established for the education of the children. The education of a lesser number could be provided for in separate schools or in any other manner that the district board might provide. This law allowed the board the right to set up separate schools and provided mandatory education for the children. What had happened in San Francisco occurred in varying degrees elsewhere in the state. Black schools were taken for granted in Sacramento and the Sacramento Board of Education established them. In 1855 the black school was located at Fourth and K streets in Sacramento, but one year later it was relocated at Fifth and Ohio streets. The first teacher was J. B. Sanderson, who was prominent in the Convention of Colored Citizens of California. This school was a private school established by the blacks themselves, but in May 1856 the Sacramento Board of Education appropriated twenty-five dollars a month for the school. This was the first aid which was given black schools; Sanderson remained as a teacher even though the school was now publicly supported.[6] In some other communities, black children continued to attend the public schools. Such was the case in Woodland School in Yalo County, but their presence was a matter of such difficulty in that district that the school board eventually had to provide a separate school for them.

The black citizens of California were interested in settling the issue and thought that it could be done through the courts. As early as 1858, the *Sacramento Daily Union* carried an item in which it said that black citizens were resolved to test the right of their children to admission on equal terms with white children in the city.[7] Initially, black citizens had hoped that this question could be settled out of the courts, but the matter was eventually carried to the California Supreme Court in the case of Mary Frances Ward, a black citizen of San Francisco. She applied to Noah Flood, principal of the Broadway Grammar School, for admission. He refused the application on the ground that the board of education had established separate schools for persons of African descent. The decision in the case was rendered by Chief Justice Wallace, who vacillated. He ruled in favor of the existing law, namely, that the black children were due an education but that the school boards were not compelled to admit them to the same schools as the white children. Judge Wallace offered the usual argument—that these facilities had to be equal but separate and that separation was not a violation of the laws of the state.

Judge Wallace's decision, however, did not conclude the matter. The question was later carried to the legislature, where it was thoroughly discussed. One bill, introduced in the Assembly on December 15, 1873, was entitled "An Act to Amend the Political Code of the State of California." This proposed bill arose from the conviction that black children were being reared in ignorance as a result of the state administrative policy, and it provided that every school in the state should be open to all children between the ages of five and twenty who were United States citizens. The bill's merits were argued in the Assembly on January 31, 1874. Governor Booth had expressed views that coincided with the intent of the bill and had been elected United States senator by a large majority because of them. His election seemed indicative of what the people were thinking. One representative favored the repeal of the present law and the passage of a positive law which would admit all children to the same schools. It was thought that blacks were not getting the financial support due them. In a dozen counties, the money that should have gone to the black schools had gone instead to the white schools.[8] However, the opposition stated that the people had not requested a change in the law and that it was doubtful that the citizens of the state would accept such a change. This position was closer to the desires of the people. Nothing was done about the enactment of a positive law, and the matter was left to the discretion of the communities.

Despite the change in the law of 1872 and the decision in the case of *Ward v. Flood,* black citizens were still fighting for admission to the schools after the turn of the century. In Los Angeles, black children were admitted in the same way as in several other cities. The school trustees set aside part of the school fund for the benefit of black children and made provision for the employment of persons to teach in these black schools. This arrangement was not satisfactory to the black citizens. They did not think that the black school was as well-equipped and as well-manned as the regular schools in the city. In Oakland, a reverse policy was followed, and black children were admitted to the public schools along with other children. The editor of the *Elevator* thought that it could be done in every instance.[9]

Another way in which blacks hoped to resolve this problem was through building schools for blacks. In this way, the authorities would realize the high cost of separate education. For example, in Woodland District in Yalo County, the different races at first attended the same school. Then the school board provided a separate school for black children. The editor of the *Elevator* said that the establishment and operation for one year probably cost $1,000, that is, an outlay of $100 of taxpayers' money per pupil. He felt that the people of the county would soon tire of such expensive luxury.[10]

The issue continued to flare up. In 1873 a black pupil applied for admission to the night school of Sacramento, and at the same time two other black pupils applied to the day school. On June 7, 1874, the superintendent of schools sent a notice to J. F. McDonald, instructing him to admit no pupils of African or Indian descent. Since the board had previously admitted the black pupils, the principal could not obey this order. He was brought before the Board of Education for insubordination but was not punished. The board upheld its previous resolution, and an effort was made to provide separate schools.[11] It did not prove profitable and was dropped. Thus, black children were admitted to the schools of Sacramento. But they were admitted under special conditions, and they continued to request certain special courses. Moreover, black children were not admitted in every case to white public schools. At one meeting of the Yalo County Board of Education in 1874, Horace Cady asked for permission to send his children to a school other than the one set aside for black children, but his request was merely filed.[12]

The question of black children in the schools of California had therefore not been fully resolved, and blacks continued their fight for the education of their children in the common schools. They asked for a ruling from the state attorney general, but he replied that unless the state was willing to build schools equal to those of the whites, nothing could be done.[13] Neither the California Supreme Court nor the legislature had given positive directives, and the admission of blacks in the regular schools of California continued to be resolved by the boards of the various districts and cities. In some cities in the Imperial Valley, separate schools were still in operation as late as 1930. However, most of the school districts found separate schools impractical and admitted black pupils.

Black citizens had been able to prepare few to teach in the schools of California because most of their efforts had been channeled into getting their children into the public schools. Some black teachers taught in the schools which were set up exclusively for black pupils. One of the first teachers trained in the schools of California was Alice Rowan Johnson. She was the daughter of Charles H. and Elizabeth Rowan, who were among the first black pioneers to locate in the San Bernardino Valley. A native Californian, Alice Rowan received her education in the public schools of San Bernardino. She entered the State Normal School, located in Los Angeles, and graduated on December 25, 1888, in a class of sixteen. When she graduated, Ira Moore, principal of the school, wrote an unsolicited recommendation describing her potential as a teacher. He indicated that she had ranked high in her class, that she had been particularly successful in teaching and managing the practice school, and that she was a young woman of excellent character. He was sure that she would be successful if her color was ignored. After graduation, Alice successfully taught in a separate school in the Trujillo School District of Riverside. After two years, she earned the Normal School Post Graduate Certificate, and her work was praised by her superintendent, Edward Hyatt.[14]

During the years when it was difficult for black students to obtain an education in the regular public schools, J. W. Bier, the Reverend J. J. Moore, and several other black citizens attempted to build an institution known as Livingston Institute.[15] This school was to be of collegiate level for the benefit of black students on the West Coast. Nothing would be done until the committee had raised $10,000, however. The amount actually collected was only $1,600. Interest lagged and for several years no money was collected nor pledges made. Lots were later bought and sold at a profit until finally $5,000 was in the treasury. In 1867 the treasurer, Nathan Gray, asked that those interested collect $4,000 in order that the plan might be executed, but this was not done.

The project failed, probably because the black citizens felt that they should not have to pay for their children's education; instead, their children should be admitted to the state schools. On January 7, 1873, a special meeting of the Livingston Institute Committee was held at Merchants' Exchange Bank in San Francisco. Since it was now evident that the plan could not be brought to completion, it was decided at this meeting to return the money collected to the subscribers upon their presentation of the proper credentials.[16]

These Afro-American citizens of California made another attempt to organize a school for the benefit of black students. The school, called Phoenixonian Institute, was organized on December 2, 1862, and incorporated on January 5, 1867. Located in San Jose, the institute consisted of a large building, and there were shade trees and an artesian well on the grounds. The hope was to raise the necessary $1,000 and to secure the property by June of that year.[17] To meet this goal, the committee solicited the aid of the public; it mailed resolutions to the people, urging them to contribute money. The first resolution promised that an auxiliary organization would be set up to aid the institute.[18]

On August 10, 1868, the institute began its eleventh term, and the rates were published as sixty to one hundred dollars a term, in advance. These rates did not cover everything that a student needed; he or she was expected to furnish his or her own sheets, pillow cases, towels, knives, forks, and spoons.[19] Money collected for Livingston Institute was not turned over to the Phoenixonian Institute Committee. If that had been done, an important school might have devloped. Phoenixonian Institute was not a great school, but it did show that black citizens were determined that their children should have at least a minimum education.

The difficulties experienced in California were similar to those encountered in other states west of the Mississippi. The statutes by which Nevada was admitted into the Union, for example, provided for the education of white children only. During the mining boom and at the time the state entered the Union, the other racial elements were Indians, blacks, and Chinese, yet no education was provided for them.[20] The first school for blacks in Nevada was a private school designed to provide for those children excluded from the regular school. Dr. Waterman, a white man, opened this school in Virginia City. The school consisted of a building on Pine Street which had been purchased and neatly fitted and equipped for that purpose.[21]

Those in charge of education in Nevada advised the minority groups that it was not wise to press their claims and that all would be well if they waited.[22] The editor of the *San Francisco Elevator* did not share this opinion. He thought that it was unnecessary to wait since the black people were requesting only the rights of citizens—a view with which blacks in Nevada agreed. They were determined to secure the right to attend the public schools and consulted legal authorities. In an important case, David Stoutmyer, represented by his father and natural guardian, Nelson, sought a writ of mandamus against James Duffy, S. H. Wright, and M. C. Gordon, who comprised the Board of Trustees of the public school in District One of Ormsby County. The Stoutmyers based their case on the laws and customs of the state of Nevada.[23] The writ asked that the trustees be forced to admit the boy to the school, but it also had a wider application. If Stoutmyer was admitted to the school, all the schools in Nevada would be open to black pupils. The petition described David as seven years of age, a resident of the district, clean and neat in his habits, orderly in his deportment, and ready to obey and to conform to all rules, usages, customs, and disciplines of the school. The petition also stated that on April 10, 1871, the petitioner, through his father, had requested admission from the trustees and had been refused.

Chief Justice J. F. Lewis and Justice B. C. Whitman gave the de-

cision of the court. Justice John Garder rendered the dissenting opinion. Although justices Lewis and Whitman agreed in their conclu-
sion, they did not agree in their reasoning. Justice Whitman claimed
that power to admit to the public school was not conferred upon the
trustees but was instead provided by the laws of the state. However,
he agreed with the chief justice that the writ of mandamus should be
granted and David should be admitted to the regular school.[24] This
action ended the struggle over separate schools in Nevada.

Black pupils in Oregon were legally restricted as much, if not
more so, than they were in some of the slave states. Yet despite such
restrictions, the admission of black children to the public schools was
not as serious a problem in Oregon as in some other western states.
For one thing, the state did not have a large black population,
perhaps because of the nature of the country and the demands of its
industries. As late as 1925, the black population was less than 1 percent of the total population of the state. Moreover, in 1870 the Fifteenth Amendment to the United States Constitution conferred citizenship upon the blacks, who in turn were able to vote in the Oregon
school election. Thus, after 1870 blacks were admitted to the schools
in Oregon.

Nevertheless, integration was not altogether a bloodless affair. In
1874 J. B. Mitchell, a resident of Pendleton and parent of two children, ages nine and twelve, sent them to the city public school, but
they were refused admission. Mitchell persisted, claiming his right as
a taxpayer. An effort to silence him, by establishing a barber shop to
rival his, failed. Mitchell insisted that his children be educated in the
public school.[25] Two directors on the Pendleton School Board felt
that they could not exclude black children from the schools because
of unforeseeable public opinion. Two years earlier, there had been a
black public school in Portland, but in the election for school direc-
tor, black leaders there had asked their friends to vote for any person, regardless of party, who would agree to abolish the black
schools. In his report to the Portland Board of Education, the
superintendent of schools had declared that the black school was an
unnecessary expense. A motion that the black school be abolished
was passed, and this ended separate public schools in Portland.[26]

There was no notable opposition to black pupils in the schools of
Minnesota, again perhaps because of the smallness of the black population there. The Quakers initiated the establishment of education

facilities for black children and founded the first day school for them in St. Anthony.[27] It is possible that blacks were not encouraged to attend the public schools and that for this reason the Quakers established schools for them.

There were no laws against the attendance of black students in the public schools of Wisconsin; nevertheless, there is a case on record in which an effort was made to prevent black pupils from attending a private school. In 1859 a black girl applied for admission to Rockford Academy. In the absence of the principal, Josiah L. Pickard, who was ill at the time, the trustees hastily met and, to appease southern students, denied the girl admission because of her color. Pickard heard of this action, left his sickbed, and notified the Board of Trustees that they must find another principal. A majority of the board was in favor of continuing their course of action, but Pickard ordered the teachers to stop work until a new principal could be found. Realizing that he meant to implement his threat, the trustees met and rescinded their earlier action.[28] The girl was admitted.

In Kansas, opposition to the right of black students to enter the public schools was more severe. The procedures for admission of black children to the schools of Kansas differed from those in other states in the Midwest. Constantly changing, some of the laws were local and applied only to a particular town. In 1855 the proslavery legislature provided for public schools open to whites and excluded all other racial groups in the state at the time.[29] The law was changed in 1861 when Kansas had definitely joined the northern states in the contest over slavery. Although hostilities had not yet begun, this accounts for the change in the admission of black children to public schools. The law declared that all districts must provide education which was equally free and accessible to all residents over five and under twenty-one years of age.[30] This act was nullified by a private act, passed the same year, which authorized Maryville to prohibit black and mulatto children from attending the public schools. In 1862 an act amending the law of 1861 was passed; it authorized organized cities to make any rules they deemed proper for the separate education of white and colored children which would secure equal education for both groups.[31] This law required that all districts establish educational facilities for black pupils. By 1867 the lawmakers had passed a law which forbade the district board to refuse any children admission to the public school. It assessed against the district or the board of education a penalty of $100 for each child for each month he was excluded from the school during the term.[32] In 1876 the legislature reaffirmed the conditions of the law of 1869 and declared that the common schools were equally free and accessible to all.[33] This remained a principle of the school law of Kansas for many years. There are, however, some exceptions to this general rule, and in several towns separate elementary schools existed.

Private laws passed by the state legislature for the benefit of certain cities give some idea of the way in which the school laws operated regarding the admission of black children to the public schools of Kansas. In 1889 an act passed for the Wichita schools specifically stated that there should be no discrimination because of race or color.[34] This act was consistent with the laws of 1867 and 1876. In 1905 the legislature passed a private law for Kansas City which was opposed in principle to both of these acts and to the private act for Wichita. This act gave Kansas City the authority to establish both separate elementary and high schools, and this situation obtained in Kansas City until recent times.[35]

The migration of blacks in 1879 had its influence on the educational adjustment of blacks in Kansas.[36] An association called the Freedmen's Aid Society was organized on May 8, 1879, and was incorporated under the laws of the state on September 19, 1881. The president was the Reverend John M. Snodgrass, the treasurer was E. D. Bulen; other members of the committee were the Reverend M. Bell, A. Atchison, and C. M. Johnson.[37] The purpose of the Freedmen's Aid Society was to relieve destitute black people who immigrated to Kansas, but the immigrants, like pioneers everywhere, were able to adjust and care for themselves. The society then turned its attention to the establishment of a school. The site was a plot eight miles west of Baxter Springs—640 acres of choice land. The section was chosen because of its proximity to Missouri and Indian Territory.[38] How well the school operated and served the people of the state is not clear. It was organized not because blacks lacked schools, but because the Freedmen's Aid Society felt that some of them needed special industrial education not offered by the public schools.

There were other efforts by the Freedmen's Aid Society to provide a school for the black students who had come to Kansas from the South. In 1881 the Reverend Mr. Snodgrass and Mr. Atchison attempted to organize a literary and business academy at Dunlop, in

Morris County. After much hard work, this was accomplished and the Colored Academy began operation. The principal was Andre Atchison, a talented and faithful man who was worthy of the confidence of the friends of the Freedmen's Aid Society.[39] The *Topeka Weekly Tribune* carried an advertisement by P. H. Smith, business manager of the academy. The candidate who sought admission to the academy was asked to pass an examination in reading, writing, arithmetic, and elements of geography. Those who had more training could enter higher classes. The courses offered by the school were literary, normal, and business. Unlike the school at Baxter Springs, the purpose of the Colored Academy was to prepare students to enter the state university. The school year consisted of three terms of twelve weeks; the fee was two dollars and fifty cents per week.[40] In 1885 the academy was still continuing its service. This is revealed by a public statement that the academy had taught an average of 150 students a year; a contribution of $500 was now needed to meet the expenses of the boarding house. It was felt that the school was doing practical work and that the people should respond to it because the state needed its service.[41] The people did respond, the academy flourished, and several of those who went to Kansas in the migration studied there.

The fight of blacks in Iowa for admission to the public schools was similar to the struggle in the other states of the West. In 1847 the Iowa General Assembly passed a regulation which made the schools of the state open and free to all white persons between the ages of five and twenty-five.[42] But at least seventeen black children attended school in 1850, and a Miss Leola Nelson Bergmann thought that either they were taught in the home of a Quaker family or perhaps some local school boards admitted them despite the school law. In 1851 the state passed another law which exempted black property owners from tax payments for school purposes.[43] The state constitution of 1857 gave the State Board of Education authority to formulate school regulations. This grant of power was in conflict with a law passed by the state legislature in 1858 which was comprehensive and had a section providing for separate schools for the education of black youth except in cases where patrons unanimously consented to the admission of blacks to the public schools. The law was declared unconstitutional, and since that time no mention of race discrimination has been made in the school laws of Iowa.[14]

This did not give blacks admission to all the schools, however. Consequently, they had to resort to the courts to secure that privilege. In 1868 Alexander Clark, one of the prominent black men in the state, brought suit against the school board of Muscatine because his daughter Susan was refused admission to the white grammar school. The court ruled that the school board had no authority to require children to attend a separate school because of race, religion, or economic status. This case was not enough to bring the practice to a close, and in some instances there were schools for blacks despite the ruling of the Iowa Supreme Court.[45] In 1874 the matter came into court again in Keokuk, another town which provided separate educational facilities for black children. Two black boys, Gerald Smith and Charles Dove, residents of Keokuk, were denied admission to the public schools because certain citizens objected to their presence. The Iowa State Supreme Court decided that black children could not be excluded from the public schools, nor could they be compelled to attend separate schools. This decision ended the separate schools in Iowa.[46]

In 1867 Colorado, still a territory, had in force a statute which decreed that whenever there were fifteen or more colored children in any district, the board of directors, with the approval of the county superintendent of schools, might provide the necessary facilities for a separate school for the instruction of such colored children. When the state constitution was drafted, sentiment had changed, and Article IX, Section 8, stated that no sectarian tenets should be taught in the public schools, nor should any distinction or classification of pupils be made on account of color.[47] Since the adoption of this constitution, Colorado's schools have been open to all persons, and if there has been any confusion, it has not come to light.[48]

During the territorial days of Arizona, no distinction was made because of color; schools were open to all students. Arizona does not appear in the census report until 1870, and at that time the number of black people was only twenty-six. But by 1910 the figure was 2,009, and by 1930 it had reached 10,749. With this increase in population, the opinion concerning black students who attended school with whites changed. In 1928 the Revised Code of Arizona stated that whenever there were twenty-five students of African descent in a high school and 15 percent of the patrons objected to their presence, the matter of their remaining in that school had to be submitted to the voters of all school districts to determine whether they could remain in the school. The board of education was to be guided by the vote. The matter of the cost of separate education had to be submitted to the voters at the same time so as to determine whether blacks would be educated in separate schools or with all the school children of the district.[49] Thus, until recent years there were in some districts of Arizona separate schools for black students.

Oklahoma was not a state until 1907, but in 1893 Oklahoma Territory made provision for separate education of white and black children. The question was to be submitted to every county in the territory. If the majority voted for separate schools, they were to be established. If the majority voted against separate schools, they could not be established, and all the children in that county must then attend the same school.[50] The remedy in each case for those who did not agree with the decision reached by the voters was to resort to mandamus proceedings. When the state entered the Union, the state constitution provided for separate schools and the legislature made this provision operative. After statehood, Oklahoma maintained separate schools for the races and defined penalties for the teacher who allowed the races to mix. In the aftermath of the 1954 U.S. Supreme Court decision outlawing segregation, the University of Oklahoma was opened to black students; the public schools followed slowly.

The other states had little trouble regarding black students who entered the schools. No information has been unearthed to show that there was any confusion about black children's entering the public schools of Montana, Wyoming, Washington, New Mexico, Idaho, Utah, North Dakota, South Dakota, and Nebraska. The small number of black people. This consciousness stimulated old and persistent prejudices that have yielded only grudgingly and partially to the estabgroup had as many as 3,000.

So it was, then, that between the close of the Civil War and the turn of the century, the claim of blacks to equality in education was opposed most strongly in those areas with a relatively large black population—areas, in short, where white people were most conscious of black people. This consciousness stimulated old and persistent prejudices that have yielded only grudgingly and partially to the establishment of laws guaranteeing freedom of education to blacks. Indeed, despite laws enacted during the nineteenth century and other farther-reaching laws that have followed in the twentieth, the struggle of black Americans to obtain an education of a quality equal to that available to white Americans continues. Many blacks experience de facto segregation and inadequate schools. Prejudice lingers, and intermittent outbreaks of violence display, all too clearly, the seriousness of this flaw in the American social fabric.

NOTES

1. William W. Ferrier, *Ninety Years of Education in California, 1846–1936* (Berkeley, Ca., 1937), p. 97.

2. Ibid., p. 99.

3. *San Francisco Daily Globe,* March 2, 1858. This same paper carried a protest from a high school student.

4. *San Francisco Daily Evening Bulletin,* February 24, 1858.

5. Ferrier, *Education in California,* p. 98.

6. William L. Willis, *History of Sacramento County, California* (Los Angeles, 1913), p. 170.

7. *San Francisco Daily Evening Bulletin,* February 24, 1858.

8. *Sacramento Daily Union,* January 30, 1874.

9. *San Francisco Elevator,* May 4, 1872.

10. Ibid., August 22, 1874.

11. Willis, *History of Sacramento County,* p. 178.

12. *San Francisco Elevator,* September 5, 1874.

13. Ibid., March 7, 1878.

14. *Los Angeles Times,* February 12, 1909.

15. *San Francisco Elevator,* December 18, 1867.

16. Ibid., January 25, 1873. Members of the committee were N. Gray, H. W. Collins, R. T. Huston, Peter Anderson, John Barber, and S. D. Simmons.

17. Ibid., July 5, 1867.

18. Ibid., August 16, 1867.

19. Ibid., August 28, 1867.

20. Myron Angel, ed., *History of Nevada* (1881; rpt., Berkeley, Ca., 1958), p. 230.

21. Edwin Bean, comp., *History and Directory of Nevada County, California* (Carson City, Nev., 1867), p. 107.

22. *San Francisco Elevator,* January 10, 1874.

23. *Reports of Cases Determined in the Supreme Court of the State of Nevada, State v. Duffy* (San Francisco: Bancroft Whitney Co., 1911), vol. 7, p. 343.

24. Ibid., p. 345.

25. *San Francisco Elevator,* December 20, 1873.

26. Ibid., May 4, 1872.

27. Thomas E. Drake, "Quakers in Minnesota," *Minnesota History* 18 (1937), p. 264.

28. Josiah L. Pickard, "Experiences of a Wisconsin Educator," *Wisconsin Magazine of History* 7 (December 1923), p. 134.

29. Clyde L. King, "The Kansas School System—Its History and Tendencies," *Kansas State Historical Society Collections* 11 (1909–10), p. 427.

30. *Laws of Kansas* (1861), Chapter 76, Article 4, Section 6 (St. Paul, Minn.: West Publishing Co., 1884).

31. Nina Swanson, "The Development of Public Protection of Children in Kansas," *Kansas State Historical Society Collections* 15 (1919–22), p. 243.

32. *Laws of Kansas* (1867), Chapter 125, Section 1.

33. *Laws of Kansas* (1876), Chapter 122, Article V, Section 3.

34. *Laws of Kansas* (1889), Chapter 227, Section 4.

35. *Laws of Kansas* (1905), Chapter 414, Section 1.

36. The question of the migration to Kansas is treated elsewhere.

37. *Articles of Incorporation and By-Laws in Topeka* (1879).

38. Isaac O. Pickering, "The Administration of John P. St. John," *Kansas State Historical Society Collections* 9 (1905–06), p. 385; announcement sent out by Elizabeth T. Comstock, April 15, 1881.

39. *Topeka Weekly Tribune,* January 14, 1882.

40. Ibid., January 21, 1882.

41. *Statement of Kansas Freedman's Academy at Dunlop* (Lawrence, September 22, 1885), Kansas State Historical Society Library, Topeka.

42. *Laws of Iowa* (1846–47).

43. *Census Report of 1850,* Code of 1851, Chapter 71, Section 1160.

44. Leola N. Bergmann, "The Negro in Iowa," *Iowa Journal of History and Politics* 46 (January 1948), p. 20.

45. *Reports of Iowa,* No. 24, p. 266.

46. Ibid., No. 40, p. 518.

47. *Colorado Revised Statutes of 1867,* "Schools," Article 5, Section 25.

48. *Constitution of Colorado,* Article 60, Section 8.

49. *Revised Code of Arizona* (1938), Section 1085.

50. *Oklahoma Statutes* (1893), Section 5862.

9 • Social life

One of the problems that faced blacks who settled in the West was that of finding a suitable social life. For the most part they had been slaves whose social life was limited. That which they did enjoy was restricted among themselves. The one institution which was always held in high esteem by the black citizen, whether in the East or in the West, was the church. In most instances, he took this institution with him to the frontier. The church was not only a place of worship; it also became a social center and served as a meeting place for other organizations. The Convention of Black Citizens, fighting for civil rights in northern California, held most of its meetings at churches. Ministers were among the leaders in the fight for full citizenship.[1] The first black church on the frontier was the African Methodist church, organized by the Reverend Mr. Charles Stewart, who left New York in December 1851 and reached San Francisco in February 1852. On his first Sunday in California he conducted a meeting at the rooming house of Edward Gomez, whom he had met in St. Thomas on his way to the Pacific Coast. The first members of this church were James Wilkerson, Harry Butler, James Barton, and Henry Luns. They subsequently rented a vacant house and began holding services. It was not long before they raised enough money to erect a church building, and thus began the first black church in California.[2]

The African Methodist Episcopal church grew to such an extent in California that it was necessary to form a conference, designated as the California Conference, organized in the Union Bethel A.M.E. church in 1865 and presided over by Bishop Jabez Pitt Campbell. In addition to the Reverend Thomas M. D. Ward, a missionary elder who later became a bishop in the church, the following ministers were present: Peter Green, Edward Tappan, James Hubbard, Charles Wesley Broadley, Peter Killingworth, James C. Hamilton, and John T. Jenifer. Two others who deserve special mention were the Reverend Barney Fletcher, who later became important in the Masonic Lodge in the northern part of California, and J. B. Sanderson, who taught for several years in the black school in Sacramento. The number of Methodists increased in that section of the country, and several other Methodist congregations were organized in other parts of California. In 1854, a few years after the Methodists began their organization in San Francisco, they set up a church in Los Angeles. At that time, the church conducted its services in the homes of Biddy Mason and Robert Owens, familiarly known as "Uncle Bob." The first members of this church were Robert Owens, Winnie Owens, Biddy Mason, and Alice Coleman. The first pastor was the Reverend Moulton, and the church was formally organized and dedicated by Bishop T. M. D. Ward.[3]

African Methodism spread to other parts of the West and by 1900 the church was established wherever there was a considerable number of blacks. In 1864 an African Methodist church was dedicated in Carson City, Nevada.[4] The first African Methodist church in Colorado was Shorter Chapel in Denver, erected in the 1880s.[5] It was most active on the frontier, providing a social as well as religious center for its members.

Other denominations extended the influence of the black church on the frontier. In 1854 Samuel Shelton established the First Baptist church in San Francisco. He purchased a warehouse, using his personal funds, and fitted it up as a church. There were churches of that faith in Marysville, Rozenville, and Los Angeles.[6] The Presbyterian and the Episcopal churches attempted to establish themselves among blacks but did not secure many members because such ritualistic churches did not flourish on the frontier. One writer says that these churches were not popular there because the desire was for a religion that was more adaptable to the needs of everyday living.[7]

Another social outlet for the black in the West was the camp meeting conducted by the black churches. This was no doubt a part of the religious revival of 1801, which reached the West much later. These backwoods meetings were rather frequent along the East Coast up to 1900, and it was one such meeting which enabled Nat Turner to stage his insurrection.[8] Meetings of this type had great influence on the black population and the black church. Dr. Dan E. Clark feels that the camp meetings were peculiarly fitted to a pioneer people and were adopted by the settlers in the West as a means of self-expression.[9] One such meeting was held in August 1874 at Berryhill's Grove in the south end of Iowa City. People from many miles away came to witness and participate in this meeting, which lasted two days and was characterized by the usual singing and preaching.[10] There is reason to think that these meetings were conducted in many other towns, but, like other phases of the passing frontier, the camp meetings eventually became less popular. The basket dinner, which is still held by some rural churches today, is a carry-over of this type of meeting.

Nonsectarian social organizations on the frontier included the many conventions and celebrations held at various times. For example, Emancipation Proclamation celebrations were held in various parts of the West. A meeting of this kind was held in Turner Hall in Leavenworth, Kansas, in November 1864. It was in honor of the emancipation of the slaves in the state of Maryland and was one of the largest ever held in Leavenworth. Some of the most outstanding people of the city attended.[11] Another of these celebrations was held in Denver in August 1865 in commemoration of the anniversary of the emancipation of the blacks in the British West Indies. The editor of the *Rocky Mountain News* reported that no pains had been spared to make it one of the greatest events of the season. The program made a favorable impression, and the procession was thought to be one of the finest things that had ever been undertaken in Denver. So impressive was it that it brought out almost the entire black population, revealing a much larger number of blacks than was thought to be in Denver and its outlying territory. The affair was a gala one with fifty or more beautifully decorated carriages and men and women on foot carrying costly banners. The activities closed with a picnic and platform speaking, with the well-known William J. Harden, a politician of considerable importance, as principal speaker.[12] Similar celebrations were held in San Jose, Sacramento, and San Francisco.

Another group which provided a social outlet was the fraternal organization. One of the most important of those which exerted great influence among the blacks of the West was the Masonic Lodge, which held a Regional Grand Lodge in St. Paul in 1898. It passed strictly enforced educational qualifications for its members.[13] One of the most important persons in the early lodges was Alexander Clark, who at one time was deputy grand master and grand master of the Most Worshipful Grand Lodge of Free and Accepted York Masons, State of Missouri and the West, embracing the states of Minnesota, Iowa, Tennessee, and Arkansas. The lodges so increased in number and membership that by 1870 there were seventy of them in Clark's jurisdiction, with a membership of 2,700. The jurisdiction was extended to include Colorado, and at the same time Clark was elected grand treasurer of the National Grand Lodge and the chairman of the Committee of Foreign Correspondence.[14] Travelling from place to place, Clark did much to organize such lodges, and they grew into an important social outlet for the blacks of the West.

The Knights of Liberty was organized in Illinois in 1846 and spread to other parts of the West. According to its historian, the Reverend Moses Dickson, its purpose was to prepare for a general uprising for the extension of civil rights during slavery days. Nothing came of the protest movement, and the organization became one of the many lodges which fought for the improvement of the social life of blacks.[15] Before 1890 there were 47,000 blacks enrolled in this organization.

The social clubs organized by women constitute another part of the social history of the West. The effort by the women of the West in organizing and developing clubs and lodges did much to make life on the frontier more liveable. One of the most active clubwomen was Josephine Leavell Allensworth. She was the wife of the well-known chaplain, Lieutenant Colonel Allensworth, the man for whom the town of Allensworth, California, was named. She had some experience in furnishing entertainment for the soldiers and their wives while her husband was on duty with the army, and she used this to good advantage for the benefit of the community when the town of Allensworth was organized in the San Joaquin Valley. With the aid of the other women of the town, Mrs. Allensworth organized a Women's Improvement Club which provided, among other things a public reading room—not an easy task, for both the building and the books had to be obtained. This club included in its objectives a playground for children.[16]

Many other women took part in club work in California. Mrs. John M. Scott, president of the Sojourner Truth Club of Los Angeles, was leader of a group that erected a clubhouse to furnish entertainment and recreation for young women before the turn of the century. Mrs. Archie Wall was one of the most active workers in the California Federated Colored Women's Clubs. Such clubs in California furnished both recreation and entertainment for those persons who came to the West to establish homes.

One means of contact between blacks and whites was interracial marriage. Early in the history of the West, states set up legal restrictions designed to confine social intercourse of blacks to their own racial group. In many of the western states, interracial marriages were prohibited by law. California prohibited mixed marriages as early as 1850. The regulation, passed when the state came into the Union, indicated the attitude of the people on this matter. It is understandable, for a large part of the population originally came from the South, where the idea of intermarriage was unthinkable. In California, the prohibition applied only to the marriage of whites and blacks, although other races were represented in the population.

The same problem of intermarriage appeared in the early history of Oregon. At first it was of little concern, and there was no opposition because there were few blacks in the state, since the law prevented both slaves and free blacks from entering. The law against intermarriage was not passed until 1862, but it went further than the California law in that it included Orientals (or Mongolians) as well as blacks. The law stated that when a marriage was consummated between one party who was white and another party who was black or Mongolian (defined as a person having at least one-fourth black or Mongolian blood), the marriage was void in Oregon.[17] The reason for such a law grew out of the attitude of the citizens of the state rather than the number of blacks in the population. In 1860, after all, there were only 128 blacks listed in the state, a decrease from the previous decade of 25 percent.

In most cases, other states and territories, as they were organized, also prohibited mixed marriages by statute. In 1865 the Montana Territorial Legislature passed a law which made intermarriage a misdemeanor punishable by any court of competent jurisdiction. If convicted, the offender was to be sent to prison for three years. It also provided that those who performed such a marriage should also be punished.[18] The Idaho Territorial Legislature passed a similar act, making intermarriage a misdemeanor and such a marriage void.[19] The attitude on this question in Idaho did not change in two decades, and such a law was still in the revised statutes of Idaho in 1887, carrying with it the same penalties as in 1867. There was a similar law in Arizona Territory, but it extended the prohibition to Indians and Orientals as well as blacks. In Colorado, the law applied strictly to marriages of blacks and whites. Such marriages were declared void, and, if the law was not obeyed, there was a penalty, although the penalty was not specified.[20]

By 1920 most western states still had laws which prevented mixed marriages. Only Washington, Minnesota, Wisconsin, and California (which had abolished its former law) permitted such marriages. Some states took no notice of racial groups other than blacks, perhaps because there were so few Orientals among the population and perhaps too because there was little hostility toward the Indians. Whatever the cause, not many states and territories had prohibitory laws against other racial groups, but they did have them against blacks, regardless of the sparsity of the black population. There were those who did not agree with these laws, and they made efforts to have them repealed. In 1878 a bill was introduced in the California legislature to make the law prohibiting the marriage of white persons with blacks, mulattoes, and Chinese null and void. Although the bill aroused some interest, it did not pass and the prohibition remained.[21]

Of course mixed marriages did occur, despite prohibition. In 1871, for example, William Nicholas toured the Indian agencies and resided for a short time in the home of a white man named Smith who lived among the Creek Indians. Smith had a black wife, a practice common among the Indians, and the family was apparently doing well in a section in which mixed marriages were prohibited.[22] In the 1880s, the *Rocky Mountain News* carried a story of another such marriage. A black man named Frank Shannon married a white woman. They had moved to Acapulco after their marriage, and the law there was not clear as to whether or not they must separate. The marriage became news when she deserted him and their six children.[23] Later, other cases arose, such as the one carried in the news the following year which caused excitement in Denver because a white woman married a black man named Thomas Lounsay. The woman was the daughter of an Englishwoman who had herself married a black man. In Oakland, David L. Thompson, a black, married a white woman. Thompson's family opposed the marriage and threatened a law suit. The law was clear: blacks and whites could not marry in California, and if it could be proved that Thompson was a black, a suit could be brought against him and won by his family. Thompson, however, maintained that he did not have more than one-quarter black blood and that he was also part Spanish, German, and English. His contention had to be considered, because his half-sister, Hortense Thompson, was definitely Caucasian. A committee was appointed to consider the matter of racial origins, but this could not be done until it was evident that Thompson was a black and would fall under the law. The final outcome of the case is not available.[24]

The problem of mixed marriages arose repeatedly throughout this period, and wherever it appeared, it created confusion. The laws were specific in all cases of mixed marriages, but they did occur despite the laws. Such instances reveal the forces of democracy as much as any phase of western history, for such marriages could not have happened in the South. It was against the law in the West; there were demonstrations; but nothing happened. The people waited for the law to take its course, which would not have been the case in some other sections of the nation.

One of the best efforts toward socialization in the West was that of blacks who banded together for the purpose of settlement in the West. One of the organizations formed on the frontier to induce the relatives of the settlers to leave the South and come west was the African Society, founded at San Bernardino, California, in the late 1890s. It was the intention of the society not to remain wholly local but to become a state group with the local units eventually under one head. The society was capitalized at $10,000, of which $1,000 in gold had been readily subscribed. There were objections, for some people felt that black citizens would become wards of the public, perhaps because at that time nineteen aged women from Georgia, Mississippi, and Alabama had been brought to the West and placed in the Riverside County Hospital. But objections notwithstanding, the African Society must have had some influence because the black population of San Bernardino more than doubled in six months.[25]

The efforts of black people in the West to provide an adequate social life for themselves was characteristic of the larger black experience in the West. Facilities which were open to the general public were closed to blacks, and they had therefore to furnish their own religious, cultural, and recreational outlets. Laws prohibiting interracial marriage were only one more dimension of the white American's effort to prevent free congress with his black fellow citizen. And yet such obstructions, real though they were, lacked the rigidity that they had in the South and East. Although the social life of the black people in the West was not at one with the social life of whites, neither was it as clearly circumscribed as that which blacks had known before moving to the frontier.

NOTES

1. *Sacramento Daily News,* October 26, 1865.

2. Delilah L. Beasley, *Negro Trail Blazers of California* (Los Angeles, 1919), p. 158.

3. *An Illustrated History of Los Angeles* (Chicago, 1889), p. 297.

4. Edwin F. Bean, comp., *History and Directory of Nevada County, California* (Carson City, Nev., 1867). p. 186.

5. James H. Baker and Leroy R. Hafen, eds., *History of Colorado* Denver, 1927), vol. 3, p. 1224.

6. Beasley, *Negro Trail Blazers,* p. 160.

7. Dan E. Clark, *The West in American History* (New York, 1937), p. 388.

8. Ibid., p. 389. Dr. Clark says that the greatest of these meetings was held at Cain Ridge in Kentucky, where it was estimated that 25,000 persons gathered from all parts of Kentucky and Tennessee, even from north of the Ohio.

9. Ibid., p. 390.

10. Leola N. Bergmann, "The Negro in Iowa," *Iowa Journal of History and Politics* 46 (January 1948), p. 49.

11. *Leavenworth Daily Conservative,* November 27, 1864.

12. *Denver Rocky Mountain News,* August 1, 1865.

13. *St. Paul Pioneer Press,* August 5, 1898.

14. *United States Biographical Dictionary and Portrait Gallery of Eminent and Self-Made Men in Iowa* (Chicago, 1878), p. 540.

15. Moses Dickson, *Manual of the International Order of the Twelve of the Knights and Daughters of Tabor,* privately printed, p. 10.

16. Beasley, *Negro Trail Blazers,* p. 226.

17. William P. Lord, *Oregon Laws,* (Salem, Ore.: W. S. Duniway, 1910), vol. 1, p. 375, Sections 502–504.

18. *Territorial Papers of Montana,* vol. 2, Bill 27, 1865.

19. *Territorial Papers of Idaho,* vol. 1, July 11 to July 17, 1867.

20. *General Laws of the Legislative Assembly of the Colorado Territory* (1864), p. 108.

21. *Sacramento Daily Record-Union,* January 11, 1878.

22. William Nicholson, "A Tour of Indian Agencies in Kansas and the Indian Territory in 1870," *Kansas Historical Quarterly* 3 (August 1934), p. 358.

23. *Rocky Mountain News,* August 15, 1883.

24. *San Francisco Call,* October 24, 1893.

25. *San Francisco Chronicle,* September 11, 1904. This is so near the period under study that it probably started earlier.

Conclusion

Blacks began moving to the West before it was acquired by the United States. While some of those who came to this new land were slaves seeking freedom, in most cases they were free men seeking a better opportunity to improve their living conditions. By and large, then, the same factors which brought other racial groups to the West brought the black population.

After the West had been acquired by the United States, the rate of immigration of black people to this region increased. The numbers were small until after the Civil War, and one factor responsible for this was slavery, which prevented blacks from going west unless they were brought by their masters or escaped. Most of those who did move west were free men, but before the Civil War there were not many free blacks. A second factor which delayed the movement of blacks to the West until after the Civil War was the limited number of occupations which were available to them. Western occupations were not in the long run those which attracted slave labor.

The first citizens who came to this section after it had been acquired by the United States explored and tested the purchase for the quality of the land and its suitability for settlement, and there were black men with these early explorers. A number of explorers were also active in the fur industry, since at this time the demand for fur was being noted in the markets of the world and fur companies were being formed to ascertain if there were furs of importance in the new land. Some of them who played an important part in this industry were Jedediah Smith, James Bridger, and Kit Carson. Blacks too were active in the fur industry throughout its period of importance, and outstanding among them were Edward Rose, James Beckwourth, and George Bonga. Military operations in the West constituted another factor which added to the black population. A few black soldiers fought in the Mexican War, and when it was over, some of them settled in the West. A large number of blacks fought in the Civil War, and when it ended, most of them were employed to bring the Indians under control. When their period of enlistment was over, many of them also settled in the West.

One of the dramatic movements of the black population was the exodus to the Middle West. Immediately following the Civil War, the condition of the black population in the South was very difficult. That section had to reestablish its economy, which had been almost destroyed by the war. No longer was a large number of slaves required. The farmers who wished to reestablish their farms did not have the funds to hire labor, which left a large number of black laborers unemployed. Many blacks felt that, because of both the economic and social conditions, it would be well to move to the West where the land was cheap and fertile. Most went to Kansas and Nebraska. At first conditions were difficult, and many found it necessary to work for white farmers who were established in the area. Soon, however, they were able to adjust themselves with good results. Some of them had excellent farms. In fact, the black men in agriculture were among the most prosperous farmers in Kansas. One of them, Junius Grove, became a "Potato King" of Kansas. He was able to produce more potatoes per acre than anyone else. Other blacks had similar results in other areas of agriculture.

Black people were interested in improving conditions and providing for their economic and social needs. Consequently, black towns developed toward both these ends. They provided merchandise for black people and were also of great value to their social needs, especially in the agricultural sections of Kansas, Oklahoma, and Nebraska. But significant though they were to the blacks who settled on the agricultural frontier, these towns were small and ephemeral. Most of them have disappeared, existing today only as ghost towns.

The mining industry was one of the most important factors in increasing the population—including the black population—of the West. People came to the gold fields from all over America because they saw an opportunity to get rich quickly. Not all of them were able to get rich, but many of them settled in California and Colorado and increased the population of whites and blacks in the West.

Black men worked in every aspect of the mining industry: they were cooks and washers as well as miners, and they worked in any other capacity wherever they were needed. Some engaged in quartz mining, but the majority worked at placer mining. Those blacks who came to the mines were not all freemen. In spite of laws in some states stipulating that slavery could not exist in them, there were slaves, often brought in with the agreement that they could purchase their freedom by working for a certain period. The owners were careful of those slaves they brought west, and in most instances they brought only those who could be depended upon to be satisfied in slavery. Even so, some slaves either escaped or carried their cases to the courts. Some found freedom almost despite themselves when they were driven from the gold fields by those who did not own slaves and felt that slaves gave their owners an unfair advantage.

Some black men in the West were employed in the various businesses that sprang up to serve the miners. Howard Barnes, for example, had come west with the Boggs family, one of whom was Lilburn Boggs, later governor of Missouri. Barnes made and sold pies to the miners for one dollar each, a price which at that time in the West would have been considered exorbitant. He was especially interested in securing enough money to complete the payments for his freedom; he still owed some payments at the close of the Civil War. Barnes was sued in the 1870s and was forced to pay the balance after slavery had been abolished. He went back to Missouri and opened a restaurant in Jefferson City. Like most blacks in this and other businesses, his success was, at best, modest. A few black businessmen, however, were quite prosperous. The San Francisco firm of Lester and Gibbs is an example of the more successful black business.

A few black people were able to enter the professions. Some practiced medicine before the turn of the century—a considerable achievement, considering the difficulties that blacks had in obtaining a decent education. In general, these professionals moved with the population from East to West and were to be found in the larger cities.

The one profession in which blacks were well represented was the clergy. Wherever the black population was found in any considerable numbers, churches were established, the Methodist and Baptist churches being most prominent. These churches were largely the same as those to which blacks had belonged in the sections where they had lived before. Because some of the hostility which they had experienced in the South also beset them in the West, they organized their own churches. Some of the leaders were such men as Reverend T. M. D. Ward of the A.M.E. church, who rose to become a bishop. Reverend J. B. Sanderson was also active in the A.M.E. church, and he served also as a teacher in the public schools of Sacramento, California.

Black people who moved west in order to escape the restrictions of the South found that some of those restrictions had moved west along with them. This was especially true in California and Oregon. In fact, black persons were prohibited by law from settling in Oregon. Thus George Washington Bush, being unable to enter Oregon, settled at Bush Prairie, Washington, a place named in his honor. The son of this sturdy citizen was a member of the first legislature of Washington and no doubt exerted some influence on state law because Washington never had the restrictions which Oregon had.

By 1890 the black population in California was the largest of any in the states under consideration. From the time the state was admitted into the Union there were restrictions placed upon black citizens, and Governor Peter Burnett recommended that black men and women be excluded from the state. This did not come to pass, but several of the leading black citizens left the state and went to Canada. One of the most significant restrictions was that which prohibited black citizens from giving testimony in the courts. Such a law left blacks without protection from criminals. It was so unfair that some judges ignored it even before the law was changed by the legislature.

The black population fought for their rights in many of the conventions called by their leaders and the churches. Conventions were held with more frequency where the population was largest. Resolutions were passed and sent to state legislatures, pointing out the many discriminations against blacks and asking that they be abolished and that black citizens be treated in the same way as other citizens of the state. Blacks also attempted to overcome some of the conditions against them by resorting to the courts, and at times they were successful.

The right of blacks to an education had to be fought for just as much as any other aspect of civil rights. Black citizens were extremely concerned about education, partly because it had been denied them before the Civil War, and partly because they saw how necessary it was in order for them to adjust to their new role. Before the Civil War they had to depend upon their masters, but now they had to depend upon their own efforts.

The black population was so small in some of the states and territories that black pupils in the schools created no problem at all and they attended school with the other students. It was different in sections like California, where black students could not attend classes with white students. The black population tried to meet this situation by using what influence they had; they sent petitions to the legislature and made use of the news media to expose the educational condition of black people. The black leaders in California established weekly newspapers which they used to acquaint their fellow citizens with the problems which faced them in both education and civil rights and with the efforts which were being made to combat these conditions. In some places, whites established separate schools for blacks which were in no sense equal to the schools established for whites. Consequently, black citizens made an effort to establish their own schools. One of the projected California schools did not materialize because officials had decreed that it could not begin operation until a specified amount was raised; the blacks were unable to meet this requirement. Another institution set up by the black citizens of California flourished for several terms.

The same problem in education faced the black citizens of Kansas. There were many changes in the laws of the state which created difficulty for black students. Black parents, like those in California, had to fight to get their children into school. In most of the small towns in Kansas the black population was so tiny that it was not possible to set up separate schools, and so the schools were integrated. The one section of the state that had separate schools was Kansas City, which continued the practice until the 1954 Supreme Court decision and perhaps later. The black population of Kansas tried to solve their educational problem by organizing private schools. The hope was to establish schools to teach industrial studies and thereby prepare those who had come to Kansas to meet the industrial needs of the area, but blacks also established a school to prepare students to enter the state university. All in all, the schools were very important and black leaders struggled to establish them so that their children could secure an education and better adjust to the communities in which they lived.

When blacks had secured the right to vote and some education, they, like all other citizens, desired to enter politics and gain offices. They were unable to win many offices because the black population was much too small to influence elections in the western states. The only states with a reasonably large black population were California and Kansas, and it was there that the greatest political effort was made by blacks to participate in politics and work for political offices. The black citizens of California were able to secure no offices of importance, but they did exert some influence on the political process. In Kansas, blacks held a number of minor offices, such as those of sheriff and justice of the peace, and several significant ones, such as that of state auditor, which was held by a black man for two terms. A black man was an assistant attorney general of the state. A major factor behind such successes was the exodus of blacks to Kansas, which provided the state with the largest black population until the 1880s.

Where their population was large, blacks were able to pile up a vote. This was important, but it would have been more so if they had not been so devoted to the Republican party. They no doubt would have achieved more if they had done what they threatened to do and had supported those candidates who were willing to treat them as other citizens were treated. The one opportunity came when the Populist party was very active in Kansas. However, black citizens refused to leave the Republican party because many of them felt that that party had given them their freedom. Whatever the reason, they did not give the Populist party the support which was expected from them.

There are several instances of the exertion of black political influence in Iowa, mostly in Republican state conventions. Blacks also had a little political influence in Colorado, which was remarkable because of the very small black population there. Black political influence in Colorado was exercised by means of the vote since they were unable to hold any offices there. In Oklahoma the influence of blacks was virtually limited to the small towns there. Because it is west of the Mississippi, Oklahoma is technically a western state, but its attitude is more like that of Arkansas and Missouri than Iowa and Nebraska. In the other Western states, the black population was so small that it exerted little or no influence.

The social life of black people in the West was important and it became more so as they became more educated and politically active. Most significant as social forces were black churches, which not only contributed to religious activity but to social welfare as well. Most centers of social activity, such as theaters and hotels, were closed to blacks, even in California. If they were to enjoy these things they had to be provided by black people themselves. This was very difficult and sometimes impossible because of the sparsity of the black population in many sections of the West.

Another social factor was marriage. Most of these western states passed laws which prohibited marriage between whites and blacks. In spite of these laws, there were some interracial marriages. This was possible in part because one of the states which never had such a law was Washington, and several of those who lived on the Pacific Coast and who desired intermarriage went to that state or to other places where there were no restrictions. Some interracial couples continued to live in states where they were in violation of the law. Sometimes they were prosecuted, but in general the West showed a tolerance that was lacking in the South.

For most black people, the West was not the Promised Land. But neither were its restrictions as severe as those which they had known in the South and the East. On balance, the West has given blacks an opportunity to make a better life for themselves. In return, they have given the West of themselves. In the course of their struggle toward a position of equality among the nation's people, they have helped to make the West a part of America.

Appendix

THE GROWTH OF THE BLACK POPULATION IN THE WESTERN STATES

As Reported by the Bureau of the Census

State	1840	1850	1860	1870	1880	1890	1900
Arizona				26	155	1,357	1,848
California		902	4,086	4,272	6,018	11,322	11,045
Colorado			48	436	2,435	6,215	8,570
Idaho				60	53	201	940
Iowa		333	1,069	5,762	9,516	10,485	12,693
Kansas			627	17,108	43,107	40,710	52,003
Minnesota	188	29	259	759	2,564	3,683	4,950
Montana				183	346	1,400	1,523
Nebraska			82	789	2,385	8,913	6,289
Nevada			45	367	488	242	134
New Mexico		22	85	172	1,015	1,936	1,160
North Dakota				94	113	373	455
Oklahoma						21,000	55,000
Oregon		207	128	346	487	1,186	1,106
South Dakota				94	288	541	465
Utah		50	59	118	232	588	672
Washington			30	207	325	1,602	2,514
Wisconsin	196	636	1,171	2,133	2,702	2,444	2,542
Wyoming				183	346	1,400	1,523
TOTAL	384	2,179	7,689	33,109	72,575	115,598	165,432

Bibliography

BIOGRAPHY AND AUTOBIOGRAPHY

Adams, Andy. *Reed Anthony, Cowman*. Boston: Houghton Mifflin Co., 1907.

Alter, J. Cecil. *James Bridger: Trapper, Frontiersman, Scout and Guide*. Salt Lake City: Shepard Book Co., 1925.

Barneby, William Henry. *Life and Labour in the Far, Far West*. London: Cassell and Company, 1884.

Beckwourth, James Pierson. *Life and Adventures*. New York: Harper and Brothers, 1856.

Bell, Horace. *Reminiscences of a Ranger, or Early Times in Southern California*. Los Angeles: Yarnell, Caystile & Mathes, 1881.

Bidwell, John. *Echoes of the Past: An Account of the First Emigrant Train to California*. Chicago: R. R. Donnelley, 1928.

Bonsal, Stephen. *Edward Fitzgerald Beale, a Pioneer in the Path of Empire*. New York: G. P. Putnam, 1912.

Brewer, William Henry. *Up and Down California in 1860–1864*. Ed. Francis P. Farquhar. New Haven: Yale University Press, 1930.

Bronson, Edgar Beecher. *Cowboy Life on the Western Plains: Reminiscences of a Ranchman*. New York: McClure Co., 1908.

Bryant, Edwin. *Rocky Mountain Adventures*. Philadelphia: D. Appelton, 1849.

Camp, Charles, ed. *James Clyman, American Frontiersman, 1792–1881*. San Francisco: California Historical Society, 1928.

Chardon, Francis A. *Journal of Fort Clark, 1834–1839*. Ed. Annie Abel. Pierre, S.D.: Department of History, State of South Dakota, 1932.

Cody, William Frederick. *The Life of Hon. William F. Cody, Known as Buffalo Bill, the Famous' Hunter, Scout and Guide.* Hartford, Conn.: P. E. Bliss, 1879.

Cook, John Wesley, comp. *Hands Up: Thirty-Five Years of Detective Life in the Mountains and on the Plains.* Denver: W. F. Robinson Printing Co., 1897.

Custer, Elizabeth Bacon. *Tenting on the Plains, or General Custer in Kansas and Texas.* New York: C. L. Webster Co., 1887.

Dellenbaugh, Frederick Samuel. *Fremont and the Forty-Niners.* New York: G. P. Putnam, 1914.

Drannan, William F. *Thirty-One Years on the Plains and in the Mountains.* Chicago: Rhodes and McClure, 1907.

Ellison, William Henry, ed. *Life and Adventures of George Nidever, 1802–1883.* Berkeley: University of California Press, 1937.

Ewers, John Canfield, ed. *Adventures of Zenas Leonard, Fur Trader.* Norman: University of Oklahoma Press, 1959.

Farnham, Thomas Jefferson. *Travels in the Great Western Prairies.* New York: Greeley and McElrath, 1843.

———. *Early Days of California: Embracing What I Heard and Saw There, with Scenes in the Pacific.* Philadelphia: J. E. Potter, 1860.

Favour, Alpheus. *Old Bill Williams, Mountain Man.* Chapel Hill: University of North Carolina Press, 1936.

Fawcett, Edgar. *Some Reminiscences of Old Victoria.* Toronto: W. Briggs, 1912.

Ferguson, Charles D. *Experiences of a Forty-Niner during Thirty-Four Years' Residence in California and Australia.* Cleveland: Frederick Wallace, 1888.

Field, Stephen Johnson. *Personal Reminiscences of Early Days in California.* Washington, D.C.: privately printed, 1893.

Fisher, Ezra. *Correspondence.* Ed. Sarah Fisher Henderson, Nellie Edith Latourette, and Kenneth Scott Latourette. Portland, Ore.: privately printed, 1919.

Fremont, John Charles. *Life, Exploration and Public Service.* New York: Miller, Orton and Mulligan, 1856.

———. *Memoirs of My Life.* New York: Belford Clarke and Co., 1887.

Gibson, George Rutledge. *Journal of a Soldier under Kearney and Doniphan, 1846–47.* Glendale, Ca.: Arthur H. Clark and Co., 1935.

Gibson, J. Watt. *Recollections of a Pioneer.* St. Joseph: Nelson Hanne, 1912.

Glasscock, Carl Burgess. *Lucky Baldwin: the Story of an Unconventional Success.* Indianapolis: Bobbs Merrill, 1933.

Goodlander, Charles W. *Memoirs and Recollections of the Early Days of Fort Scott.* Fort Scott: Monitor Printing Co., 1900.

Gorham, George Congdon. *Biographical Notice of Stephen J. Field.* Privately printed, 1892.

———— and Stephen J. Field. *Personal Reminiscences of Early Days in California.* 1893; rpt., New York: Da Capo Press, 1968.

Hastings, Frank Seymour. *A Ranchman's Recollections.* Chicago: Breeder's Gazette, 1921.

Hittell, Theodore Henry. *Adventures of James Capen Adams, Mountaineer and Grizzly Bear Hunter of California.* New York: Scribner, 1926.

James, George Wharton. *Heroes of California.* Boston: Little, Brown, 1910.

Karsner, David. *John Brown, Terrible "Saint."* New York: Dodd, Mead, 1934.

Kelley, Charles and Hoffman Birney. *Holy Murder: the Story of Porter Rockwell.* New York: Monton, Balch, 1934.

Kelly, Charles and Dale Morgan. *Old Greenwood: the Story of Caleb Greenwood: Trapper, Pathfinder, and Early Pioneer.* Revised ed. Gerrytown, Ca.: Talisman Press, 1965.

Larpenteur, Charles. *Forty Years a Fur Trader on the Upper Missouri.* Ed. Elliott Coues. New York: F. P. Harper, 1899.

Lauderdale, Robert J. and John M. Doak. *Life on the Range and on the Trail.* Ed. Lela N. Pirtle. San Antonio: The Naylor Co., 1936.

Lienhard, Heinrich. *Pioneer at Sutter's Fort, 1846–1850.* Trans. and ed. Marguerite E. Wilbur. Los Angeles: the Calaffa Society, 1941.

Love, Nat. *Life and Adventures of Nat Love.* Los Angeles, 1907.

Luttig, John C. *Journal of a Fur Trading Expedition on the Upper Missouri, 1812–1813.* Ed. Stella M. Drumm. St. Louis: Missouri Historical Society, 1920.

Majors, Alexander. *Seventy Years on the Frontier.* Ed. Prentiss Ingraham. Chicago: Rand, McNally, 1893.

Maverick, Mary Ann. *Memoirs of Mary A. Maverick.* Ed. Rena Maverick Green. San Antonio: Alamo Printing Co., 1921.

Mayne, Richard Charles. *Four Years in British Columbia and Vancouver Island.* London: J. Murry, 1862.

Meeker, Ezra. *Pioneer Reminiscences of Puget Sound.* Seattle: Lorsman and Hanford, 1905.

————. *The Ox Team, or the Old Oregon Trail, 1852–1906.* New York, 1907.

————. *The Busy Life of Eighty-Five Years of Ezra Meeker.* Seattle, 1916.

————. *Seventy Years of Progress in Washington.* Seattle, 1921.

Mooso, Josiah, *Life and Travels.* Winfield, Kan.: Telegram Print, 1888.

Newmark, Harris. *Sixty Years in Southern California, 1853–1913.* Ed. Maurice H. and Marco R. Newmark. 4th ed. Los Angeles: Zeitlin and Ver Brugge, 1970.

Patterson, Lawson B. *Twelve Years in the Mines of California.* Cambridge, Mass.: Miles and Dillingham, 1862.

Potter, Theodore Edgar. *The Autobiography of Theodore Edgar Potter.* Concord, N.H.: The Ramford Press, 1913.

Powell, Lawrence Clark. *Philosopher Pickett.* Berkeley: University of California Press, 1942.

Quaife, Milo Milton, ed. *John Askin Papers*. 2 vols. Detroit: Detroit Library Commission, 1928–1931.

———, ed. *Narrative of the Adventures of Zenas Leonard, Written by Himself*. Chicago: R. R. Donnelley, 1934.

———, ed. *Kit Carson's Autobiography*. Chicago: R. R. Donnelley, 1935.

Robinson, Philip Steward. *Sinners and Saints*. Boston: Roberts Brothers, 1883.

Ruxton, George Frederick. *Adventures in Mexico and the Rocky Mountains*. New York: Harper and Brothers, 1848.

———. *Life in the Far West*. New York: Harper and Brothers, 1859.

Sherman, Edwin. *Biographical Material*. Bancroft Library, University of California.

Shuck, Oscar Tully, ed. *Representative and Leading Men of the Pacific*. San Francisco: Bacon and Company, 1870–1875.

Siringo, Charles A. *Texas Cowboy, or Fifteen Years on the Hurricane Deck of a Spanish Pony*. New York: Rand, McNally, 1886.

———, *Lone Star Cowboy*. Santa Fe, N.M., 1919.

Townsend, John Kirk. *Narrative of a Journal Across the Rocky Mountains*. Philadelphia: Perkins and Marvin, 1839.

Victor, Frances. *Eleven Years in the Rocky Mountains and Life on the Frontier*. Hartford: Columbian Book Co., 1879.

Voorhees, Luke. *Personal Recollections of Pioneer Life on the Mountains and Plains of the Great West*. Privately printed. Cheyenne, Wyo., 1920.

Williams, James. *Life and Adventures of James Williams, a Fugitive Slave*. San Francisco: Women's Union Print, 1873.

Wood, John. *Journal of John Wood*. Columbus: Nevins and Myers, 1871.

Woods, Daniel B. *Sixteen Months at the Gold Diggings*. New York: Harper and Brothers, 1851.

MANUSCRIPTS

Aldrich, Frank J. "Diary of a Trip across the Country in 1876." Typed copy in Huntington Library, San Marino, California.

Beckwourth, James. "Documents." Bancroft Library, University of California.

Brown, John H. "Manuscript." Bancroft Library, University of California.

Brown, John. "Papers." Charles B. Tunnell Collection, California Historical Society, San Francisco.

Carpenter, William O. "A California Pioneer of the Fifties." Bancroft Library, University of California.

Clyman, James. "Papers." Huntington Library, San Marino, California.

Damon, John F. "Papers." Huntington Library, San Marino, California.

Davis, William H. "Papers." Huntington Library, San Marino, California.

Folson, Joseph L. "Papers." Bancroft Library, University of California.

"Fort Sutter Papers." Huntington Library, San Marino, California.

Grimshaw, William R. "Narrative of Life and Events in California during Flush Times." Bancroft Library, University of California.

Harvey, James Rose. "The Negro in Colorado." M.A. thesis, University of Denver, 1941.

"History of the Negro in Los Angeles." W.P.A., Federal Writers Project, 1936. Manuscript in Sacramento State Library, California.

Larkin, Thomas. "Papers." Bancroft Library, University of California.

Lassel, Stanlus. "Diary of an Overland Journey." Bancroft Library, University of California.

Leidesdorff, William A. "Biographical Sketch." Bancroft Library, University of California.

——. "Papers." Bancroft Library, University of California.

——. "Papers." Huntington Library, San Marino, California.

McKinstry, George. "Documents of the History of California." Bancroft Library, University of California.

Mack, Effie M. "Life and Letters of William Morris Steward, 1887–1909." University of California, Berkeley, 1930.

Manning, James F. "William Alexander Leidesdorff's Career in California." M.A. thesis, University of California.

Robinson, Alfred. "Statement of Recollections on Early Years in California." Bancroft Library, University of California.

Savage, W. Sherman. "Workers of Lincoln University." Lincoln University, Missouri, 1951.

Waldron, Nell Blyth. "Colonization in Kansas from 1861–1890." Dissertation, Northwestern University, 1932.

Wilson, Benjamin D. "Observations on Early Days in California and New Mexico." Bancroft Library, University of California.

STATE DOCUMENTS

COMPILED LAWS:

U.S. State Department. *Arizona Territory Acts, 1804–1871*. National Archives, Washington, D.C.

Arizona Secretary of State. *Arizona State Legislature Acts, 1887*. Prescott.

California State Legislature Acts, 1853. San Francisco: Franklin Printing House, 1853.

Kansas State Legislature Acts, 1857.

Lord, William P. *Oregon Laws*, 3 vols. Salem, Ore.: W. S. Duniway, 1910.

Secretary of State of Missouri. *Revised Statutes of Missouri, 1825–1848*. St. Louis: Chambers and Knapp, 1848.

GENERAL STATUTES:

General Laws of the Legislative Assembly of Colorado Territory, 1864. Denver: Byers and Dudley, 1864.

Kansas General Laws, 1868. Lawrence: John Speer, 1868.

Kansas General Laws, 1861–1885. Carson City

Kansas. vol. 7, St. Paul, Minn.: West Publishing Co., 1884.

Nebraska. vol. 2, Callaghan and Co.: Chicago, 1873.

Nevada. vol. 7, Bancroft Whitney Co.: San Francisco, 1911.

Reports of Cases Determined in the Supreme Court of the State Of: California. Vols. 2, 4, 5, 9, 14, 15, 17, 34, 36, St. Paul, Minn.: West Publishing Co., 1860–1864.

FEDERAL DOCUMENTS

Richardson, James Daniel. *Messages and Papers of the Presidents.* 1787–1897, 10 vols. Washington, D.C.: Government Printing Office, 1896–1899.

U.S., Department of War. *Monthly Reports* of the Ninth and Tenth Cavalry Units and the Twenty-Fourth and Twenty-Fifth Infantry Units, 1866–1890. National Archives, Washington, D.C.

Northwestern Reporter, Vol. 91. St. Paul, Minn.: West Publishing Co., 1910.

U.S., Congress, Senate. *Report of Select Committee on Exodus.* Forty-Sixth Congress, 2nd session. National Archives.

U.S. Census Office:

    5th Census, 1830. Washington, D.C.: F. P. Blair, 1832.

    6th Census, 1840. Washington, D.C.: Blair and Rives, 1841.

    7th Census, 1850. Washington, D.C.: Globe Office, 1851.

    8th Census, 1860. Washington, D.C.: Government Printing Office, 1864.

    9th Census, 1870. G.P.O., 1872.

    10th Census, 1880. G.P.O., 1883–1888.

    11th Census, 1890. G.P.O., 1896.

Reports of the Adjutant General of the United States. G.P.O., 1866–1890.

Report of U.S Bureau on Indian Affairs, 1869. G.P.O., 1869.

Reports of the General of the Army, 1860–1890. National Archives

Territorial Papers of:

    California, 1846–1847. Vol. 1. State Department and National Archives.

    California and Colorado, 1861. State Department and National Archives.

    Dakota, March 28, 1861–January 7, 1873. State Department and National Archives.

    Idaho, July 3, 1867–December 1, 1872. Vol. 2. State Department and National Archives.

    Montana, 1865. State Department and National Archives.

    Nevada, 1861. Vol. 1. State Department and National Archives.

    New Mexico. 1861–1864. Vol 2 State Department and National Archives.

    Oregon, 1848–1859. State Department and National Archives.

    Washington, February 1859–December 1872. State Department and National Archives.

    Wyoming, 1866–1872. State Department and National Archives.

SECONDARY WORKS

BOOKS

Alexander, Charles. *Battles and Victory of Allen Allensworth*. Boston: Sherman, French and Co., 1914.

Altrocchi, Julia C. *The Spectacular San Francisco*. New York: E. P. Dutton, 1949.

Angel, Myron, ed. *History of Nevada*. Oakland, Ca.: Thompson & West, 1881; rpt., Berkeley, 1958.

Armstrong, Moses Kimball. *Early Empire Builders of the Great West*. St. Paul, Minn.: E. W. Potter, 1901.

Asbury, Herbert. *The Barbary Coast: an Informal History of the San Francisco Underworld*. New York: A. A. Knopf, 1933.

Atherton, Gertrude. *Golden Gate Country*. New York: Duell, Sloan and Pearce, 1945.

Bailey, Robert Gresham. *River of No Return*. Lewiston, Idaho: Bailey and Blake, 1935.

Baker, James Heaton and Leroy R. Hafen, eds. *History of Colorado*. Denver: Linderman Co., 1927.

Bancroft, Hubert Howe. *History of California*. 7 vols. San Francisco: The History Company, 1884.

————. "History of Nevada, Colorado, and Wyoming, 1840–1888." *The Works of Hubert Howe Bancroft*. Vol. 25. San Francisco: The History Company, 1890.

Bard, Floyd C. *Horse Wrangler: Sixty Years in the Saddle in Wyoming and Montana*. Norman: University of Oklahoma Press, 1960.

Barry, Theodore A. *Men and Memories of San Francisco, in the "Spring of '50."* San Francisco: A. L. Bancroft, 1873.

Batty, Joseph. *Over the Wilds to California: or, Eight Years from Home*. Ed. John Simpson. Leeds: J. Parrot, 1867.

Beadle, John Hanson. *The Undeveloped West; or, Five Years in the Territories*. Philadelphia: National Publishing Co., 1873.

Bean, Edwin F., comp. *History and Directory of Nevada County, California*. Carson City, Nev.: Daily Gazette Printing Co., 1867.

Beasley, Delilah Leontium. *Negro Trail Blazers of California*. Privately printed. Los Angeles, 1919.

Beattie, George William. *Heritage of the Valley San Bernardino's First Century*. Pasadena: San Pasqual Press, 1939.

Bechdolt, Frederick R. *Giants of the Old West*. New York: The Century Co., 1930.

Bennett, Estelline. *Old Deadwood Days*. New York: J. H. Sears, 1928.

Berry, Don. *A Majority of Scoundrels: an Informal History of the Rocky Mountain Fur Company*. New York: Harper and Co., 1961.

Blankenship, Georgiana, comp. and ed. *Early History of Thurston County, Washington*. Privately printed. Olympia, Wash., 1914.

Blegen, Theodore Christian. *Minnesota History.* Vol. 7. St. Paul: University of Minnesota Press, 1928.

Borthwick, J. D. *Three Years in California.* London: W. Blackwood and Sons, 1857.

————. *The Gold Hunters.* Cleveland: Onting Publishing Co., 1917.

Boyd, David. *History of Greeley and the Union Colony of Colorado.* Greeley: Greeley Tribune Press, 1890.

Brackenridge, Henry M. *Journal of a Voyage up the River Missouri.* 2nd ed. Baltimore: Coate and Maxwell, 1816.

Bradley, Glenn D. *Story of the Pony Express.* Chicago: McClury and Co., 1913.

Bratt, John. *Trails of Yesterday.* Chicago: University Publishing Co., 1921.

Brewerton, George Douglas. *Overland with Kit Carson.* New York: McCann, 1930.

Briggs, Harold Edward. *Frontiers of the Northwest.* New York: Appleton-Century, 1940.

Brown, Jesse and A. M. Willard. *The Black Hills Trails: a History of the Struggle of the Pioneers in the Winning of the Black Hills.* Ed. John T. Milek. Rapid City, S.D.: Rapid City Journal Co., 1924.

Buckbee, Edna Bryan. *The Saga of Old Tuolumne.* New York: Press of the Pioneers, 1935.

Buffum, Edward Gould. *Six Months in the Gold Mines.* London: R. Bentley, 1850.

Burnett, Peter Hardeman. *Recollections and Opinions of an Old Pioneer.* New York: Appleton and Co., 1880.

Burton, Richard Francis. *The City of the Saints and Across the Rocky Mountains to California.* London: Longmans, Green and Roberts, 1861.

Butler, James Davie. *The Pony Express.* Privately printed. Oregon City, Ore., 1928.

Bryant, Edwin. *What I Saw in California.* Santa Ana, Ca.: Fine Arts Press, 1936.

Byington, Lewis Francis, and Oscar Lewis, eds. *History of San Francisco.* Vols. 1–3. San Francisco: S. J. Clarke, 1931.

Calkins, Ernest Elmo. *They Broke the Prairie.* New York: Scribner and Sons, 1937.

Cameron, Marguerite. *This is the Place.* Caldwell, Id.: Caxton Printers, 1941.

Camp, William Martin. *San Francisco: Port of Gold.* Garden City, N.Y.: Doubleday, 1947.

Carr, Harry. *Los Angeles, City of Dreams.* New York: Appleton-Century, 1935.

Carroll, John Millar, ed. *Black Military Experience in the American West.* New York: Liveright, 1971.

Cashin, Herschel C. et al. *Under Fire with the Tenth United States Cavalry.* New York: American Publishing Co., 1899.

Catteral, Helen Tunnicliff, ed. *Judicial Cases Concerning American Slavery and Negroes.* 5 vols. Washington, D.C.: Carnegie Institute, 1926–1937.

Chapman, Arthur. *The Pony Express: the Record of a Romantic Adventure in Business.* New York: Putnam and Sons, 1932.

Chapman, Charles E. *History of California: The Spanish Period.* New York: Macmillan, 1921.

Chittenden, Hiram Martin. *History of Early Steamboat Navigation on the Missouri River.* New York: E. P. Harper, 1903.

———. *American Fur Trade of the Far West.* Vols. 1–2. New York: Press of the Pioneers, 1935.

Christianson, T. *Minnesota, or the Land of the Sky Tinted Waters.* Vols. 1–5. Chicago: American Historical Society, 1935.

Clark, Dan Elbert. *The West in American History.* New York: Thomas Y. Crowell, 1937.

Clark, Robert. *History of the Willamette Valley.* Chicago: S. J. Clarke, 1927.

Cleland, Robert Glass. *History of California: The American Period.* New York: Macmillan, 1922.

———. *This Reckless Breed of Men: The Trappers and Fur Traders of the Southwest.* New York: A. Knopf, 1950.

Clyman, Charles L. *James Clyman, American Frontiersman, 1792–1881.* San Francisco: California Historical Society, 1928.

Coman, Katherine. *Economic Beginnings of the Far West.* New York: Macmillan, 1912.

Cordley, Richard. *Pioneer Days in Kansas.* Boston: Pilgrim Press, 1903.

Cross, Ralph Herbert. *Early Inns of California, 1844–1869.* Privately printed. San Francisco, 1954.

Custer, Elizabeth Bacon. *Following the Guidon.* New York: Harper and Brothers, 1890.

Dale, Edward Everett. *The Range Cattle Industry.* Norman: University of Oklahoma Press, 1930.

Dale, Harrison. *The Ashley-Smith Explorations and Discovery of a Central Route to the Pacific.* Glendale, Ca.: Arthur H. Clarke, 1941.

Dana, Julian. *Sutter of California.* New York: Press of the Pioneers, 1934.

Davis, William Heath. *Seventy-Five Years in California.* San Francisco: J. Howell, 1967.

———. *Sixty Years.* San Francisco: A. J. Leary, 1889.

Delano, Alonzo. *Across the Plains and Among the Diggings.* 1854; rpt., New York: Miller, Orton, and Mulligan, 1936.

Dick, Everett. *Sod House Frontier, 1854–1890.* New York: Appleton-Century, 1937.

Dixon, Olive King. *Life of Billy Dixon, Plainsman, Scout, and Pioneer.* Dallas: P. L. Turner, 1927.

Dobie, Charles Caldwell. *San Francisco: A Pageant.* New York: Appleton-Century, 1943.

Dobie, James F. *The Longhorns*. Boston: Little, Brown, 1941.

Dorsey, John Morris. *Thoughts for Careful Consideration*. Topeka, 1906.

Downie, William. *Hunting for Gold*. San Francisco: Press of California Publishing Co., 1893.

Drake, Charles Clayton. *Who's Who in Coffeyville*. Coffeyville, Kan.: Coffeyville Journal Press, 1943.

Dunbar, Seymour. *History of Travel in America*. Vols. 1–4. Indianapolis: Bobbs-Merrill, 1915.

Eldredge, Zoeth Skinner. *The Beginning of San Francisco from the Expedition of Anza, 1774, to the City Charter of April 15, 1850*. Vols. 1–2. New York: Century History Co., 1915.

Espinosa, Jose Manuel. *Crusaders of the Rio Grande*. Chicago: Institute of Jesuit History Publications, 1942.

Faris, John Thomas. *On the Trail of the Pioneers*. New York: H. Doran, 1920.

Farish, Thomas Edwin. *History of Arizona*. 8 vols. Phoenix: Filmer Brothers Electrotype Co., 1915–1918.

Ferrier, William Warren. *Ninety Years of Education in California, 1846–1936*. Berkeley: Sathergate Book Shop, 1937.

Fleetwood, Christian A. *The Negro as a Soldier*. Washington, D.C.: Howard University, 1895.

Foreman, Grant. *Pioneer Days in the Early Southwest*. Cleveland: Arthur H. Clark, 1926.

———. *The Five Civilized Tribes*. Norman: University of Oklahoma Press, 1934.

Fowler, Arlen L. *Black Infantry in the West, 1869–1891*. Westport, Conn.: Greenwood Publishing Co., 1971.

Fritz, Percy Stanley. *Colorado, the Centennial State*. New York: Prentice Hall, 1941.

Gard, Wayne. *The Chisholm Trail*. Norman: University of Oklahoma Press, 1954.

Gaston, Joseph. *Portland, Oregon: Its History and Builders*. Chicago: S. J. Clarke, 1911.

Ghent, William James. *The Road to Oregon: A Chronicle of the Great Emigrant Trail*. New York: Longman, Green and Co., 1929.

Gibbs, Mifflin. *Shadow and Light*. Privately printed. Washington, D.C., 1902.

Gilbert, Douglas. *American Vaudeville, Its Life and Times*. New York: McGraw, Hill, 1940.

Gilbert, Frank T. *History of California from 1513 to 1850*. Vol. 1 of *History of Butte County, California*. San Francisco: Harry L. Wells, 1882.

Gillespie, William Henry. *Laws of the Territory of Nevada*. San Francisco: printed under supervision of Martin Gillespie, 1862.

Gladstone, Thomas H. *The Englishman in Kansas; or, Squatter Life and Border Warfare*. New York: Macmillan Co., 1914.

Gould, Charles N. *Oklahoma Place Names*. Norman: University of Oklahoma Press, 1933.

Graves, Jackson. *My Seventy Years in California, 1857–1927*. Los Angeles: Los Angeles Times Press, 1927.

Greenhow, Robert. *History of Oregon and California, and the Other Territories on the North-west Coast of North America*. Boston: Little, Brown, 1844.

Gregg, Josiah. *Commerce of the Prairies*. New York, 1854.

Grinnell, George B. *Beyond the Old Frontier*. New York: Charles Scribner, 1913.

Hafen, LeRoy, and C. C. Rister. *Western America*. New York: Prentice-Hall, 1941.

Hall, Frank. *History of the State of Colorado*. Chicago: Blakely Printing Co., 1889–1895.

Hammond, George Peter. *Coronado's Seven Cities*. Albuquerque: Coronado Exposition Commission, 1940.

Hanna, Phil Townsend. *California Through Four Centuries*. New York: Farrar and Rinehart, 1935.

Harlan, Jacob Wright. *California '46 to '88*. San Francisco: The Bancroft Co., 1888.

Harris, Theodore, ed. *Negro Frontiersman: The Western Memoirs of Henry O. Flipper, First Negro Graduate of West Point*. El Paso: Texas Western College Press, 1963.

Hart, Ann Clark, ed. *Clark's Point*. San Francisco: The Pioneer Press, 1937.

Hawgood, John Arkas, ed. *First and Last Consul: Thomas Oliver Larkin and the Americanization of California*. San Marino, Ca.: Pacific Company, 1962.

Hawkins, William George. *Lunsford Lane; or, Another Helper from North Carolina*. Boston: Crosby and Nichols, 1863.

Hayes, Benjamin. *Pioneer Notes from the Diaries of Judge Benjamin Hayes, 1849–1875*. Ed. Marjorie Tisdale Wolcott. Privately printed. Los Angeles, 1929.

Heap, Gwinn Harris. *Central Route to the Pacific*. Philadelphia: Lippincott, Grambo Co., 1854.

Hebard, Grace Raymond, and E. A. Brininstool. *The Bozeman Trail*. 2 vols. Cleveland: Arthur H. Clark, 1922.

Helper, Hinton Rowan. *Land of Gold: Reality vs. Fiction*. Baltimore: H. Taylor, 1855.

Henry, Stuart Oliver. *Conquering Our Great American Plains: A Historical Development*. New York: E. P. Dutton, 1930.

Hill, Alice Polk. *Tales of Colorado Pioneers*. Denver: Pierson and Gardner, 1884.

Hill, J. L. *The End of the Cattle Trail*. Long Beach, Ca.: George W. Moyle, 1925.

Hill, Laurence. *La Reina: Los Angeles in Three Centuries*. Los Angeles: Security Trust and Savings Bank, 1929.

Hittell, John Shertzer. *The Resources of California.* 6th ed. San Francisco: A. Romain, 1874.

Hittell, Theodore Henry. *History of California.* Vols. 1–4. San Francisco: Pacific Press Publishing House and Occidental Publishing Co., 1897.

Hubbard, Lucius, James H. Baker, William P. Murray, and Warren Upham, eds. *Minnesota in Three Centuries, 1655–1908.* Vols. 1–4. New York: Publishing Society of Minnesota, 1908.

Hulbert, Archer, ed. *Southwest on the Turquoise Trail.* Denver: Denver Public Library, 1933.

Hunt, Rockwell D. *California Firsts.* San Francisco: Fearon Publishers, 1957.

Hunter, John Marvin, comp. and ed. *Trail Drivers of Texas.* 2nd ed. Nashville: Cokesbury Press, 1925.

An Illustrated History of Los Angeles County, California. Chicago: Lewis Publishing Co., 1889; rpt. Berkeley, 1959.

Ingalls, Sheffield. *History of Atchison County, Kansas.* Lawrence: Standard Publishing Co., 1916.

Ingersoll, Luther A. *Ingersoll's Century Annals of San Bernardino County, 1769–1904.* Privately printed. Los Angeles, 1904.

Inman, Henry. *The Old Santa Fe Trail.* Topeka: Macmillan Co., 1912.

Irving, Washington. *Adventures of Captain Bonneville.* Ed. Edgeley W. Todd. Norman: University of Oklahoma Press, 1961.

————. *Astoria.* Ed. Edgeley Todd. Norman: University of Oklahoma Press, 1964.

Isely, Elise. *Sunbonnet Days.* Caldwell, Id.: Caxton Printers, 1935.

Johnston, Abraham Robinson, M. B. Edwards, and P. G. Ferguson. *Marching With the Army of the West.* Ed. Ralph Bieber. Glendale, Ca.: Arthur H. Clark, 1936.

Katz, William Loren. *The Black West.* Garden City, N.Y.: Doubleday, 1971.

Kelly, William. *An Excursion to California over the Prairie, Rocky Mountains, and Great Sierra Nevada.* London: Chapman and Hall, 1851.

Kelsey, D. M. *Our Pioneer Heroes and Their Daring Deeds.* San Francisco: H. L. Bancroft, 1890.

Kendall, Reese P. *Pacific Trail Camp-Fires.* Chicago: Scroll Publishing Co., 1901.

Kennedy, Elijah Robinson. *The Contest for California in 1861: How Colonel E. D. Baker Saved the Pacific States to the Union.* Boston: Houghton-Mifflin, 1912.

Knowland, Joseph R. *California, a Landmark History.* Oakland: Tribune Press, 1941.

Lang, Herbert O. *History of Tuolumme County, California.* Privately printed. San Francisco, 1881.

Langford, Nathaniel P. *Vigilance Days and Ways.* Boston: J. G. Cupples Co., 1890.

Larimer, William, and William H. H. Larimer. *Reminiscences of General William Larimer and of His Son, William H. H. Larimer, Two of the Founders of Denver City.* Privately printed. Lancaster, Pa.: New Era Printing Press, 1918.

Laut, Agnes Christina. *Pilgrims of the Santa Fe*. New York: F. A. Stokes, 1931.

Lawson, John D., ed. *American State Trials*. 17 vols. 1914; rpt., Wilmington, Del.: Scholarly Resources, 1971.

Leckie, Wolliam H. *Buffalo Soldier: A Narrative of the Negro Cavalry in the West*. Norman: University of Oklahoma Press, 1967.

Lewis, Oscar, and Carroll D. Hall. *Bonanza Inn, America's First Luxury Hotel*. New York: A. Knopf, 1945.

Lindquist, Maude Lucille, and James W. Clark. *Early Days and Ways in the Old Northwest*. New York: Scribner, 1937.

Lockley, Fred. *Oregon Trail Blazers*. New York: Knickerbocker Press, 1929.

Lowther, Charles C. *Dodge City, Kansas*. Philadelphia: Durrance and Co., 1940.

McClintock, John S. *Pioneer Days in the Black Hills*. Deadwood, S.D.: John McClintock, 1939.

McCoy, Joseph G. *Historic Sketches of Cattle Trade of the West and Southwest*. Ed. Ralph Bieber. Glendale, Ca.: Ramsey, Millett, and Hudson, 1940.

McFie, Matthew. *Vancouver Island and British Columbia*. London: Longman, Green, 1865.

McGroarty, John S. *Los Angeles from the Mountains to the Sea*. Vol. 1. Chicago: American Historical Society, 1923.

McNeal, Thomas A. *When Kansas Was Young*. Topeka: Capper Publication, 1934.

Meeker, Ezra. *Kate Mulhall: A Romance of the Oregon Trail*. New York: E. Meeker, 1926.

Merk, Frederick. *Economic History of Wisconsin During the Civil War Decade*. Vol. 1. Madison: Madison Soceity, 1916.

Mitchell, William Ansel. *Linn County, Kansas: A History*. Privately printed. Kansas City, Mo., 1928.

Morgan, Dale Lowell. *Jedediah Smith and the Opening of the West*. Indianapolis: Bobbs-Merrill, 1953.

———. *The West of William S. Ashley, 1822–1838*. Denver: Old West Publishing Co., 1964.

Morgan, Murray, *Northwest Corner: The Pacific Northwest, Its Past and Present*. New York: Viking Press, 1962.

Morgan, Neil Bowen. *Westward Tilt: The American West Today*. New York: Random House, 1963.

Nankivell, John Henry, comp. and ed. *History of the Twenty-Fifth Regiment, United States Infantry*. Fort Collins, Colo.: Old Army Press, 1972.

Napton, William Barclay. *Over the Santa Fe Trail, 1857*. Kansas City, Mo.: Franklin Hudson, 1905.

Neihardt, John Gneiseman. *The Splendid Wayfaring*. New York: Macmillan, 1920.

Nevins, Allan. *Fremont, the West's Greatest Adventurer*. New York: Harper and Brothers, 1928.

O'Brien, Robert. *This is San Francisco*. New York: Whittlesey House, 1948.

Oklahoma: a Guide to the Sooner State. Norman: University of Oklahoma Press, 1945.

Osgood, Ernest Staples. *The Day of the Cattleman*. Minneapolis: University of Minnesota Press, 1929.

Packard, Wellman. *Early Emigration to California, 1849–1850*. Rpt., M. Custer, 1928.

Parkman, Francis. *Oregon Trail*. Boston: Little, Brown, 1955.

Parrish, Randall. *The Great Plains: the Romance of Western American Exploration, Warfare, and Settlement, 1527–1870*. Chicago: McClury and Co., 1907.

Paxson, Frederick Logan. *History of the American Frontier, 1763–1893*. Boston: Houghton-Mifflin, 1924.

Penn, Irvine Garland. *The Africo-American Press and Its Editors*. Springfield, Mass.: Willey and Co., 1891.

Peters, Harry Twyford. *California on Stone*. Garden City, N.Y.: Doran and Co., 1935.

Phillips, Catherine Coffin. *Portsmouth Plaza, the Cradle of San Francisco*. San Francisco: J. H. Nash, 1932.

Phillips, Paul Chrisler. *The Fur Trade*. Norman: University of Oklahoma Press, 1961.

Pie, Sophie Alberding. *Buckboard Days*. Ed. Eugene Cunningham. Caldwell, Id.: Caxton Printers, 1936.

Porter, Kenneth Wiggins. *The Negro on the American Frontier*. New York: Arno Press, 1971.

Prosch, Charles. *Reminiscences of Washington Territory*. Seattle: Charles Prosch, 1904.

Quaife, Milo Milton, ed. *Death Valley in '49*. Chicago: R. R. Donnelley and Sons, 1927.

————, ed. *The Border and the Buffalo*. Chicago: R. R. Donnelley and Sons, 1938.

Quiett, Glenn Chesney. *They Built the West: An Epic of Rails and Cities*. New York: Appleton-Century, 1934.

Riesenberg, Felix. *Golden Gate: The Story of San Francisco Harbor*. New York: A. Knopf, 1940.

Rister, Carl Coke. *Land Hunger: David L. Payne and the Oklahoma Boomers*. Norman: University of Oklahoma Press, 1942.

Rodenbough, Theophilus Francis, and William L. Haskin, eds. *The Army of the United States*. New York: Maynard Merrill and Co., 1896.

Rollins, Philip Ashton. *The Cowboy*. New York: Scribner and Sons, 1922.

Romero, Patricia, comp. and ed. *I Too Am America: Documents from 1619 to the Present*. Washington, D.C.: Association for the Study of Negro Life and History, 1968.

Root, Frank Albert. *The Overland Stage to California*. Topeka: by the author, 1901.

Rothert, Otto Arthur. *The Outlaws of Cave-In Rock*. Cleveland: Arthur H. Clark, 1924.

Russell, Charles. *Back Trailing on the Old Frontier*. Great Falls, Mon., Cheely Rahan, 1922.

Rye, Edgar. *The Quirt and the Spur; Vanishing Shadows of the Western Frontier*. Chicago: W. B. Conkey Co., 1909.

Sabin, Edwin Legrand. *Kit Carson Days (1809–1868)*. New York: A. C. McClury, 1914.

Saxton, Charles. *The Oregonian: or, History of the Oregon Territory*. Washington, D.C.: Ward and Sons, 1846.

Scherer, James. *The Thirty-First Star*. New York: G. P. Putnam and Sons, 1942.

Scott, Harvey Whitfield. *History of the Oregon Country*. Cambridge, Mass.: Riverside Press, 1924.

Scrugham, James Graves, Ed. *Nevada*. 3 vols. New York: American Historical Society, 1935.

Shelby, Charmion, ed. *Revolt of the Pueblo Indians of New Mexico and Otermin's Attempted Reconquest, 1680–1682*. Part 1. Albuquerque: University of New Mexico Press, 1942.

Shinn, Charles Howard. *Mining Camps, a Study in American Frontier Government*. New York: Scribner and Sons, 1885.

———. *The Story of the Mine, as Illustrated by the Great Comstock Lode of Nevada*. New York: D. Appleton, 1898.

Smiley, Jerome Constant, ed. *History of Denver, with Outlines of the Earlier History of the Rocky Mountain Country*. Denver: Denver Times and Times Sun Publishing Co., 1901.

Smith, Herndon, comp. *Centralia, the First Fifty Years, 1845–1900*. Centralia, Wash.: Daily Chronicle and F. H. Cole Printing Co., 1942.

Sonnichsen, Charles Leland. *Cowboys and Cattle Kings*. Norman: University of Oklahoma Press, 1950.

Soule, Frank, John H. Gihon, and James Nisbet. *Annals of San Francisco*. New York: D. Appleton, 1855.

Streeter, Floyd Benjamin. *Prairie Trails and Cow Towns: the Opening of the Old West*. Boston: Devin Adair Co., 1936.

Sullivan, Maurice S. *The Travels of Jedediah Smith*. Santa Ana, Ca.: Fine Arts Press, 1934.

Switzler, William Franklin. *Switzler's Illustrated History of Missouri, from 1541 to 1877*. St. Louis: C. R. Barns, 1879.

Talbot, Theodore. *Journals, 1843 and 1849–52*. Ed. Charles Carey. Portland, Ore.: Metropolitan Press, 1931.

Taylor, Paul Schuster. *An American-Mexican Frontier, Nueces County, Texas*. Chapel Hill, N.C.: University of North Carolina Press, 1934.

Tenny, Edward Payson. *Colorado and Homes in the New West*. Boston: C. Dillingham, 1880.

Texas: A Guide to the Lone Star State. New York: Hasting House Publishers, 1940.

Thurman, Sue B. *Pioneers of Negro Origin in California*. San Francisco: Acme Publishing Co., 1949.

Thwaites, Reuben Gold. *A Brief History of Rocky Mountain Exploration, with Especial Reference to the Expedition of Lewis and Clark*. New York: D. Appleton, 1904.

Tinkham, George Henry. *A History of Stockton*. San Francisco: W. M. Hinton, 1880.

———. *California Men and Events*. Stockton, Ca.: Record Publishing Co., 1915.

Triplett, Frank. *Conquering the Wilderness*. New York: N. D. Thompson, 1883.

Trotter, James M. *Music and Some Highly Musical People*. Boston: Dillingham, 1878.

Tuthill, Franklin. *History of California*. San Francisco: H. H. Bancroft, 1866.

Twitchell, Ralph Emerson. *Leading Facts of New Mexican History*. Vol. 2. Cedar Rapids, Iowa: The Torch Press, 1912.

———. *Old Santa Fe: The Story of New Mexico's Ancient Capital*. Santa Fe: New Mexican Publishing Corporation, 1925.

Tyson, Philip T. *Geology and Industrial Resources of California*. Baltimore: W. Minifie and Co., 1851.

Underhill, Reuben Lukens. *From Cowhides to Golden Fleece*. Palo Alto, Ca.: Stanford University Press, 1939.

Vandiveer, Clarence A. *The Fur-Trade and Early Western Exploration*. Cleveland: Arthur H. Clark, 1929.

VanDyke, Theodore Strong. *San Diego County, California*. San Francisco, 1883.

Van Tramp, John C. *Prairie and Rocky Mountains Adventures; or, Life in the West*. St. Louis: J. H. Miller, 1859.

Vestal, Stanley. *Mountain Men*. Cambridge, Mass.: Houghton-Mifflin, 1937.

Violette, Eugene Morrow. *History of Missouri*. Boston: D. C. Heath, 1918.

Warner, Juan Jose, et al. *An Historical Sketch of Los Angeles County, California . . . September 8, 1771, to July 4, 1876*. Rpt., Los Angeles: O. W. Smith, 1936.

Washington: a Guide to the Evergreen State. Portland, Ore.: Binfords and Mort, 1941.

Webb, Walter Prescott, and H. Bailey Carroll, eds. *Handbook of Texas*. Austin: Texas State Historical Association, 1952.

Westermeier, Clifford, ed. *Trailing the Cowboy, His Life and Lore as Told by Frontier Journalists*. Caldwell, Id.: Caxton Printers, 1955.

Wheeler, Homer Webster. *The Frontier Trail: or, from Cowboy to Colonel*. Los Angeles: Los Angeles Times-Mirror Press, 1923.

Willard, Charles Dwight. *The Herald's History of Los Angeles City*. Los Angeles: Kingsley-Barnes, 1901.

Willard, James. *Colorado: Short Studies of Its Past and Present*. Boulder: University of Colorado, 1927.

Willis, William Ladd. *History of Sacramento County, California*. Los Angeles: Historic Record Co., 1913.

Wilson, John Albert. *History of Los Angeles County, California*. 1880; rpt., Berkeley: Thompson and West, 1959.

Winks, Robin Williams. *The Blacks in Canada: A History*. New Haven: McGill Queen's University Press, 1971.

Workman, Boyle. *The City That Grew*. Los Angeles: Southland Publishing Co., 1936.

Wright, George Frederick, ed. *History of Sacramento County, California*. Oakland: Thompson and West, 1880; rpt., Berkeley: Howell-North, 1960.

Wright, Robert Marr. *Dodge City, the Cowboy Capital*. Wichita: Wichita Eagle Press, 1913.

Young, Francis. *Echoes from Arcadia*. Denver: Lansing Brothers, 1903.

Zornow, William Frank. *Kansas: A History of the Jayhawk State*. Norman: University of Oklahoma Press, 1957.

PERIODICALS

Alvord, Clarence W., and Clarence E. Carter, eds. "Business Affairs in the Illinois Country, July 7, 1768–September 15, 1768." *Illinois State Historical Library Collections* 16 (1921), 341–413.

Ayer, John E. "George Bush, the Voyageur." *Washington Historical Quarterly* 7 (1916), 40–45.

Baker, Gen. James H. "Address at Fort Snelling in the Celebration of the Centennial Anniversary of the Treaty of Pike with the Sioux." *Minnesota Historical Society Collections* 12 (1905–08), 291–301.

Beach, James H. "Old Fort Hays." *Kansas State Historical Society Collections* 11 (1909–10), 571–581.

Beasley, Delilah L. "Slavery in California." *Journal of Negro History* 3 (January 1918), 33–44.

———, and M. N. Work, comps. "California Freedom Papers." *Journal of Negro History* 3 (January 1918), 45–54.

Beller, Jack. "Negro Slaves in Utah." *Utah Historical Quarterly* 2 (October 1929), 122–126.

Bergmann, Leola N. "The Negro in Iowa." *Iowa Journal of History and Politics* 46 (January 1948), 3–90.

"Biographical Sketches of North Dakota Pioneers: Frank Viets." *North Dakota State Historical Society Collections* 7 (1925), 61–79.

Bliss, Colonel John H. "Reminiscences of Fort Snelling." *Minnesota Historical Society Collections* 6 (1894), 335–353.

Brown, John. "Pioneer Journeys: From Nauvoo, Illinois, to Pubelo, Colorado, in 1846, and Over the Plains in 1847." *Improvement Era* 13 (July 1910), 802–810.

Carleton, Mary T., comp. "The Byrnes of Berkeley: From Letters of Mary Tanner Byrne and Other Sources." *California Historical Society Quarterly* 17 (March 1938), 41–48.

Carroll, H. Bailey. "Texas Collection." *Southwestern Historical Quarterly* 48 (July 1944), 87–125.

Coffin, Nathan E. "The Case of Archie P. Webb, a Free Negro." *Annals of Iowa*, 3rd series, 11 (July-October 1913), 200–214.

Connelley, William E. "The Lane-Jenkins Claim Contest." *Kansas State Historical Society Collections* 16 (1923–25), 21, 176.

Cowan, Robert E. "The Leidesdorff Estate: a Forgotten Chapter in the Romantic History of Early San Francisco." *California Historical Society Quarterly* 7 (June 1928), 105–111.

Coy, Owen C. "Evidences of Slavery in California." *Grizzly Bear* 19 (October 1916), 1–2.

Davenport. T. W. "Slavery Question in Oregon." *Oregon Historical Society Quarterly* 8 (September 1908), 189–253.

Davidson, John N. "Negro Slavery in Wisconsin." *Proceedings of the State Historical Society of Wisconsin,* Fortieth Annual Meeting (December 8, 1892), pp. 82–86.

Dawson, James. "Major Andrew Dawson, 1817–1871." *Montana Historical Society Contributions* 7 (1910), 61–72.

Dee, Henry D., ed. "The Journal of John Work, 1835." *British Columbia Historical Quarterly* 9 (January 1945), 49–69.

Dick, Everett. "The Long Drive." *Kansas State Historical Society Collections* 17 (1926–28), 27–97.

"Documentary: The Fremont Episode [Larkin's Circular "to Several Americans," Telling of the Happenings at Sonoma and the Mobilization of the "Californian Forces"]." *California Historical Society Quarterly* 7 (March 1928), 79–80.

"Dr. W. H. Ward's Colony Plan Frustrated." *Minnesota History Bulletin* 2 (August 1917), 215.

Drake, Thomas E. "Quakers in Minnesota." *Minnesota History* 18 (1937), 249–266.

Flandrau, Charles E. "Reminiscences of Minnesota during the Territorial Period." *Minnesota Historical Society Collections* 9 (1898–1900), 197–222.

Foreman, Grant. "Early Post Offices of Oklahoma." *Chronicles of Oklahoma* 6 (September 1928), 271–298.

Foster, Stephen C. "Los Angeles Pioneers of 1836." *Publications of the Historical Society of Southern California* 6, Part 1 (1903), 80–81.

Frazee, George. "The Iowa Fugitive Slave Case." *Annals of Iowa,* 3rd series, 4 (July 1899), 118–137.

Garvin, Roy. "Benjamin, or 'Pap,' Singleton and His Followers." *Journal of Negro History* 33 (January 1948), 7–23.

Giddens, Paul H. "News from Kansas in 1870." *Kansas Historical Quarterly* 7 (May 1938), 170–182.

Gillespie. Archibald H. "Further Letters, October 20, 1845, to January 16, 1846, to the Secretary of the Navy." *California Historical Society Quarterly* 18 (September 1939), 217–228.

Grignon, Augustin. "Seventy-Two Years' Recollections of Wisconsin." *Wisconsin State Historical Society Collections* 3 (1857; rpt. 1904), 197–295.

Grinnell, George B. "Bent's Old Fort and Its Builders." *Kansas State Historical Society Collections* 15 (1919–22), 28–91.

"Grizzly" (pseud.). "Capt. Joseph L. Folsom." *Grizzly Bear* 1 (July 1907), 15–16.

Hafen, LeRoy R. "The Last Years of James P. Beckwourth." *Colorado Magazine* 5 (August 1928), 134–139.

Harrington, W. P. "The Populist Party in Kansas." *Kansas State Historical Society Collections* 16 (1923–25), 403–450.

"Henry County District Court." *Annals of Iowa* 11 (July-October 1913), 179.

Henry, Francis. "George Bush." *Oregon Pioneer Association Transactions,* Fifteenth Annual Reunion (1887), pp. 68–69.

Herriott, F. I. "Transplanting Iowa's Laws to Oregon." *Oregon Historical Society Quarterly* 5 (June 1904), 139–150.

Howay, F. W. "The Negro Immigration into Vancouver Island in 1858." *British Columbia Historical Quarterly* 3 (April 1939), 101–113.

Kellogg, Louise P. "The Story of Wisconsin, 1734–1848." *Wisconsin Magazine of History* 3 (1919–20), 189–208.

King, Clyde L. "The Kansas School System—Its History and Tendencies." *Kansas State Historical Society Collections* 11 (1909–10), 424–455.

"Letters of George Bonga." *Journal of Negro History* 12 (January 1927), 41–54.

"List of Citizens Living at Ft. Benton, Montana, during the Winter of 1862 and 1863." *Montana Historical Society Contributions* 1 (1876), 347–348.

"List of Voters Registered in Redlands, Lugonia, and Crafton School Districts." *Citrograph* 3 (Saturday, September 22, 1888), [9].

"Local History Items." *Minnesota History* 8 (December 1927), 446–453.

Lockley, Fred. "Some Documentary Records of Slavery in Oregon." *Oregon Historical Society Quarterly* 17 (June 1916), 107–115.

———. "Facts Pertaining to Ex-Slaves in Oregon, and Documentary Record of the Case of Robin Holmes vs. Nathaniel Ford." *Oregon Historical Society Quarterly* 23 (June 1922), 111–137.

Lowe, Percival G. "Recollections of Fort Riley." *Kansas State Historical Society Collections* 7 (1901–02), 101–113.

Meehan, Thomas A. "Jean Baptiste Point du Sable, the First Chicagoan." *Illinois State Historical Society Journal* 56 (Autumn 1963), 439–453.

Meeker, Moses. "Early History of Lead Region of Wisconsin." *Wisconsin State Historical Society Collections* 7 (1872; rpt. 1908), 271–296.

Meyers, Augustus. "Dakota in the Fifties." *South Dakota Historical Collections* 10 (1920), 130–194.

"Minnesota as Seen by Travelers: A Danish Visitor of the Seventies, II." Trans. and ed. Jacob Hodnefield. *Minnesota History* 10 (September 1929), 309–325.

"Minnesota as Seen by Travelers: A Pennsylvanian Visits the West in 1855." *Minnesota History* 7 (December 1926), 336–339.

Nicholson, William. "A Tour of Indian Agencies in Kansas and the Indian Territory in 1870." *Kansas Historical Quarterly* 3 (August 1934), 289–326.

"Official Roster of Kansas [Officials], 1854–1925." *Kansas State Historical Society Collections* 16 (1923–25), 658–745.

Pelzer, Louis. "The History of Political Parties in Iowa from 1857 to 1860." *Iowa Journal of History and Politics* 7 (April 1909), 179–229.

———. "The Negro and Slavery in Early Iowa." *Iowa Journal of History and Politics* 2 (October 1904), 471–484.

Perry, Dan W. "The First Two Years." *Chronicles of Oklahoma* 7 (September 1929), 278–322; (December 1929), 419–457.

Pickard, Josiah L. "Experiences of a Wisconsin Educator." *Wisconsin Magazine of History* 7 (December 1923), 125–147.

Pickering, Isaac O. "The Administration of John P. St. John." *Kansas State Historical Society Collections* 9 (1905–06), 378–394.

Porter, Kenneth W. "Relations between Negroes and Indians within the Present Limits of the United States." *Journal of Negro History* 17 (July 1932), 287–367.

Ramsdell, Charles W. "The Natural Limits of Slavery Expansion." *Mississippi Valley Historical Review* 16 (September 1929), 151–171.

Reid, Robie L. "How One Slave Became Free: An Episode of the Old Days in Victoria." *British Columbia Historical Quarterly* 6 (October 1942), 251–256.

Savage, W. Sherman. "The Negro in the Westward Movement." *Journal of Negro History* 25 (October 1940), 531–539.

———. "The Role of the Negro Soldiers in Protecting the Indian Territory from Intruders." *Journal of Negro History* 36 (January 1951), 25–34.

Scott, Leslie M. "Soil Repair Lessons in Willamette Valley." *Oregon Historical Society Quarterly* 18 (March 1917), 55–69.

Shirk, George H. "First Post Offices within the Boundaries of Oklahoma." *Chronicles of Oklahoma* 26 (Summer 1948), 179–244.

"Slavery among the Saints." *Millenial Star* 13 (February 15, 1851), 63.

Swanson, Nina. "The Development of Public Protection of Children in Kansas." *Kansas State Historical Society Collections* 15 (1919–22), 231–278.

Sweet, Oney F. "An Iowa County Seat." *Iowa Journal of History and Politics* 38 (October 1940), 339–407.

Swisher, Jacob A. "The Rise and Fall of Buxton." *Palimpsest* 26 (June 1945), 179–192.

Taliaferro, Maj. Lawrence. "Auto-Biography." *Minnesota Historical Society Collections* 6 (1894), 189–255.

Thorpe, Francis N. "The Political Value of State Constitutional History." *Iowa Journal of History and Politics* 1 (January 1903), 17–45.

Thwaites, Reuben G. "The Territorial Census for 1836." *Wisconsin State Historical Society Collections* 13 (1895), 247–270.

———. "Notes on Early Lead Mining in the Fever (or Galena) River Region." *Wisconsin State Historical Society Collections* 13 (1895), 271–292.

———, ed. "The Mackinac Register of Marriages—1725–1821." *Wisconsin State Historical Society Collections* 18 (1908), 469–513.

Turnbull, Thomas. "Travels from the United States across the Plains to California." Ed. Frederic L. Paxson. *Wisconsin State Historical Society Proceedings* (January 1913), pp. 137–225.

Warner, Louis H. "Wills and HijuelasnVew *Mexico Historical Review* 7 (January 1932), 75–89.

Warren, William W. "History of the Ojibways, Based upon Traditions and Oral Statements." *Minnesota Historical Society Collections* 5 (1885), 21–394.

Watson, Douglas S. "The Great Express Extra of the *California Star* of April 1, 1848: The Forerunner of California Promotion Literature." *California Historical Society Quarterly* 11 (June 1932), 129–137.

Wells, Harry L. "Beckwourth's Ride." *Pony Express Courier* 2 (October 1935), 16.

Wheat, Carl I., ed. " 'California's Bantam Cock': The Journals of Charles E. De Long, 1854–1863." *California Historical Society Quarterly* 10 (March 1931), 40–78; (September 1931), 271–297.

Wheeler, William F. "Sacajaweah: An Historical Sketch." *Montana Historical Society Contributions* 7 (1910), 271–296.

Williams, Mary F., ed. "Papers of the San Francisco Committee of Vigilance of 1851." *Academy of Pacific Coast History Publications* 4 (1919).

Wilson, George Jr. "George Wilson: First Territorial Adjutant of the Militia of Iowa." *Annals of Iowa,* 3rd series, 4 (January 1901), 563–576.

Wright, R. M. "Personal Reminiscences of Frontier Life in Southwest Kansas." *Kansas State Historical Society Collections* 7 (1901–02), 47–83.

Yost, Genevieve. "History of Lynchings in Kansas." *Kansas Historical Quarterly* 2 (May 1933), 182–219.

NEWSPAPERS

(Note: The dates following newspaper entries indicate that the newspapers for those years were consulted.)

Afro-American Advocate (Coffeyville, Kansas). 1890–1893.
Amarillo Press. 1944.
Atchison Free Press. 1879.
Atchison Globe. 1914.
Boston Evening Transcript. April 1879.
California Examiner (San Francisco). 1858–1868.
California Mail Bag. 1860.
California Weekly Chronicle (San Francisco). 1857.
Coffeyville Journal. December 1942.
Comfort (Augusta, Maine). 1903.
Denver Daily Evening News. 1862.
Denver Rocky Mountain News. 1855, 1879–1900.
Emporia [Kansas] *Gazette.* 1890, September 8, 1915.
Garnett [Kansas] *Plaindealer.* April 1880.
Kansas City [Missouri] *Call.* August 19, 1941.
Kansas City [Missouri] *Star.* May 1900, May 1910.
Lawrence Home Journal. 1878–1879.

Lawrence Western Home Journal. 1879.

Leavenworth Times. 1879.

Los Angeles Star. 1857–1879.

Los Angeles Times. 1909.

Milwaukee Sentinel. 1862.

Milwaukee Sentinel Gazette. 1850–1851.

Mirror of the Times (San Francisco). 1857–1858.

Nordlysit (New York). May 12, 1938.

Oakland Graphic. 1927.

Oakland Tribune. 1916.

Olympia [Washington] *Daily Tribune.* 1890–1893.

Oregon Spectator (Oregon City). Nearly complete collection in the library of the Historical Society of Portland; scattered in the Bancroft Library, University of California, Berkeley.

Oregonian (Portland). 1865–1875.

Pacific Appeal (San Francisco). 1863.

Pacific Tribune (Seattle). 1862.

Pandex of the Press (San Francisco). 1902.

Pony Express Courier. May 1930, October 1935.

Redlands [California] *Daily Facts.* 1929.

Rocky Mountain Sentinel (Santa Fe, New Mexico). 1879.

Sacramento Daily California Statesman. 1858.

Sacramento Daily Globe. 1856.

Sacramento Daily Union. 1850–1870, 1874, 1878.

Sacramento Democratic State Journal. 1851–1857.

St. Louis Globe Democrat. 1879–1880.

St. Paul Weekly Pioneer Press. 1898.

San Francisco Call. 1890–1904.

San Francisco Daily Alta Californian. 1851, 1857, 1858, 1860.

San Francisco Daily California Chronicle. 1856.

San Francisco Elevator. 1852, 1865, 1867, 1868, 1870–1874, 1885.

San Francisco Evening Post. 1904.

San Francisco Pacific News. 1843, 1851.

San Francisco State Register. 1871–1873.

Texas Livestock Journal. April 21, 1883.

Topeka Advocate. May 1896.

Topeka Capital. 1888, 1937.

Topeka Journal. March 20, 1916.

Topeka Weekly Tribune. 1882.

University of Arizona Bulletin (Tucson). November 3, 1896.

Weekly New Mexican (Santa Fe). March 1878.

Weekly Oregonian (Portland). 1846–1870.

Weekly Pacific News (San Francisco). 1849.

Yankton [South Dakota] *Press.* 1872.

Index

About the Author

Professor emeritus at Missouri's Lincoln University, W. Sherman Savage has published extensively on the topics of abolition and slavery. Among his books are *Controversy over Abolition* and *History of Lincoln University*.